BLACK BASEBALL, BLACK BUSINESS

BLACK BASEBALL, BLACK BUSINESS

Race Enterprise and the Fate of the Segregated Dollar

Roberta J. Newman and Joel Nathan Rosen

University Press of Mississippi / Jackson

www.upress.state.ms.us

The University Press of Mississippi is a member
of the Association of American University Presses.

First printing 2014

∞

Library of Congress Cataloging-in-Publication Data

Newman, Roberta J.
Black baseball, black business : race enterprise and the fate of the
segregated dollar / Roberta J. Newman and Joel Nathan Rosen.
pages cm
Includes bibliographical references and index.
ISBN 978-1-49680-457-0 (cloth : alk. paper) — ISBN 978-1-61703-955-3
(ebook) 1. Negro leagues—Economic aspects. 2. Business enterprises, Black—History—20th century. 3. Discrimination in sports—United
States—History—20th century. I. Rosen, Joel Nathan, 1961– II. Title.
GV875.N35N49 2014
796.357'64—dc23   2013033564

British Library Cataloging-in-Publication Data available

For Monte Irvin
and Our Families

CONTENTS

HEADING DOWNTOWN

Monte Irvin, Hall of Fame, 1973

In my ninety-five years, I have been asked all manner of questions about my experiences playing Negro League ball. And a lot of those questions come with follow-ups regarding my move to the Majors with the Giants in 1949. I've been asked pretty much everything about what I saw, how I felt, who I knew, who I liked, and so on. But these questions always had something to do with my life on the field.

All these years later, I'm still delighted to discuss baseball with fans and scholars alike. So when Professors Newman and Rosen first approached me about the work they were doing on the Negro Leagues, I was happy to help, especially because their questions were so different from what I am used to hearing. While they were obviously fans of the game, they were much more interested in what was happening outside the ballparks rather than inside, and that made me all the more curious. But it wasn't until they asked me to reminisce about my social life during my transition from Negro Leaguer to Major Leaguer that got me thinking about what had been and the flood of memories that came with it.

But in addition to the memories (good memories, mostly), revisiting their questions got me to thinking about the changes I went through—what we all went through—during this remarkable time. I, my friends, my colleagues, and our fans had spent the majority of our adult lives Uptown, in the clubs and cafés of Harlem and similar places in Newark as well as elsewhere around Negro League cities, but by the turn of the 1950s, the lives that we had come to know had taken a pretty sudden turn. A lot of us simply came to find ourselves spending much more time Downtown rather than Uptown. Where once I used to see the great musicians of my youth performing at Smalls Paradise and the Savoy, by the 1950s I was spending nearly the same amount of time at places like Toots Shor's. And this was true for a lot of my fellow former Negro Leaguers as well as the many young men who began arriving in the Majors around the same time. Now, it wasn't exactly balanced there. Willie Mays and I rarely sat all that close to Joe DiMaggio's or Mickey Mantle's table over at Toots's place, but we were there. They'd seat us, they'd serve us, and while we may have been close to the kitchen door or had an obstructed view of the room, through these experiences we actually started to feel like celebrities in what was for us a much bigger pond than we were used to. It was certainly different, and I think back on it now and realize it was probably about that time that my world was starting to change—slowly perhaps, but changing just the same. I may have been too young to notice or even care all that much, but I can see now how much that period affected not only my life but the lives of the other ballplayers and those who were connected to us in quite dramatic ways.

Making the transition to Major League Baseball was a part of this challenge. But as Newman and Rosen have shown throughout this work, being a professional ballplayer always came with challenges, much of which happened as much on the field as off it. Thinking back to those Negro League days—and these were mostly great days—they were also difficult times. Squabbling with owners while trying to make ends meet, trying to take care of our families, learning how to fall asleep sitting up on a bus. Every day was an adventure. We loved the game, but it got harder and harder to play "the game" that came before the first pitch and after the last out.

One of our biggest complaints was that while we were supposed to be the big attractions, too often the owners thought they were the show, and so did many of the promoters. We certainly didn't have much recourse. We were playing baseball and getting paid for it, and because the Major Leagues weren't yet an option, most of us resigned ourselves to making the best of our situation. It's not like we didn't know. We knew that it was as much about survival as anything else. We had to survive travel restrictions in the North as well as in the South. We had to figure ways around the foolishness and injustice when it came to food and accommodations. But we also knew that on the worst day, playing baseball was still a much better life than working on the line or some other regular job, so we pushed through it like soldiers wearing a different sort of uniform than the one I wore in France.

As I continue to look back, I find it funny, too, how many times we talked about not just baseball strategy but how shortsighted the owners seemed to be when it came to day-to-day operations. We'd been to Major

League parks. We'd seen them selling scorecards with players' photo-graphs, people buying food and eating it in the stands, but we couldn't seem to understand why fans over at the stadium in Newark weren't being offered the same experience as those watching the ball games in the Bronx at Yankee Stadium. It wasn't until Mr. Pompez started making some real money with concessions by selling food and scorecards where his Cubans played that my owner, Mrs. Manley, and a couple of other team owners started to see the light. Too bad, too, as by that time, the Negro League run was just about over. With the war coming to an end and all the rumors flying about that Major League scouts were looking at us, we knew that opportunities were starting to open themselves up for us. And we knew that change was just around the corner. But we also knew that it wasn't going to be easy for any of us. We watched as Jackie Robinson got knocked about, but we also saw our friends and teammates beating a similar path out of town while listening to the owners complain about their money moving down the road and the disloyalty of their players as it all was com-ing apart.

Yes, playing Negro League baseball had its ups and downs, but we did our best to make the most of a difficult situation. When it was over, it gave some of us a chance to move on to the Major Leagues—not enough of us, but a select few who did what we could to make the most of the opportu-nity. A lot of my teammates and friends had the talent to play in the big leagues but just never got the chance because they were either too old or there was no room on a roster for that many former Negro Leaguers in what used to be white ball. Too many folks didn't get to see Mule Suttles or Buck Leonard or Josh Gibson or Satchel Paige in his prime. My dear friend Ray Dandridge ended his career playing in Minneapolis, but even in his advancing age, he still had the talent to help out any ball club. We all knew it as much as we knew most everything else that was going on around us. But mostly, we knew about change. We knew what was fair and unfair, but we also knew that we were playing baseball and were getting paid to do it.

As these authors show, desegregation in baseball was hard on every-body. It was certainly hard on Jackie Robinson, but it was difficult for the other men that came up after him, too. It was certainly tough on Satchel Paige and my old teammate, Larry Doby, when they came up with Cleve-land in '48. But we could also see how tough it was in Harlem, around the Hill in Pittsburgh, along Chicago's South Side, Vine Street in Kansas City, and other places where we used to play. Barbershops, restaurants, clean-ers, beauty shops—they all depended on the same customers who used to come watch us play. So when our baseball was no longer the big draw, all these businesses suffered. But many weren't just businesses. These were our friends, and we watched helplessly as their livelihoods started to vanish. Great hotels struggled, some of our favorite night spots also struggled or closed down all together, and a lot of the great old neighborhoods started to look empty and a lot more beat up than we remembered.

The chance to play in the Major Leagues was a dream come true for many of us, but we also knew it was never going to be easy—for any of us. Change never is.

REDISCOVERING A TOTAL INSTITUTION

Earl Smith, Ph.D., Wake Forest University

The Negro Leagues are an interesting and often perplexing phenomenon in the history of American sports. On one hand, the Negro Leagues make sense as a place for devalued American men to partake in the leisure time activity of baseball. Yet on the other hand, the Negro Leagues make no sense at all for the simple reason that all men interested in playing the game of baseball should be able to do so together; even more important, in the world of competitive athletics, all players should want to play against the very best players. Empirically analyzing this conundrum is the task taken on by Professors Roberta J. Newman and Joel Nathan Rosen in this exciting new book, *Black Baseball, Black Business: Race Enterprise and the Fate of the Segregated Dollar.*

A great deal has changed in the twenty-first century that could not have been predicted even twenty-five years ago. There is now a wing at the National Baseball Hall of Fame and Museum in Cooperstown, New York, that is dedicated to heroes of the Negro Leagues. Approximately eighteen former Negro League players have been enshrined in this wing—led by Satchel Paige—heeding a call first sounded by the great Ted Williams in his induction speech back in 1966. All of this represents progress. Or does it? Is a segregated wing an appropriate tribute to a segregated period in history, or does it simply re-create the segregation that Jackie Robinson and so many others worked so hard to move beyond? Or is this yet another footnote to the much more complex question of what the Negro Leagues continue to represent many years after their demise?

Black Baseball, Black Business explores such matters. But it is not just another one of the many Negro League–related books. It does not merely chronicle the stories of the many men we know who played in the Negro Leagues, from Satchel Paige to Grant "Home Run" Johnson to James "Cool

Papa" Bell to Larry Doby to Josh Gibson to Buck Leonard to Monte Irvin and so many others. Rather, undertaken in the mode of analysis pioneered by the late theorist Erving Goffman, this book offers a serious examination of the larger world of the Negro Leagues as what Goffman once termed a total institution, which the authors approach from the standpoint of the interconnection of linkages of men (and a few women) who paid for, owned, and otherwise controlled the Negro Leagues.

Many of these stories will force the reader to ask why it took so long for this authoritative social history of the Negro Leagues to be published in light of the fact that so many books have been written about the subject. It is a good question, and part of the answer might be that previous authors were less committed than Newman and Rosen are to move beyond mere hagiography to look for more than a list of the all important names associated with Negro League baseball, thus uncovering assumptions as well as destroying the social stereotypes that keep us from a full and true understanding of how the world of Negro League baseball really worked. In short, the authors offer a full-blown social science analysis, not just sound bites about a great player here and there or some amazing feat of athleticism.

Newman and Rosen approach their subject with a deep knowledge of the backstories of control, corruption, deals gone bad, and, yes, exploits on the field of play that packed stadiums year after year until the cherry-picking of integration started to rob the Negro Leagues of their best players, ultimately leading to the financial disasters that killed the leagues. No two scholars are better equipped to bring us this fascinating tour de force that will soon be the standard source on the significance and legacy of the Negro Leagues.

BLACK BASEBALL,
BLACK BUSINESS

1

Black Business and Consciousness in Context

Introduction

As has been well documented, baseball's color line, drawn in 1883, led to the formation of a series of loosely organized leagues and independent teams generally referred to collectively though not entirely accurately as the Negro Leagues. Composed of African American players along with a contingent of dark-skinned Latinos, the various iterations of organized black baseball represented a vibrant if not always thriving business enterprise. But the Negro Leagues and black baseball in general did not emerge in a vacuum. Nor did they disintegrate in a vacuum in the seasons immediately following the desegregation of the Major Leagues on April 15, 1947. Seemingly in the shadow of mainstream professional sports, black baseball was a nexus in a web of businesses that made up a segregated economy, both de facto and de jure. It and a handful other ventures such as black-owned insurance companies, the black press, and the "ethnic" beauty industry, as exemplified by the empires of Madam C. J. Walker and Annie Turnbo Malone's Poro Colleges of Hair and Beauty Culture, as well as illegal numbers and policy rackets fueled an economic engine that powered a system comprised of more modest enterprises.

While the tendrils of Jim Crow's reach extended far beyond the limits of the South, for the millions of African Americans who lived under its thumb, Jim Crow meant more than just signs on water fountains and bathroom doors. Jim Crow was an economy based primarily on the speculation that "separate but equal" was not a temporary condition but rather a fixed

3

and permanent fact of doing business in America. The omnipresence of the color line in post-Reconstruction America helped sketch a secondary line that offered a strange degree of salvation to some while articulating quite forcibly to others that their place in the order would be marked through a narrowly defined back door. Such was the case with the business of black baseball and the system within which it functioned. Though limited in comparison with mainstream ventures, the money nonetheless flowed back and forth within this economy that had been forced into existence by the prevailing social and political climate in urban centers such as Pittsburgh, Kansas City, Chicago, New York, Indianapolis, and Philadelphia.

But what happened to black baseball and the other businesses enterprises in this urban, African American economy when the foundation of segregation upon which they were built proved to be made of shifting sands? What were the implications for businesses created by self-professed race men and women who outwardly demanded progress while at the same time depended on the status quo for their livelihoods? Moreover, how did African American entrepreneurs respond when faced with the fading of the color line? And what were the implications for the larger African American economy, built as it was on an illusory foundation of segregation, after the tide had inexorably turned?

Race Businesses and the Great Migration

"Ethnic businesses," write Ivan Light and Steven J. Gold, "are not simply places where customers purchase goods and services and owners earn a living. Instead, they are embedded in a wide variety of commercial and personal relationships that are central to collective life. Business is the means whereby community is originated."[1] African American businesses established during the first half of the twentieth century certainly fit this description. Black baseball was at times one of the more profitable businesses in urban African America, making a considerable contribution to what Light and Gold define as an "ethnic economy," a system that "consists of co-ethnic self-employed and employers and their co-ethnic employees."[2] Light and Gold use the term *ethnic enclave economy* to identify this type of community-based and community-building economy composed of interrelated businesses whose owners and employees share a single ethnicity or in this case race—or perhaps more accurately color—and that are clustered together geographically in a segregated community.[3] This form of aspiring entrepreneurship sought to exploit markets typically ignored by mainstream business practices.

Despite popular assumptions to the contrary, African American enterprise has a long history in the United States, reaching back to the colonial period. Small slave-owned stores such as the one operated by the Montgomerys of Davis Bend, Mississippi, provided goods to the surrounding plantation community.[4] Other African Americans operated successful ventures in the service industry: Samuel Fraunces, for example, was the proprietor of a revolutionary-era eatery in New York City that was best known not for its owner's race but because it was the site of George Washington's farewell speech to his troops. African American entrepreneurship is thus deeply ingrained in American life. An article in *Ebony*'s special edition marking two hundred years of the African American experience notes, "The overall history of the black American business has been gradual and continuous."[5]

Nevertheless, early African American entrepreneurship was limited in scope. According to historian Juliet E. K. Walker, "Despite some successes, most antebellum black businesses remained marginal enterprises, earning minimal profits. Black business people were confronted with both legal and societal constraints that restricted their participation in many occupations. Antebellum black entrepreneur John Malvin, who established a business in Great Lakes shipping[,] said, 'I found every door was closed against the colored man in a free state, excepting the jails and penitentiaries.'"[6] Even though limited black entrepreneurship stretches back to the period prior to the nation's founding, the African American ethnic enclave economies, of which black baseball was a vital part, were not a significant presence in the fabric of America's cities until the Great Migration.

While a small but steady stream of African Americans began to trickle up from the rural South to the urban North throughout the second half of the nineteenth century and first years of the twentieth, especially after the failure of Reconstruction, what has come to be called the Great Migration began in earnest when Europe went to war in 1914. This demographic shift resulted from a simultaneous increase in employment in war industries and constituent businesses and a decrease in the availability of cheap labor, fueled to that point by a steady influx of white European ethnic immigrants. In addition, the cotton crop suffered significant damage as a consequence of a boll weevil infestation, reducing the amount of work available for African American laborers in the South. Migrating north appeared to offer huge economic as well as personal advantages. "Over the course of six decades," writes Isabel Wilkerson, "some six million black southerners left the land of their forefathers and fanned out across the country for an uncertain existence in nearly every other corner of America. The Great Migration would become a turning point in history. It would transform urban America and recast the social and political order of every city it touched."[7] Furthermore, "it was the first big step the nation's servant class ever took without asking."[8]

What Wilkerson identifies as a vast, leaderless movement and "perhaps the biggest under-reported story of the twentieth century" was encouraged if not initiated by Robert S. Abbott, founder, owner, and editor of the *Chicago Defender*, which essentially functioned as African America's paper of record during the first decades of the twentieth century and helped fuel the developing ethnic enclave economies of the urban North.[9] Abbott began publishing his paper in 1905 and initially encouraged his readers to stay in the South, where they could fight for their due. But as perceived economic opportunities increased, he changed his tune quite emphatically. The *Defender* published articles, editorials, poems, cartoons, and advertisements urging readers to migrate and even included one-way schedules for trains headed to Chicago.[10]

But Abbott's enthusiasm did little to mitigate the challenges most new migrants faced in the North. Concerned about the untutored behavior of rural southerners, unused to the demands and vicissitudes of industrial work and the required decorum of urban life, the *Defender* published advice for the newcomers. The sage wisdom Abbott and his staff passed on included, "Do not appear on streets in house slippers, boudoir caps and aprons. Don't allow your children to play in windows with dirty, greasy hands. Keep both your children and your windows presentable." And "Keep your business to yourselves. Wait until the proper time to talk, and talk to the proper person. If you happen to be arrested for some alleged misdemeanor, talk to a lawyer, or the judge: don't broadcast to the policeman and the neighbors—none of them can help you."[11] Abbott and company also offered migrants advice regarding the workplace. In "Take Heed and Make Good at Your Work," the *Defender* counseled its readers, "This is a new section of the country, living conditions you will find vastly different. Money will be made easier and temptations will, of course, become greater. This is not the biggest worry. The main thing is to [adapt] yourself to whatever line of work that you take up and make yourself proficient in that line. . . . Work with the sole idea to make yourself wanted and not to be cast aside when the tide changes."[12]

White southerners considered the *Defender*'s content subversive, and the paper was not sold in the South. Instead, it was carried along rail lines by Pullman porters and other railroad employees. Its dispersal in this manner was not serendipitous but rather appears to have been orchestrated by Abbott and his editorial staff. A regular column, "Railroad Rumblings by Jack," likely penned by Abbott himself, not only chronicled news and notes from the rails but included regular items such as, "The editor of the *Chicago Defender* congratulates the railroad men for the circulation of the *Chicago Defender* throughout the country. Keep it up boys, for old fifty and the *Defender* staff of writers are with you."[13] "Railroad Rumblings" also reminded readers of the paper's dedication to serving as what had come to be called a race business run by a race man—that is, an enterprise and an entrepreneur specifically dedicated to the well-being of African American consumers.

An item appearing in "Railroad Rumblings" on November 6, 1915, for example, reads, "The *Chicago Defender*'s staff of writers abounds in men who are superior to all temptation; whom nothing can divert from a steady pursuit of the interests of their race. We have our eyes open to their interest. We nourish them in our own thoughts for love of liberty[;] we hold them dear and true to all. It is our belief that the railroad men as well as others know that *The Chicago Defender* is the only fearless race paper published in the United States."[14] The item also admonished readers to subscribe. Such pieces served several functions. They informed potential migrants that the paper was presumably altruistic, maintaining that its only goal was their liberty and economic salvation in the North. Moreover, these words implied that the railroad men transporting the paper's vital messages were trustworthy. At the same time, these items took on the other entries in the growing pool of black newspapers and periodicals, which included the *Pittsburgh Courier*, the *Philadelphia Tribune*, and most particularly, the rival *Chicago Broad Ax*, emphasizing the *Defender*'s fearlessness.

And Abbott's *Defender*, a model for race businesses to come, was not the only publication advocating migration. *The Messenger*, founded in 1917 by A. Philip Randolph and Chandler Owen, was and continues to be generally associated with the Harlem Renaissance, which, like black baseball, would not have been possible without the Great Migration. Still, in the paper's early days, it, too, admonished its readers to leave the South, urging, "Fellow Negroes of the South, leave there. Go North, East, West—anywhere—to get out of that hell hole. There are better schools here for your children, higher wages for yourselves, votes, if you are 21, better housing, and more literacy. All is not rosy here, but it is a Paradise compared with Georgia, Arkansas, Texas, Mississippi, and Alabama. . . . Stop buying property in the South, to be burned down and run away from over night. Sell your stuff quietly, saying nothing to the Negro lackeys, and leave! Come into the land of at least incipient civilization."[15]

During the 1920s, *The Messenger* had influential black writers compose a series of articles about conditions for African Americans in each of the forty-eight states. Looking back in 1926, civil rights activist and African Methodist Episcopal minister Robert W. Bagnall Jr. represented African American Detroit as a haven, heaping on hyperbole in what had become a typical fashion for the times: "When the Migration came, Negroes poured forth into Detroit at the rate of 100 a day from all parts of the South. Jobs begged for men. Wages were sky-high. Labor was king. Night and day, the factories were kept at full speed. Money was plentiful, and the Negro got his full share. He saved money so that later, when unemployment came, it was found that his group was the last to ask for charity. He made good; established bank accounts and bought homes. He broke into semi-skilled and skilled work. The masses of him were followed by doctors, lawyers, and businessmen, and a great company of preachers. Negro Detroit jumped from 8,000 in 1914 to 85,000 in 1926, for Detroit became the Mecca of the Negro."[16] Indeed, the first wave of the Great Migration, touted as it was by Abbott's *Defender* and the *Messenger*, necessarily led to the establishment of black enclaves such as Bagnall's Detroit and Chicago's Bronzeville, among others, all of which became homes to teams in the incipient Negro Leagues.

New migrants might have followed Abbott's advice about dress, cleanliness, and comportment of children, but they did not heed his suggestion that they "not segregate yourselves by moving into districts populated wholly by the Race. Scatter out: select your homes according to your means and position, not according to color."[17] Of course, such self-segregation was often not a matter of choice. Few migrants had either the means or the position to obtain unfettered access to housing. And when they did, the majority were prevented from exercising this freedom by residential segregation ordinances imposed by a number of municipalities. Declared unconstitutional by the Supreme Court in 1917, municipal residential segregation ordinances were replaced by restrictive covenants on property. Restrictive covenants, which remained in place until the passage of the Fair Housing Act of 1968, were legal agreements by property owners, developers, and other real estate professionals not to sell or lease homes to potential residents not of a specified race and/or ethnicity. Covenants generally meant that only Caucasian Protestants were welcome.[18] Restrictive covenants affected members of a number of ethnic groups, leading to the establishment of urban America's many Little Italys and Chinatowns, but the covenants' control over availability of housing for African Americans was the most visible and the most intractable.

Thus, despite Abbott's well-meaning advice, migrants from the Mississippi Delta found themselves relocating to Chicago's Black Belt, which came to be known as Bronzeville in the 1920s.[19] Abutting the city's notorious Levee vice district, Bronzeville was home to more than fifty brothels (including the Everleigh Club, where heavyweight champion Jack Johnson took up with Belle Schreiber, a white prostitute, leading to his public downfall) as well as to pickpockets, rollers of drunks, and saloon keeper Mickey Finn. The Black Belt also bordered the Union Stock Yards, an area so polluted that the flow of the Chicago River had to be reversed in 1900 to save the water supply after repeated cholera, dysentery, and typhoid fever outbreaks. The area was also characterized by a lingering cloud of smoke belched out by the chimneys of its coal-burning factories, trains, and power plants.[20] In short, it was hardly Chicago's most desirable real estate. Undesirability was in many cases a salient feature of the soil in which the new African American enclave economies took root.

Though it was true of many of African America's new urban enclaves, not every black neighborhood was located in an environmental disaster zone. Harlem became the center of New York City's African American life as the result of the actions of an enterprising entrepreneur, Philip A. Payton Jr., founder of the Afro-American Realty Company. Formed in 1904, prior to the Great Migration, and capitalized with shares sold to the public at ten dollars each, Payton's real estate empire began with the purchase of five four-story buildings originally intended for occupation by upwardly mobile ethnic white New Yorkers. When they refused to pay exorbitant rents, however, African American migrants with few options for decent housing stepped in, often taking in lodgers to make the rent and leading to overcrowded conditions.[21] Although Payton's enterprise folded in 1907, the victim of recession as well as shady business practices, he laid the foundation for the creation of Harlem's African American economy. John E. Nail and Henry C. Parker, two black entrepreneurs involved in Payton's enterprise, followed in his footsteps during the migration, laying the groundwork for the growth of a large, cohesive community.[22] In Light and Gold's words, "The establishment of communal centers favored shops and professional offices, vital to the creation of an ethnic economy in geographic space."[23]

So why did certain migrants go to Bronzeville, others to Harlem, and still others to Kansas City's 18th and Vine district, to Detroit's Black Bottom, to North Philadelphia, or to Pittsburgh's Hill, among other areas? To a great extent, they followed jobs, rail lines, and kin, tending to end up in the same communities populated by their family, friends, and neighbors from back home. In this way, patterns of migration followed those of earlier generations of European immigrants. In New York City's notorious Five Points, for example, it was not unusual to find the ethnic makeup of residents differing from block to block, with contiguous tenements made up of immigrants from the same town in County Kerry or the same Polish shtetl. The same held true in the urban African American neighborhoods that welcomed southern migrants, though not always with open arms.

In their landmark study of Bronzeville, *Black Metropolis*, St. Clair Drake and Horace R. Cayton address the growth of the idea of community there and in other African American enclaves, writing, "The pattern of residential segregation inevitably gives rise to an intense community consciousness among Negroes. They begin to think in terms of gaining control of their own areas, and the struggle for this control is the dominant motif of economic and political action within Black Metropolis."[24] For all intents and purposes, these communities may be identified as what Light and Gold call "institutionalized ghettos," which "are characterized by an extensive degree of social organization and feature strong, independent social networks, personal responsibility for neighborhood problems and participation in voluntary and formal organizations."[25] Indeed, race businesses such as black baseball arose within these areas.

Baseball as Race Business

But defining black baseball, including the organized Negro Leagues, as purely a race business poses a problem. The majority of the founders of the first Negro National League—most specifically Rube Foster and C. I. Taylor—as well as the consumers who made up the league's fan base were African American. The industry, born in 1920 at Kansas City's Paseo YMCA, however, was never entirely black-owned and -operated. As Neil Lanctot observes in *Negro League Baseball: The Rise and Ruin of a Black*

Institution, black baseball regularly relied on infusions of white capital and with it white involvement.[26] The general assumption is that white involvement in the business of black baseball took the form of incursion by booking agents, such as the much-reviled Nat Strong and his sometime partner, H. Walter Schlichter. Strong not only promoted games but also owned the Brooklyn Royal Giants of the Eastern Colored League as well as Dexter Park, home of the white semi-professional Bushwicks. Dexter Park was also an oft-used Negro League venue near the border of Brooklyn and Queens. Strong routinely helped himself to a sizable cut of revenue from the ball clubs—black as well as white—that played there. Yet as is so often the case, the reality is much more complicated.

Writing specifically about Chicago's Bronzeville, Adam Green observes, "Classic mechanisms of migrant socialization, from machine politics to industrial welfare, mandated that virtually all manifestations of cultural and social life among Chicago's blacks carry some determinate sense of obligation to the surrounding population of white folk. . . . [E]ven in the dense cultural world of black music, the racial vector presumed to be impossible to eradicate in fact traced a dense web of interracial associations."[27] The same may be said of black baseball. The august Kansas City Monarchs, for example, one of the original teams in the Negro National League, were owned and operated by James Leslie Wilkinson. Wilkinson's partner, T. Y. Baird, brought on board in the early 1930s to finance the portable lighting system that helped keep the team alive during the depression, bought Wilkinson's share in 1948. Both men were white. So was Joe Tito, a bootlegger who with his brothers purchased Pennsylvania's Latrobe brewery during the waning days of Prohibition. Tito gave Gus Greenlee his start in the bootlegging business and later essentially functioned as his silent partner. Greenlee, who would emerge as a powerful numbers racketeer and entrepreneur, owned the Crawford Grill, a center of black Pittsburgh's nightlife, which served as a laundering facility for his profits. More significantly, he owned the Pittsburgh Crawfords, one of the few Negro League teams with control over its ballpark, however briefly. Nevertheless, taking into account white interests, whether predatory like those of Strong or cooperative like those of Wilkinson and Tito, Negro League baseball is conventionally termed a black business institution, born of segregation and aimed primarily at African Americans. To borrow from the language of the twenty-first-century marketplace, the Negro Leagues offered baseball "for us, by us."[28] As such, black baseball may still be seen as a vital component of the black enclave economy.

In a very real sense, Greenlee was an exemplar of the successful African American entrepreneur operating in the segregated economy. He had interests in a number of ventures—legal and illegal alike—and all of his businesses were closely intertwined. He certainly enjoyed a productive working partnership with Tito, himself a member of an ethnic group that had faced its fair share of discrimination and formed its own ethnic enclave economy. At the same time, Greenlee's public face was that of a race man, dedicated to promoting the interests of his fellow African Americans. Looking at Greenlee and his entrepreneurial cohort in this way, it seems appropriate to define the milieu in which they functioned—the web of black business of which baseball was an important nexus—as an African American economic ecosystem not only affected by the broader, seemingly exclusionary, mainstream economy but also a separate, functioning entity surviving in the shadow of the mainstream.

Even a cursory glance at Greenlee's empire, centered on Pittsburgh's Wylie Avenue ("Deep Wylie" to the readers of the *Pittsburgh Courier*), serves to point out another important feature of black baseball's role in the wider ecosystem. Black baseball, like white, organized baseball and indeed every other spectator sport, regardless of the race of its owners or the community from which it draws its fan base, is first and foremost part of the entertainment industry. Greenlee operated during the 1930s, but his entrepreneurial activities still serve as a case in point. "The transportation, leisure, and entertainment enterprises during the turn of the century," writes Walker, "were also a direct response to the era's climate of racial separation and exclusion. . . . In virtually every American city with a black population of sufficient size and enterprise, there was increasing construction of black hotels, theaters, and other buildings that provided space for black civic and cultural activities."[29] And in many ways, black baseball's fortunes may be seen as tied, though not inextricably, to those of the wider entertainment industry catering to African American consumers.

Professional black baseball was positioned as a "show" from the outset. Like the *Defender* and other exemplars of the black press, the black baseball industry depended on the patronage of communities built during the Great Migration and was rooted in the late-nineteenth- and early twentieth-century North and Midwest. As early as 1886, mainstream daily newspapers such as the *New York Times* ran advertisements under "Amusements" for "colored" baseball contests involving the Cuban Giants, the Gorhams, and other teams. It is instructive to note that black baseball's first chronicler, Sol White, felt it necessary to clarify that the Cuban Giants "were neither Cubans nor Giants, but thick-set and brawny colored men."[30] In the *Times*, the baseball ads were sandwiched between those for other spectacular amusements: "Imre Kirafly's latest, greatest, and supreme triumph, NERO: OR THE FALL OF ROME," and "Pain's 1666 GREAT FIRE OF LONDON" and "THE BIGGEST SHOW ON EARTH! America's Most Mighty Exhibition, BUFFALO BILL'S WILD WEST." In this regard, the Cuban Giants positioned themselves as a baseball enterprise "by us, for them," making them something of a marketing curiosity.[31] Observes Negro League historian Jerry Malloy, "In part, the Cuban Giants were successful because of this commerce between wealthy whites and ball-playing blacks. This mixture [consisted] of America's most and least favored classes." The Cuban Giants, the first professional black baseball club, were founded initially in 1885 by African American employees of the Argyle Hotel, a summer resort in Babylon on New York's Long Island, where they entertained guests. The team eventually chose a southern resort for its home base, moving in a direction opposite to the currents of the future Great Migration. Henry Morrison Flagler, Florida's original land baron, constructed the 540-room Ponce de Leon resort in St. Augustine in 1888. There and at the Royal Poinciana and Breakers in Palm Beach, other resorts in Flagler's empire, the Cuban Giants became the show for members of the "most favored classes."[32]

Another example of the use of early black baseball as a business decidedly "by us, for them" for the commercial purposes of attracting a white clientele is that of the Page Fence Giants. Formed by two white businessmen along with two nonwhite players, Grant "Home Run" Johnson and Bud Fowler, both of whom played in organized white baseball before the color line was drawn in 1883, the Page Fence Giants were little more than a traveling advertisement for the Page Wire Fence Company of rural Adrian, Michigan, and another sponsor, Monarch Bicycles. The team traveled throughout the Upper Midwest in a private Pullman coach bearing the fence company's name on its side, riding from the train to games on Monarch bikes and distributing trade cards, an ancestor of baseball bubble gum cards, to promote the sponsors' products.[33]

Pre-migration black baseball was an altogether different ball game from the vital industry that developed in response to demand from fans of color and became an important cog in the wheel of the African American ecosystem. "For them, by us" is clearly not the same thing as "for us, by us," and that distinction differentiates the game prior to the Great Migration from the game that emerged during that era. Nevertheless, recognizing the foundations of black baseball in the entertainment business is

important for a more complete understanding of the enterprise, exemplifying the cooperation between black and white entrepreneurs operating in
and around the black game.

Looking at the historic link between black baseball and more broadly
conceived traveling amusements connects barnstorming, a practice that
continued unabated from early black baseball until the demise of the
Negro Leagues, with that of another arm of the entertainment industry,
black vaudeville. Unlike the origins of black baseball or vaudeville, however, the origins of barnstorming remain obscure. According to various
accounts, barnstorming originally referred either to the practice by theatrical troupes of traveling from town to town in rural, nineteenth-century
America, and performing in barns or to campaign tactics by politicians
who held court in rural areas, orating while standing atop sawed-off trees,
quite literally making "stump speeches." But in the 1920s, the term came to
refer to the business of stunt pilots and flying circuses, often accompanied
by airplane salesmen, performing at county fairs and the like.[34] *Barnstorming*, in general terms, came to indicate any form of traveling entertainment
exhibition baseball. Even in its heyday, Negro League baseball depended
at least in part on barnstorming to capitalize its business.

Given the importance of both traveling black baseball and traveling
black vaudeville to the ecosystem established as a result of the Great
Migration, it is similarly instructive to look at the latter industry. Though
majority white-owned, the Theatre Owners Booking Association
(TOBA), colloquially known by the performers who labored therein as
"Tough on Black Asses," operated venues east of the Mississippi River—
North and South—that employed entertainers of color. As such, it fueled
constituent enterprises including hotels, rooming houses, restaurants,
gas stations, and saloons in much the same way that black baseball would.
Indeed, TOBA and its successor, the Chitlin' Circuit of musical and comedy venues, which counted African Americans among their most visible
owners, offered a counterpoint to the business of black baseball. This
industry also played an important role in the overarching story of black
entrepreneurship. So, too, did the race record business, which exposed
TOBA and Chitlin' Circuit artists to a wider audience. Indeed, later in
the twentieth century, the African American record industry, facing
many of the same obstacles as black baseball, not least among them the
blurring of the color line, forged a response that departed significantly
from that of the Negro Leagues.

Modernity and the New Negro

The growth of urban African America was fueled not only by the Great Migration but also by competing political philosophies. Contextualizing his subject's background in *Malcolm X: A Life of Reinvention*, Manning Marable writes,

> On the eve of America's entry into World War I, black American political culture was largely divided into two ideological camps: accommodationists and liberal reformers. Divisions in tactics, theory, and ultimate goals concerning race relations would persist through the century. Led by the conservative educator Booker T. Washington, the accommodationists accepted the reality of Jim Crow segregation and did not openly challenge black disenfranchisement, instead promoting the development of black-owned businesses, technical and agricultural schools, and land ownership. The reformers, chief among them the scholar W. E. B. Du Bois and the militant journalist William Monroe Trotter, called for full political and legal rights for black Americans, and ultimately the end of racial segregation itself.[35]

While Malcolm X lies beyond the scope of this work, Marable's explanation certainly applies to the earlier period. As he suggests, political ideology was hotly contested terrain at a time when the building of economic edifices such as black baseball, the Chitlin' Circuit, and other race enterprises remained a work in progress. Moreover, as Marable makes clear, the locus of this discourse lies in the collective words and works of Booker T. Washington.

Born a slave in 1856, Washington's story is the stuff of legend and inspiring children's books. As has often been recounted, he rose from an impoverished childhood to found the Tuskegee Normal and Industrial Institute in 1881 and to become what we would now call a motivational speaker. A firm believer in the notion that economic improvement, however limited, provided a barometer of success and therefore progress, Washington delivered a landmark address at the September 18, 1895, opening of the Cotton States and International Exhibition in Atlanta, one in a series of international exhibitions and World's Fairs that showcased capitalist economic progress. In what is commonly referred to as the Atlanta Compromise Speech, Washington proclaimed,

A ship lost at sea for many days suddenly sighted a friendly vessel. From the mast of the unfortunate vessel was seen the signal: "Water, water, we die of thirst." The answer from the friendly vessel at once came back, "Cast down your bucket where you are." . . . The captain of the distressed vessel, at last heeding the injunction, cast down his bucket and it came up full of fresh, sparkling water from the mouth of the Amazon River. To those of my race who depend on bettering their condition in a foreign land, or who underestimate the importance of cultivating friendly relations with the Southern white man who is their next door neighbor, I would say cast down your bucket where you are[;] cast it down in making friends in every manly way of the people of all races by whom we are surrounded.

Cast it down in agriculture, in mechanics, in commerce, in domestic service and in the professions. And in this connection it is well to bear in mind that whatever other sins the South may be called upon to bear, that when it comes to business pure and simple, it is in the South that the Negro is given a man's chance in the commercial world. . . .

. . . Our greatest danger is, that in the great leap from slavery to freedom we may overlook the fact that the masses of us are to live by the productions of our hands, and fail to keep in mind that we shall prosper in proportion as we learn to dignify and glorify common labor and put brains and skill into the common occupations of life. . . . No race can prosper till it learns that there is as much dignity in tilling a field as in writing a poem. It is at the bottom of life we must begin and not the top. Nor should we permit our grievances to overshadow our opportunities.

Washington concluded, "The wisest among my race understand that the agitation of questions of social equality is the [extremist] folly and that progress in the enjoyment of all the privileges that will come to us, must be the result of severe and [constant] struggle, rather than of artificial forcing. . . . It is important and right that all privileges of the law be ours, but it is vastly more important that we be prepared for the exercise of these privileges. The opportunity to earn a dollar in a factory just now is worth infinitely more than the opportunity to spend a dollar in an opera house."[36] Washington's "go slow" gospel of progress via economic success within the parameters of Jim Crow laid the groundwork for many of the businesses that comprised the urban African American ecosystem in the century to come. However, it also helped fuel the segregationist fire, leading the U.S. Supreme Court to uphold Louisiana's law requiring segregated railroad accommodations in an 1896 decision, *Plessy v. Ferguson*.

The law read, in part, "All railway companies carrying passengers in their coaches in this state, shall provide equal but separate accommodations for the white, and colored races, by providing two or more passenger coaches for each passenger train, or by dividing the passenger coaches by a partition so as to secure separate accommodations."[37] *Plessy* made "separate but equal" the law of the land. Both the intended and unintended consequences of Washington's Atlanta Compromise Speech would have a direct effect on the business of black baseball and the world in which it functioned. The speech became the baseline for how African Americans came to view their place in the larger economic picture.

To encourage the growth of black entrepreneurs willing to "cast down their buckets" where they were, Washington formed the National Negro Business League (NNBL) in 1900.[38] More often than not, those buckets were cast down in places such as Bronzeville, Harlem, the Hill, and 18th and Vine. And the NNBL provided support to the community-building businesses of these enclaves and others in urban African America. Several decades after its founder's death, the NNBL ultimately became one of the harshest critics of the black business establishment.

Equally storied, William Edward Burghardt Du Bois followed a path quite different from Washington. Du Bois was born in 1868 in Great Barrington, Massachusetts, and was educated at Fisk University and Harvard University. More importantly, he was also one of the founders of the National Association for the Advancement of Colored People (NAACP) in 1909. Once a supporter of Washington's ideas of progress, Du Bois broke intellectually with the Tuskegee founder, respectfully referring to him as "a compromiser between the South, the North, and the Negro."[39] The accommodationist rhetoric at the heart of the Atlanta Compromise Speech precipitated this rift. And in his landmark work, *The Souls of Black Folk*, Du Bois responded directly to Washington's appeal for accommodation:

> Mr. Washington represents in Negro thought the old attitude of adjustment and submission; but adjustment at such a peculiar time as to make his programme unique. This is an age of unusual economic development, and Mr. Washington's programme naturally takes an economic cast, becoming a gospel of Work and Money to such an extent as apparently almost completely to overshadow the higher aims of life. Moreover, this is an age when the more advanced races are coming in closer contact with the less developed races, and the race-feeling is therefore intensified; and Mr. Washington's programme practically accepts the alleged inferiority of the Negro races.[40]

Du Bois went on to ask, "Is it possible, and probable, that nine millions of men can make effective progress in economic lines if they are deprived of political rights, made a servile caste, and allowed only the most meagre chance for developing their exceptional men? If history and reason give any distinct answer to these questions, it is an emphatic NO."[41] Moreover, he argued, "We have no right to sit silently by while the inevitable seeds are sown for a harvest of disaster to our children, black and white."[42] Du Bois took the position that anything less than full enfranchisement and integration was unacceptable.

However, as Marable suggests, the ideas espoused by black nationalist Marcus Garvey, the founder of the Universal Negro Improvement Association (UNIA), stem not from Du Bois's line of reasoning but from Washington's. Garvey's calls for African American self-reliance had a considerable effect on the business of the black ecosystem, so the idea that they originated with Washington is somewhat unexpected. According to Marable,

> Central to Garvey's appeal were his enthusiastic embrace of capitalism and his gospel of success; self-mastery, willpower, and hard work would provide the steps to lift black Americans. "Be not deceived," he told his followers, "wealth is strength, wealth is power, wealth is influence, wealth is justice, is liberty, is real human rights." The purpose of the African Communities League was to set up, in his words, "commercial houses, distributing houses, and also to engage in business of all kinds, wholesale and retail." Starting in Harlem, the league opened grocery stores and restaurants, and even financed the purchase of a steam laundry. In 1920, Garvey Incorporated the Negro Factories Corporation to supervise the movement's growing list of businesses. His best-known and most controversial start-up, however, was the Black Star Line, a steamship company backed by tens of thousands of blacks who bought five- and ten-dollar shares. Ironically, all this activity depended on the existence of *de facto* racial segregation, which limited competition from white businesses, all of which refused to invest in urban ghettos.[43]

Research has yet to find that any of black baseball's entrepreneurs were members of UNIA, nor was UNIA one of the fraternal organizations that fronted a baseball team. But the owners who went on to form the Negro National League (NNL) in 1920, like Garvey and his followers—indeed, like the virulently anti-Garvey Du Bois himself—might be seen as what Alain Locke in 1925 called the "New Negro." In fact, Locke's edited book of that title, originally published that year, remains one of the central texts of the Harlem Renaissance.

Locke's New Negro is characterized by "the belief in the efficacy of collective effort, in race co-operation. This deep feeling of race is at present the mainspring of Negro life. It seems to be the outcome of the reaction to proscription and prejudice; an attempt, fairly successful on the whole, to convert a defensive into an offensive position, a handicap into an incentive."[44] Cultural critic Gerald Early suggests that in addition to its importance in the Harlem Renaissance, Pan-Africanism as preached by Garvey may also be seen as one component of the New Negro movement. Early cites as another component

> the rise of a new racial entrepreneurism exemplified by the founding of the Negro baseball leagues by Rube Foster, the hair care products of Madam C. J. Walker and Annie Malone, and Marcus Garvey's ill-fated Black Star Line. Clearly, these last activities indicate that if some members of the black elite were interested in attracting white philanthropy, other blacks were trying to devise economic schemes that would free the race of white support. In this sense, the New Negro Movement was a new phase of the institution-building and collective identity-construction work that marked African American endeavors since the end of the Civil War, a phase where blacks began to throw off the shackles of both a shallow Victorian-oriented sense of virtue (although most of Garvey's grander ideas were strictly inspired by Victorianism) and an isolated rural folk-life that constrained as much as it enabled.[45]

Negro League entrepreneurs thus positioned themselves as race men and women, outwardly bucking against white support. In this respect, the members of the NNL cohort were indeed New Negros. Nevertheless, faced with the realities of doing business behind a color line under circumstances in which their access to operating capital was habitually limited, they often depended on white support more than they would admit out loud. Still, central to Locke's idea of the New Negro is the notion of black solidarity, of community building in the wider sense. In this regard, Garvey's separatism and Du Bois's integrationism would seem to be clearly at odds. And in many ways they were.

So where do black baseball's entrepreneurs fall on this spectrum? As American culture has come to imagine, sports build community, and participation in baseball, America's iconic sport, whether as a player, an owner, or a fan, helps the participant self-identify as a participant in

America.[46] In the case of the Negro Leagues, participation reinforced the idea of what it meant to be an American under the thumb of Jim Crow, perhaps leading to some sense of solidarity.

There is, however, another way to look at the position of black baseball's owners as well as many of the African American ecosystem's other entrepreneurs. In a 1947 essay in *Survey Graphic* magazine entitled "Human, All Too Human," sociologist E. Franklin Frazier wrote, "The segregated community, which is essentially a pathological phenomenon in American life, has given certain Negroes a vested interest in segregation—involving more than dollars and cents considerations."[47] But is it possible to suggest that black baseball's entrepreneurs, proprietors of a business that was integral to the segregated African American ecosystem, somehow maintained a vested interest in segregation? Or were they true race men and women, New Negroes and their offspring, dedicated to the improvement of the quality of life in segregated urban African America? Did they, like the *Chicago Defender*'s Abbott and other representatives of the black press, come down firmly on the side of integration, or were they in their own way adherents to Washington's admonition to "cast down their buckets" where they were, staying behind the color line? An examination of the Negro Leagues and their role in the larger African American ecosystem addresses these and even more substantive questions.

The Book

This project is not intended as a comprehensive study of Negro League baseball. Rather, it is an attempt to contextualize the business of black baseball as well as to examine its role as a bellwether for the fate of the segregated dollar from the establishment of the large urban communities fed by the Great Migration to the dawn of the civil rights movement. Baseball as played between the lines is secondary to this work. For all the game's romance and importance as an American institution, it remains primarily in the background, while the clicking of the turnstiles is foregrounded. Of nearly equal importance are the industries that are either directly or indirectly informed and affected by the ebb and flow of Negro League baseball as well as contrasting enterprises. Other businesses—elsewhere in the entertainment world, in publishing, or in finance—complete a critical view of race sport and the desegregation narrative.

The chapters that follow explore in great detail the relationships between Negro League baseball and the African American ecosystem against the backdrop of the larger mainstream economic machinery. Accordingly, this work has been organized chronologically to present the Negro League story as it relates to broader socioeconomic and cultural trends in a historically coherent fashion. Chapter 1 offers an overview of the project as a whole, exploring in particular some of the theoretical underpinnings of this study while providing a brief introduction to some of the central places and personalities that drive this narrative. It also places the business of black baseball firmly in the context of the Great Migration, without which this enterprise could never have come to fruition.

Chapter 2 traces the early history of the first organized Negro Leagues as a product of the migration in progress. It also introduces the major urban centers that were the primary recipients of the migration's demographic shift. As the influx of migrants infused new cultural forms into existing communities, these communities changed inexorably. The response was an expansion of the existing economies that brought a palpable vibrancy. This chapter considers the ways in which changing populations informed and affected the development of these local economies.

Chapter 3 focuses on the particular effects of the Great Depression on the organization of the Negro Leagues as well as on the African American ecosystem as a whole. This chapter also explores the emergence of Pittsburgh as a major force in the revival of Negro League baseball following the collapse of the original leagues and looks at the challenges of reconstructing black baseball during the heart of the worldwide economic malaise, which disproportionately affected African America.

Chapter 4 takes a broad-based approach to the business of black baseball by looking specifically at the war years, with particular attention to the challenges posed by wartime business restrictions. It also considers the ways in which the music industry responded to similar challenges. Additionally, this chapter chronicles the evolving antagonisms between black baseball's entrepreneurs and the white, presumably Jewish, booking agents and others considered by some observers as interlopers with potentially sinister intent. It concludes with a brief outline of the role of the Ives-Quinn Anti-Discrimination Act of 1945 and its place in the breaching of Major League Baseball's color line.

Chapter 5 centers on the breaching of this color line in Major League Baseball. It focuses primarily on the changing landscape wrought by the end of World War II, specifically tracing the ways in which increasing calls for civic engagement combined with shifting demographic patterns and the commercial introduction of technologies pioneered during the war that altered the course of race relations and their implications for race business. Particularly important here is the theoretical work found in Gunnar Myrdal's *An American Dilemma*, which attempts to explain in part the vicissitudes of attempts by African American entrepreneurs to effect social change via economic advancement. This chapter contrasts the traditional, insular model of race business, which focused solely on the segregated dollar, with a new model that was developed by an increasingly enfranchised population looking to compete within the mainstream.

Chapter 6 examines the aftermath of the desegregation of the Major Leagues, a development that stripped black baseball of both its stars and its fan base. Moreover, the chapter traces the disintegration of the organized Negro Leagues, once a major player in the African American economy to a peripheral position as a small-scale disorganized barnstorming operation. In so doing, the chapter considers the lengths to which the remaining owners were forced to go to keep their enterprises alive, resorting not only to the divestment of their most important resources, their talent, but to engaging in novelty performance that had previously been considered below the venture's once-lofty standards. Of particular interest is way in which the gradual demise of black baseball served as a bellwether for other race industries, most specifically those in the hospitality and entertainment sectors.

As a means of contrast, Chapter 6 concludes with a brief exploration of the Chitlin' Circuit, a business built on a model that at first blush closely resembles Negro League baseball but that continued, by virtue of a new business model and the exploitation of technological advances, to function as an important node in the African American ecosystem long after the demise of the race sport. Finally, the chapter examines why businesses with a vested interest in segregation could not survive in a changing world.

Finally, to bring these matters into a contemporary context, the postscript offers a brief examination of the state of African American entrepreneurship, especially as it pertains to sports and entertainment. The chapter draws a straight line between those entrepreneurs who fired the economic engines of the ecosystem during the Great Migration and a generation of entrepreneurs who, in their own way, moved beyond the narrow confines of the race dollar and entered the main currents of the American economy.

A Note on Primary Source Material

For the most part, this research is based on articles, columns, and editorials printed in the black weeklies as well as other outlets in the broader African American press, such as *The Crisis*, *The Messenger*, and *Ebony*. The traditional black press, itself a series of business enterprises forced to operate with limited resources, often had to make due with small staffs and at times increasingly counterproductive cost-cutting measures. As a result, copyediting and proofreading frequently suffered at the expense of content. Thus, quoted material frequently includes grammatical and syntactical errors as well as inconsistent and occasionally misplaced or altogether missing punctuation. While distracting at times, these errors have been left intact for the sake of tone and accuracy.

2

Capitalizing Black Baseball and the African American Economic Ecosystem, 1914–1929

Introduction

On February 13 through 14, 1920, a cabal of baseball entrepreneurs and journalists convened at the Paseo YMCA, just one block away from the crossroads of African American Kansas City at 18th and Vine. At the urging of Robert S. Abbott's *Chicago Defender*, Chicago's Andrew "Rube" Foster and Indianapolis's C. I. Taylor were joined by representatives from Detroit and St. Louis as well as from the host city to form "a circuit for the season of 1921." "One of the big surprises of the first day's meeting," noted the *Defender*, whose "sporting editor," Cary B. Lewis, was elected secretary, "was when 'Rube' Foster uncovered the fact that he had a charter, incorporated, for a National Negro Ball League." Indeed, the revelation that the league was already incorporated in Illinois, Michigan, Ohio, Pennsylvania, New York, and Maryland "dumbfounded" those present despite the fact that the idea of the league had been some time in coming.[1] So was born the initial Negro National League (NNL), the first of what would collectively come to be known as the Negro Leagues. The largely midwestern circuit got its first official rival in 1923 with the creation of the Mutual Association of Eastern Colored Clubs, more commonly known as the Eastern Colored League (ECL). The ECL was spearheaded by Philadelphia's Edward Bolden, whose "race corporation," according to the *New York Amsterdam News*, might be "held up as a beacon of light to other

24

organizations all over the country."[2] Bolden's Darby, Pennsylvania, club was joined by teams from Brooklyn, Manhattan, Baltimore, and Atlantic City, soon to be followed by franchises from Harrisburg, Pennsylvania; Washington, D.C.; Newark, New Jersey; and Pittsburgh. In coming years, the NNL would welcome its own series of teams from Pittsburgh as well as clubs from Cleveland and other urban centers in Ohio, in addition to a southern contingent featuring teams from Birmingham, Memphis, Nashville. Milwaukee and Louisville also entered the league, albeit briefly.

Independent black baseball teams whose fans were predominantly people of color had operated in these and other locations even before the onset of the Great Migration. In fact, notably missing from this iteration of organized Negro baseball were Pittsburgh's Homestead Grays, which later became one of the stalwarts of black baseball but at the time chose to remain unaffiliated. Given the relative success of independent black baseball to date, what led the *Defender*, the African American paper of record, to call for the teams to organize? What led Foster and Taylor to convene the Kansas City meeting and Bolden to follow in their footsteps? More significantly, what interest did baseball's entrepreneurs and sports journalists have in creating a circuit made up of teams from these specific locations? The answers may be found in the locations themselves. From the start of the Great Migration to the onset of the Great Depression, the highs and lows of the black urban economy were exemplified by the shifting fortunes of the business of black baseball. In these urban centers, vibrant communities arose, complete with business districts that shadowed the mainstream economy in multiple ways.

Chicago

It is no surprise that the *Chicago Defender* spearheaded the Kansas City meeting and the resulting league or that Rube Foster was involved. After all, the *Defender* originated in one of the central hubs—if not *the* central hub—of the Great Migration, and Abbott's newspaper as well as Abbott himself were right there in the thick of things, publicizing the availability of employment and encouraging the migrants. "Chicago," sociologist Charles S. Johnson observed, "is in more than one sense the colored capital and every sense the top of the world of the bruised, crushed, and thwarted manhood of the south."[3] "One can make money in Chicago. This is its most respectable attraction," observed Johnson. In "Illinois: Mecca of the Migrant Mob," published in *The Messenger* in 1923, Johnson, concealing neither his concern nor his admiration for Chicago, continued, "No one escapes Chicago without an impression of State Street in the second ward. Tawdry stretches of brick and frame decrepitude, leaning in rather discordant obliquity, here and there snapped into order by the rigidly erect lines of a new building. Crowds—almost static crowds—a rich but impossible mixture. Each strain of this enforced homogeneity must set up its own antitoxin to indifference, for 'the stroll' appeals—in motley indiscriminateness to the Negro in Chicago."[4] Regardless of his assessment of this "rich but impossible mixture" and his propensity for linguistic gymnastics, Johnson was certainly right about the crowds. The African American population of Chicago and surrounding Cook County skyrocketed from 46,627 in 1910 to 115,238 ten years later.[5] "In a slice of city between nineteen blocks live 92,000 of them, nauseated by the stench of the stockyards on the west and revived again by the refreshing breeze off Lake Michigan in the east," Johnson could not help but editorialize.[6] Given the demographic shift, which resulted primarily from the mass influx of migrants who were generally underserved or downright ignored by Chicago's mainstream economy, an entrepreneurial spirit arose, and those it inspired sought to fill the holes left by mainstream businesses.

The "progress" of Chicago's Black Belt, Bronzeville—its "black metropolis," in the words of sociologists St. Clair Drake and Horace Cayton—"spread along the once fashionable South Parkway and Michigan Boulevard, closing up the pocket which existed in 1920 . . . taking over the stone-front houses and the apartments, buying the large church edifices and opening smaller churches in houses and stores, establishing businesses, and building a political machine as they went."[7] Of this rapidly growing ecosystem, Johnson wrote, "Here is the home of the world's greatest weekly with a circulation of more than 100,000 and a plant valued at as many dollars, the Liberty Life Insurance Company, with 3,500,000 worth of insurance in force after two years work, the only such institution in the North; two banks, two hospitals, 200 churches ranging from the air-tight storefronts of the illiterate cults, dissenters and transplanted southern churches, to the imposing structure of the Olivet Baptist Church, with a membership of ten thousand, and 1,800 business establishments varying in size from nondescript fly-traps called restaurants to the dignified Overton building."[8]

But the roots of Drake and Cayton's black metropolis as well as of the economy that made Foster's Chicago American Giants and the Negro

National League a reality extend back before the Great Migration to aspiring black entrepreneurship in the Levee, the city's most infamous vice district, from the late nineteenth century until Progressive Era reforms resulted in its cleanup in 1912.[9] Located on the Near South Side, the Levee housed high- and low-class brothels, gaming houses, and constituent businesses that catered to those engaged in local commerce and their clients. The Levee was also the seat of power of the First Ward Democratic machine of Bathhouse John Coughlin and Michael "Hinky Dink" McKenna, who provided protection for Levee entrepreneurs, essentially shielding them from legal action—at a price.[10] Among the African American businessmen and -women who set up shop in the city's wide-open vice district was an early migrant, Sam Young, a riverboat gambler from Alabama, whose two guiding passions were baseball and games of chance. "Policy Sam," as he came to be known based on his most successful enterprise, the policy rackets, enjoyed the financial backing of Italian immigrant Julius Benvenuti, thereby demonstrating an established pattern of mixed-race enterprises operating in predominantly black neighborhoods, a model that would extend to the Negro Leagues as well.[11]

Policy and its close analogue, the numbers, were illegal lotteries with similarly murky origins. According to one theory, policy, the older of the two, was originally a type of gambling insurance. Bettors on lotteries would make secondary wagers in the hopes that one would hit, hence the name, *policy*. Another version suggests that the name *policy* came from the occasional practice by African Americans of betting their insurance money. According to Ron Chepesiuk, in policy, "seventy-eight numbers . . . are wrapped in special containers and dropped in a drum-shaped receptacle or 'wheel,' from which numbers are drawn. The player selects a certain amount of numbers, the most common being three numbers, or a 'gig,' betting that the combination of numbers he has chosen will 'fall,' or win, in the next drawing."[12]

From the late nineteenth century until the 1940s, policy was the dominant game among urban blacks as well as working-class whites. Numbers, in contrast, were reputed to have come from the West Indies to Harlem, possibly imported by Carlos Duran, an operator from the Dominican Republic known as "Dominique" to the Harlemites with whom he did business. In this variant, a gig bettor wagers on three digits, 000 to 999. The house, or bank, derives its results not from a wheel but rather from some prearranged number that would be published in local newspapers, such as bank clearinghouse totals or the New York Stock Exchange numbers. Winning numbers were also occasionally generated based on Major League Baseball scores. With payoffs as high as six hundred to one on bets as low as a penny, it is easy to see why playing policy and the numbers appealed to their core constituencies.[13] Regardless of origins or rules, such illegal lotteries were big business, fueling the economic engines of urban African American ecosystems nationwide.

From the outside looking in, these rackets had the appearance of run-of-the-mill criminal enterprises. But on the inside, they functioned as neighborhood savings and loans, credit unions, and investment banks. In essence, they acted practically as the community's Small Business Administration at a time and place when such agencies did not exist. Writes Juliet E. K. Walker, "What is especially significant in 20th century black business history is the extent to which the informal, often illegal, business activities, including policy, provided venture capital for the establishment of many legitimate black enterprises. Some notable black entrepreneurs built legitimate businesses on profits made from enterprises considered less than reputable."[14] Indeed, numbers and policy banks filled the space created when mainstream banks refused to extend credit to African Americans.

On a more local level, as in Chicago, policy and the numbers also worked to support local businesses including saloons, barbershops, beauty parlors, pool halls, drugstores, and cigar shops. In these establishments as well as other dedicated facilities, bettors made their wagers, at the same time patronizing the small businesses. In this way, the informal economy of the rackets supported formal economic activity in African American ecosystems.

Policy Sam laid the foundations of the gambling and saloon businesses on which his protégé, John "Mushmouth" Johnson, built. Johnson's operations were so prominent that they even caught the attention of the mainstream press. The *Chicago Tribune*, for example, covered Johnson's base of operations in a June 1897 article headlined, "Games on the 'Levee' Wide Open. Crowds Fill 'Mushmouth' Johnson's State Street Dive." The paper claimed that "the doors leading to his gambling-house were wide open, and not even a 'lookout' was on hand to scan the faces of the visitors. In the place were 200 men."[15] Johnson's State Street "resort" is also mentioned in a *Tribune* article cataloging Chicago's most notable or notorious gambling houses—depending on one's perspective—as home to a variety of games of chance, most particularly craps as well as draw and stud poker.[16] Interestingly, the second article does not mention Johnson's race, though his nickname, Mushmouth, was a period term that would have indicated his status as African American.[17]

That a person of color owned a gambling institution in the Levee is not at all surprising. It was, after all, the Midwest's preeminent mixed-race vice district. Nor would it have been unusual for Johnson to have been the proprietor of a nightclub. In fact, his Dreamland Ballroom on South State Street, later renamed the Dreamland Cafe, was one of the central nodes of Bronzeville's music scene.[18] Rather, it is Johnson's social circle and his business associations that warrant attention. The key to Johnson's importance as a nexus in the web that would become Chicago's Black Belt ecosystem may be found in a wedding announcement in the *Defender*, important enough to have been published on the paper's front page with the headline, "Binga-Johnson Wedding the Most Brilliant Ever Held in Chicago." Why was this front page news? The groom, Jesse Binga, was the Black Belt's leading entrepreneur, while the bride, Eudora Johnson, was Mushmouth Johnson's sister.[19]

Binga was a migrant not from the South but from Detroit via Pocatello, Idaho, and points west, where he made a significant profits via land speculation. In the 1890s, Binga opened a real estate office on South State Street. Like Philip A. Payton Jr. in Harlem, Binga rented apartments to new migrants in what was then a racially mixed neighborhood, developing a reputation as a pioneer.[20] And like Payton, Binga exploited a housing glut, in this case owing to the abandonment of the neighborhood in the wake of the departure of the builders and staff of the 1893 World's Columbian Exhibition.[21] More importantly, in 1908, the real estate mogul opened the eponymous Binga State Bank on South State Street, helping to anchor the Black Belt's business district. At the time, the Binga Bank was the only one of America's approximately ten "race banks," as the *Defender* called them, located above the Mason-Dixon Line. "This is due to the fact that Illinois gives the colored man a better show than all the other Northern states," boasted the *Defender*. "The average young man here is buying more property in Chicago than in any other northern city."[22] Abbott was a member of the board of directors of Binga's bank. Although the wedding took place a year after Mushmouth Johnson's death, it was indeed Johnson's own fortune that allowed Eudora Binga to cement her place among Chicago's African American nouveau riche, while her social connections benefited her husband equally.

Johnson's place in the gambling rackets was subsequently filled by his own protégés, Robert T. Motts and Henry Teenan Jones. "Both Jones and

Motts," writes Cynthia M. Blair, "gained considerable notoriety and wealth as proprietors of both legitimate and illegal recreational enterprises. Establishments such as these provided jobs for black men who, like women, sought alternatives to low-paying, menial employment. For the black working men who frequented their back rooms, these and other gambling saloons held out the remote possibility of multiplying—and the less remote possibility of losing—the slim pay earned in the wage economy."[23]

Blair also points to another vital business that contributed to the African American ecosystem both immediately before and during the Great Migration, as it has to virtually every other economy: "Prostitution, like gambling, catered to the recreational needs of men. It rivaled gambling as one of the largest and perhaps the most visible sector of the urban informal economy. Unlike gambling, however, the sex trade offered a steady stream of jobs to women."[24] To point out the connections that swirled around operators like Johnson, Motts, and Jones, whose work centered on such areas of the informal economy, and players in the formal economy such as Binga, does not diminish Binga's contributions in any way but instead emphasizes the linkages between the two economies as inextricable parts of the same ecosystem. And as in all ecosystems, one part could not exist without the other.

Saloon keepers and gamblers such as Johnson, Motts, and Jones also played pivotal roles in the formal economic life of the Black Belt. Motts, for example, was the proprietor of Chicago's preeminent black theater, the Pekin. Billed as the "Only Negro Theater in the World," the Pekin featured vaudeville, ragtime music, and cakewalks.[25] Unlike shows promoted by the Theatre Owners Booking Association (TOBA), the Pekin presented black entertainment "for us, by us."

Motts died in 1911 and was succeeded by Jones as both Bronzeville's gambling kingpin and a legitimate businessman in the entertainment field. Jones owned and operated several nightclubs and cabarets, most notably the Elite No. 1 and the Elite No. 2. With the Great Migration well under way in 1915, the *Defender* went out of its way to remind new Chicagoans that it was in their best interest to buy black. One article written by "The Wise Old Owl" singled out Jones's Elite clubs, along with several other entertainment ventures, as "cafes of the highest class, and . . . places that any self-respecting person can visit with the full consciousness that the goods, treatment and service equals any to be found anywhere."[26] Of course, among those offering high-class services at the Elite clubs, as Blair makes clear, were Bronzeville's prostitutes.[27]

Negro ball was an intimate part of this economic whirl. Even before the Great Migration truly got under way, Jones partnered with Frank Leland, who would remain a force in the nascent world of Chicago black baseball, to organize the first semiprofessional team of color, the Chicago Unions, and Jones later helped to capitalize Foster's Chicago American Giants.[28] To be sure, Foster and his teammates were also patrons of Jones's establishments: In 1915, a small item in the *Defender*, publicizing what would now be called the team's "welcome home dinner," subtly points to the interconnectedness of the different tendrils of the Black Belt's entertainment scene, noting that following the opening game, the team would be feted at the Elite No. 2. The list of dignitaries expected to be in attendance included not only John M. Schorling, the white owner of the park where the American Giants played, and "other local celebrities" but also Jones, described as president of the City League.[29] The league routinely featured the type of high-level semiprofessional play, regardless of color, characterized by Foster's team.

The tightly woven web that was Bronzeville's business world was constantly expanding. In 1919, Chicago experienced a devastating race riot. According to a study that attempted to find a cause for it, the riot was partially the result of the rapidly expanding black community's perceived encroachment on neighborhoods and facilities formerly considered to be the territory of resentful white ethnics and partially as a result of the postwar labor glut. According the study, the number of African American business enterprises in the Black Belt "increased from 1,200 in 1919 to 1,500 in 1920," with "651 [such businesses] on State Street, the main thoroughfare, 549 on principal cross streets, and more than 300 on other streets." Moreover, the boundaries of Bronzeville were also spreading: "On Cottage Grove Avenue, Negroes have only recently established themselves in large numbers, yet between Twenty-eight and Forty-fifth streets there are fifty-seven Negro business places, including nine groceries, three drug-stores, and two undertaking establishments."[30] These enterprises included Chicago's first African American insurance company, Liberty Life (later known as Supreme Liberty Life as a result of a merger on the eve of the Great Depression), a well-capitalized and well-run venture that remained solvent until 1962. Additionally, two South Side representatives of the black press, the *Broad Ax* and the *Bee*, joined the *Defender* in spreading news of interest to Chicago's African Americans. Explains economist Robert C. Puth, "From 1910 to 1920, the proportion of Chicago Negroes employed in manufacturing rose from 17 per cent to 45 per cent, while the Negro population more than doubled. The chief sources of industrial employment were food processing (especially the stockyards), iron foundries, mail-order houses, and the railroads."[31] While hardly afflu-ent, the new migrants had some disposable income to spend on entertain-ment.[32] It is, therefore, easy to see that Chicago's role as the prime mover in the formation of the original Negro National League was fueled in large part by the economic machinery that powered Chicago's Black Belt.

Given Chicago's status as the city with the second-largest African Amer-ican population and its central role in the Great Migration both intellectu-ally as the home of the *Defender* and demographically as the destination of many former southerners, it is no surprise that Rube Foster and the Windy City cohort motivated the NNL's foundation. And yet, for all of Chicago's emergent dominance, Kansas City held the distinction of hosting the meet-ing that gave organized black baseball its structure and its charter.

Kansas City

Although the importance of the Kansas City Monarchs to the collective history of black baseball—most specifically the Negro Leagues—cannot be overlooked, the team was a Johnny-come-lately compared to Foster's American Giants. The Monarchs were not formed until 1919, specifically responding to the need for a team in Kansas City. The Monarchs repre-sented J. L. Wilkinson's first foray into black baseball, though not his first experience with the sport or his first venture involving players of color. Wilkinson was first employed by a Bloomer Girl outfit as both a promoter and a player who even appeared in drag, as more than one young man did. In 1912, he became owner of the All-Nations team, a genuinely integrated barnstorming club, and three years later, he set up shop in Kansas City, capitalizing on the potential popularity that a racially mixed team would have with the city's growing African American population.[33] Thus, despite the fact that he was not a person of color, his proven management skills and his knowledge of the marketplace seem to have made him the most likely candidate to back a Kansas City franchise.

During the Great Migration, Kansas City's black population, like that of the other cities with teams in the NNL and the ECL, certainly grew. But Kansas City's African American population did not spike between 1910 and 1920. Rather, it grew more steadily, increasing by one-third not only during this period but also during the preceding decade. In fact, significant black migration to Kansas City started in the years following the Civil War and continued through the Great Migration's second wave during and after World War II.[34]

To fully understand the development of Kansas City's African American ecosystem and hence its vital role in Negro baseball, it is useful to look at migration patterns prior to 1910. The first major influx of African Americans arrived in Kansas City from rural Mississippi and Louisiana in the aftermath of Reconstruction. Known as the "Exodusters," an estimated six or seven thousand headed to Kansas, which they perceived to be the Promised Land, hoping to substitute homesteading for sharecropping. The majority of these migrants made it as far as Wyandotte County, near Kansas City. Although some went on to join colonies founded by the self-proclaimed "Father of the Exodus," Benjamin "Pap" Singleton, others chose to stay, many on the Missouri side, thereby anchoring black Kansas City.[35] With a meatpacking industry second in size only to Chicago's and a position as a rail hub combined with the city's proximity to both the cattle ranches and hog markets of the West, Kansas City boomed. By the late 1880s, packinghouses and processing plants were major area employers, and they began to hire people of color almost immediately, unlike Chicago, where the industry did not employ great numbers of African Americans until the Great Migration.[36] "Although to an outside middle-class observer," writes Charles E. Coulter, "the work performed in the packinghouses was demeaning, it is important to remember that for many African Americans in Kansas City, the wages paid by Armour, Wilson, and others were a step toward a better future."[37] So, too, was work on the railroads and even domestic labor. As is generally the case, where there is employment, there is migration. And where there are migrants, there is usually a migrant community and a migrant economy to serve its needs. This was certainly true between 1900 and 1920 in Kansas City, where businesses catering to African Americans were clustered in two areas—around 12th Street, along Woodland and Vine, and on 18th Street, along the Paseo, and Highland, Vine, and Woodland Avenues.[38] "There are in Kansas City Missouri," wrote Asa Earl Martin in *Our Negro Population: A Sociological Study of the Negroes of Kansas City* (1913),

> four well-equipped Negro drugstores, with a stock valued at $27,500; they are doing an annual business of $57,500. Three of these stores have been in operation eight years. There are four undertaking and embalming establishments, doing an annual business of $600,000; one shoe store, one dry goods

store, about twenty-five pressing and cleaning establishments, seven saloons, eighty-five tailor shops, seventy-five pool-halls, two newspapers, and numerous restaurants, all doing an annual business of about $35,000.

The Negro is just entering the business world as a competitor for the trade of his own people, and thus far he has made a creditable showing. He is fast winning the confidence of his own race, which must be done before he can hope to receive the recognition of the white man.[39]

Black Kansas City's growing business district was served by three newspapers, the *Call*, the *Sun*, and the *American*. The *Call* and the *Sun* were edited by progressive-minded Republican race men, Chester A. Franklin and Nelson Crews, respectively.[40] The *Kansas City American*, in contrast, was founded by Felix H. Payne, who was also among the most successful businessmen in Kansas City's black music scene. His ventures also included nightclubs, and he and fellow entrepreneurs Piney Brown and Ellis Burton functioned as godfathers to local musicians, providing jobs and financial assistance.[41] Payne also dabbled in black baseball in 1909 as the owner of the Kansas City (Kansas) Giants.[42] Like Chicago's Henry Teenan Jones, Payne made his fortune in the numbers rackets, thereby straddling the line between the formal and informal economies of Kansas City's African American ecosystem.[43] At the same time that he was profiting from the rackets and underground nightclubs, he served on the board of directors of the Wheatley-Provident Hospital, Kansas City's first major black-controlled medical facility.

As might be expected of an important figure in the press, Payne wielded a great deal of political power as the major African American voice in Kansas City's Democratic machine, run by its kingpin, Tom Pendergast. A major player in that machine, Payne operated rather freely in both the formal and informal spheres from the first decade of the twentieth century until 1939, when Pendergast was imprisoned at Leavenworth for tax evasion. That the Pendergast machine ran operations in black Kansas City throughout its reign is not surprising. Unlike urban America's other major political machines, most notably New York's Tammany Hall and later Chicago's Kelly-Nash machine, the Pendergast operation did not depend entirely on support from immigrant or migrant communities but drew heavily from white middle-class constituents as well as African American voters. According to Lyle W. Dorset,

By the 1920s, Pendergast had gained the support of even more of the colored community by throwing his organization behind a Negro who was opposed by a white Democrat. Some of the Negro workers in the organization rallied support to the machine by reminding the voters that Negroes were given many jobs by the party. The editor of another local Negro newspaper felt that a debt of gratitude was owed to Pendergast for finding jobs for Negroes, who represented "a segment of the state's population small in number and influence." The jobs that the Democratic chieftain got for members of the Negro community were diverse. There were the caretaker jobs, of course; but as soon as the machine gained control of the city government in 1926, two Negro physicians were given posts in the city's colored hospital and in the Health Department.[44]

As the mouthpiece for black Democratic Kansas City and as a nightclub owner, Payne had significant connections to Pendergast and his cronies. Although Kansas City's African American ecosystem developed outside a mainstream economy that did not serve the black community's needs, it was never independent of the mainstream. While this was true of most black, urban economies, it was particularly evident in Kansas City, where Boss Pendergast's fingerprints appeared all over enterprises large and small.

Befitting an entrepreneur of his status, Payne was also involved in high-profile fund-raising efforts not related to the numbers rackets. A charter member of the Paseo YMCA, he helped spearhead the effort to build the facility. In addition to Payne and the other members of Kansas City's black bourgeoisie, Julius E. Rosenwald contributed to the construction of the Paseo YMCA as well as many other such institutions. Rosenwald had made his fortune as president and later chair of Sears Roebuck and Company. According to an article published in the NAACP's organ, *The Crisis*, Rosenwald used his money for a number of philanthropic efforts involving the country's African Americans, including schools across the South. He held that "every community with a large colored population should have a center for wholesome recreation including dormitory and restaurant facilities. Colored people alone were not able to provide such institutions. He felt it was the duty of white people 'irrespective of their religious beliefs,' to assist." Rosenwald pledged to contribute twenty-five thousand dollars toward the construction of a "colored YMCA" to any city able to raise seventy-five thousand dollars via public subscription.[45] In Kansas City, the white YMCA contributed fifty thousand dollars, while Payne and his associates contributed the remainder.

Payne was not present at the creation of the NNL but was nevertheless involved. A week before the Kansas City meeting, the *Chicago Defender* noted that Payne planned to entertain the visiting magnates with "a smoker and an auto drive."[46] While attending the conclave, Cary B. Lewis, identified as the *Defender*'s managing editor and NNL secretary, was hosted by Payne and his wife and was the guest of honor at Kansas City's Lincoln's Birthday celebration, speaking on the subject of "Opportunities for Newspaper Men."[47] As an entrepreneur, a political operative, and a prominent social figure, Payne unquestionably garnered attention in Kansas City. But the fact that the *Defender* noted his comings and goings highlights his importance to the larger African American ecosystem extending beyond Kansas City. Whether Payne participated directly in the founding of the NNL is ultimately less important than the idea that he stood at the center of black Kansas City's economic life and that the community was big enough and economically powerful enough to warrant the formation of a new team under the ownership and management of Wilkinson, a seasoned baseball man.

Indianapolis

"Indianapolis, the metropolis of Indiana," noted the *Baltimore Afro-American* in 1912, "is a thriving, hustling busy city[;] it is also the capital of the State and as full of politicians as an egg is full of meat."[48] Reporting two years later on the state of black business in "western" cities, the *Afro-American*'s Ralph W. Tyler called for the organization of an Indianapolis-based business league:

> One who makes an investigating tour over this city is gratifyingly amazed at the very great number of Negro business enterprises. The congested condition of Indiana Avenue is due to the fact that on or about this thoroughfare are located the greater numbers of business offices and that for a distance north, east, south and west of Senate street is the Negro business center....
>
> ... [W]ithin four or six blocks are located eighty-four Negro business enterprises, perhaps a greater number in a like area than can be found in any other city. And Indianapolis is one of the very few cities in the country where the Negro has developed the manufacturing idea.[49]

The African American enclave centered around Indiana Avenue and Senate Street was home to eighty-four business establishments in 1914, a testament to the growth of the city's black community and a result, once again, of the Great Migration. Over the first two decades of the twentieth century, the migration more than doubled Marion County's African American population from 17,536 to 35,634 in 1920, with most of the new arrivals settling in urban Indianapolis. There, they joined an established community that had misgivings about their new neighbors.[50] In addition to four "bright, progressive newspapers," the editors of which were "active in every effort looking to the betterment of the race," as well as a new YMCA building funded in part by Rosenwald and dedicated by Booker T. Washington in 1913, Indianapolis's black ecosystem had both a number of voices while serving as something of a spiritual center.[51] Perhaps more than in similar enclaves, the Senate Street YMCA had a centralizing effect. Its "Monster Meetings," a series of conclaves that showcased local and national black leaders and brought important issues to the fore, dealt with economic and other matters that resonated throughout African America.[52] The YMCA also hosted the NNL's second annual meeting.

But while the Senate Street YMCA provided a locus for community activities, it was not the most important institution in Indianapolis from an economic standpoint. That position was occupied by the company headquarters of one of the most prominent entrepreneurial ventures in early twentieth-century African America, Madam C. J. Walker's Beauty Systems. Though Walker is often credited with conceiving what is now known as the "ethnic beauty" industry, she was the protégé of Annie Turnbo Malone, whose St. Louis–based Poro College provided a model for Walker's enterprise. Both women not only manufactured hair care products aimed at women of color but also trained young black women in using those products. Walker, the first black female millionaire, was active in Booker T. Washington's National Negro Business League (NNBL), addressing the organization's convention more than once. Although she died in 1919, she left a formidable legacy as a business leader and more particularly as a force in Indianapolis's African American ecosystem.[53]

Indiana Avenue's Madam C. J. Walker Building opened in in 1927 as the company headquarters. On the street level, the Madam Walker Theater, with its Grand Casino Ballroom, anchored the city's black entertainment district, which also featured music clubs and "black and tan" dance halls.[54] Just a few blocks southeast of the Walker Building on Indiana Avenue, right off Senate, stood C. I. Taylor's billiard hall, which advertised with some regularity as far afield as Chicago, in the *Defender*. There is no evidence that Taylor and Walker interacted on a business level, but both were involved with the Senate Street YMCA. Taylor is best known as the owner and manager of the Indianapolis ABCs and one of the guiding forces in the formation of the NNL. The ABCs were originally sponsored by the American Brewing Company, a German American–owned producer of Bohemian-style beers marketed to Indianapolis's German population.[55] Although the team bore the brewery's name, it was never under brewery ownership; however, Taylor may have purchased a stake in the company.[56]

In 1908, Ran Butler, a saloon keeper, political leader, and self-professed race man, purchased the ABCs. The preceding year, Butler and Frank Leland, owner of another black Chicago ball club, the Leland Giants, had tried but failed to form a league.[57] In 1910, the ABCs changed ownership again, this time moving into the hands of Tom Bowser, a white man. Taylor joined the team as manager in 1914 and assumed partial ownership, forcing Bowser out within a year.[58] Following a pattern that repeated throughout the history of black baseball and to a certain extent black entrepreneurship in general, Taylor seems to have partnered with and was certainly capitalized by white entrepreneurs. At the very least, his team was sponsored by a white company and bore its name, pointing to some financial involvement. The American Brewing Company, however, did not survive Prohibition and folded before the NNL's establishment in 1920.

Detroit

Also attending the 1920 meeting at the Paseo YMCA was John "Tenney" Blount, a numbers banker who may or may not have had a large capital stake in his team, the Detroit Stars. Indeed, much about Blount's connection to the team, which Rube Foster actually organized, placing the racketeer at the helm, remains obscure.[59] What is certain, however, is the way the press initially embraced the Stars' new front man. In 1921, Frank "Fay" Young of the *Chicago Defender* crowed, "Two years ago Blount knew nothing about the game. He did know business. Making a careful survey of conditions around Detroit, he saw a good opportunity of placing a first-class baseball club in that city and backed up his belief by setting aside $2,000 with which to start his venture. In 1919 he spent $1,800 in advance salaries, uniforms, rental of park, etc., before he made one dime. At the end of the playing season he found himself $11,000 to the good."[60] Whether Blount's entrepreneurial skill leaned more toward the rackets and less toward baseball ownership, as Neil Lanctot suggests, or whether Blount was the savvy owner trumpeted by Young, his team had the potential fan base to become a financial success. Detroit's black community at the time of the NNL's founding certainly had the numbers to support a team. the other communities represented in the Negro National League, Detroit was a product of the Great Migration. Indeed, the Great Migration had a proportionally greater effect on Detroit than on either Kansas City or Indianapolis. In 1910, Detroit had only 5,741 African Americans (1.2 percent of the population); a decade later, that number had risen to 40,838 (4.1 percent), and in 1930, Detroit's 120,000 blacks accounted for 7.6 percent of the population.[61]

There is no doubt that the presence of the automobile industry accounted for much of this rapid expansion, manufacturing jobs as it manufactured cars. In "Michigan, Land of Many Waters," originally published in *The Messenger* in 1919, African Methodist Episcopal minister and civil rights activist Robert W. Bagnall Jr. wrote that Henry Ford's Detroit plant "employed around 8,000 Negroes, mostly doing heavy work. A considerable group, however, do skilled work, and there is a Negro foreman, several Negro clerks, and one Negro, Glenn Cochman, a young graduate of the University of Michigan, who is employed in the experimental department as an electrical engineer."[62] Walter F. White, writing on the "Success of Negro Migration" in *The Crisis*, observed that one automobile manufacturer employed between 1,200 and 1,500 African Americans, while another employed more than 1,100.[63]

There is no doubt that the automobile industry, which could claim thirty-seven manufacturing plants and two hundred and fifty locations making parts and accessories by the mid-1920s, produced jobs. Given the size of Detroit's African American migrant population, Bagnall and White could easily be accused of manipulating the statistics, if not downright hyperbolizing in order to boast of high black employment numbers in the automobile industry as a means of underscoring race pride. The majority of African American migrants to Detroit, however, worked neither in Ford plants nor in those of other automobile manufacturers. Rather, they were, for the most part, domestics or in the service economy.[64]

Detroit's new black population was no more integrated into the mainstream than the migrants in any other black metropolis. The majority of the city's black population was concentrated on its near east side, in the adjacent Black Bottom and Paradise Valley neighborhoods, which, according to Paul Finkelman,

> quickly came to symbolize both the promise and the painful reality of the North: Detroit revealed itself not to be the much-touted "land of milk and

honey." . . . [T]he area would become a crime- and poverty-ridden ghetto and a vibrant center of racial and cultural identity—"a mixture of everything imaginable—including overcrowding, delinquency, and disease," Gloster Current, former resident and local NAACP president, once declared. Yet it also possessed glamour, action, religion, brains, organization, and business. One contemporary counted 360 businesses populating Paradise Valley during the 1920s and the two decades that followed, including a number of prestigious theaters.[65]

Many but not all of Black Bottom/Paradise Valley's brains, organizational skills, and businesses belonged to the area's African American residents, as Blount's outfit illustrates. The Detroit Stars, like so many other black ball clubs, both organized and independent, rented their home venue from a white promoter. Blount's team played in Mack Park, conveniently located close to Paradise Valley. He leased the facility from its owner, big-time haberdasher John Roesink, who was ethnically Dutch and certainly white. According to Detroit historian Richard Bak, "Like all Hastings Street merchants, Roesink had daily contact with blacks. 'Oh, John Roesink was a household word in the black community,' recalled one Black Bottom resident." At the same time that Roesink the sports promoter provided the Stars with their park, Roesink the clothier provided the team's impressive uniforms. By 1925, he owned the team outright.[66]

Roesink's involvement with the NNL follows the pattern of white participation in the urban African American ecosystem. In this case, Blount, the racketeer, who by the time he severed his relationship with the Stars had been appointed deputy sheriff of Wayne County, seemed to be the perfect face of the team, covering for Roesink.[67] Bak observes,

> Policy banks took big losses on occasion, so bettors needed to trust racket men not to "swing with the kitty" instead of paying off. In this regard, Blount came across as someone who was as good as his word. He "was one of the squarest men," recalled one of his players. "I never worked for anyone better. If you worked, you got paid. Nothing but the best." His greatest asset may have been his very light skin, which allowed him to "pass" in white society. This was an important consideration in turn-of-the-century America, whether one was a black waiter hoping to work in a downtown white hotel or a black promoter looking to arrange a game with the owner of a white baseball team. Black newspapers of the day were filled with advertisements for Nadinola Face Powder, Dr. Fred Palmer's Skin Whitener, and other makes of bleaching cream.[68]

Blount's light skin may have benefited him in some of his business ventures, both formal and informal. It certainly would not have hindered him in his political endeavors. But Foster tapped Blount to front the Stars as a race man in a race league. At that point, Kansas City's Wilkinson was still the only white entrepreneur openly involved in the NNL. Rather, Blount's apparent honesty, his reputation for not "swinging with the kitty" and being as good as his word, probably made him a valuable business asset to the league, at least initially. Ultimately, however, Blount was forced out by Foster, the result of a feud relating to the allocation of booking fees. At the same time Roesink was collecting 25 percent of the receipts for rental of his park, Foster demanded that the league receive a 5 percent cut of the team's proceeds, which Blount contended ended up in the Chicago baseball magnate's pocket.[69]

In a sense, Blount's tenure with the Stars can be seen as a cautionary tale about the business of African America during the Great Migration. Although individual businesses—the Kansas City Monarchs, Madam C. J. Walker's beauty empire, and black insurance companies and burial societies—were certainly successful by every measure, poor capitalization and poor organization often led to questionable business practices. Blount's Detroit Stars seemed to be a success—both as a race business and a moneymaker—under the surface, but the franchise was less than stable. In this regard, it resembles the community itself. Drawn to the Motor City by jobs in the automobile industry and its constituent businesses, the migrants appeared to prosper. If Bagnall and White were to be believed, Detroit's primary industry offered the possibility of financial security, if not immeasurable wealth, for the migrants. But as Finkelman demonstrates, appearance is not always reality.

Philadelphia

Though some late-twentieth and early twenty-first century chroniclers of Negro League history are as prone to hyperbole as were Bagnall and White, the story of the first NNL as an economic enterprise is considerably more nuanced than hyperbole allows. Indeed, while Chicago, Kansas City, Indianapolis, Detroit, and St. Louis proved to be fertile ground for the business of the NNL, Dayton, Cleveland, and Pittsburgh did not.[70] According to Lanctot, "Foster and several black sportswriters attributed much of the league's financial problems to poor management and 'slack business records' of franchise owners and attempted to increase the involvement and investment of experienced black businessmen. Most prosperous black entrepreneurs, however, were reluctant to participate in such a financially risky venture that typically required a $1,000 deposit, 10 percent of the gross receipts from each game, and an additional 20–25 percent to a white park owner."[71]

Despite its shifting membership and questionable business practices, the NNL initially had success. In addition to its fluid charter membership, the NNL added two eastern "associate members," the Hilldale club of Darby, Pennsylvania, and Atlantic City's Bacharach Giants.[72] But after realizing no financial advantage and balking at Foster's leadership, Hilldale withdrew from the NNL, spearheading the formation of another circuit. In a move essentially mirroring that of the NNL two years earlier, the ECL was founded on December 16, 1922, at the Southwest YMCA in Philadelphia by representatives of the Baltimore Black Sox, the Lincoln Giants, the Brooklyn Royal Giants, and the Bacharachs as well as Hilldale, under the ownership of Ed Bolden.[73] In founding the new league, Bolden established a close working relationship with controversial white owner and booking agent Nat Strong, further angering Foster. While internecine conflict among black baseball's entrepreneurs was responsible for the formation of the competing league, social, economic, and demographic forces made that creation possible. The establishment of significant African American ecosystems in Philadelphia, New York, and Baltimore, in part as a result of the Great Migration, made black baseball economically feasible.

Beginning in 1910, Bolden's club played its home games at Hilldale Park in Darby, five miles west of downtown Philadelphia and accessible to city residents via a short trolley ride. Like Chicago and Kansas City, Philadelphia already had a significant African American population when the migrants began to arrive. In 1897, the University of Pennsylvania undertook a study, directed by W. E. B. Du Bois, to examine the conditions under which the city's black residents lived. Wrote Du Bois, "Here is a large group of people—perhaps forty-five thousand, a city within a city—who do not form an integral part of the larger social group."[74] According to 1900 census data, just three years later, Philadelphia had 62,613 Negro residents.[75]

As large as that population may have been, particularly in comparison with Indianapolis or even Kansas City, by 1920, Philadelphia's black population had soared to 134,220.[76] As in other urban centers that already had African American enclaves prior to the Great Migration, Philadelphia's established black community viewed the newcomers with suspicion. Notes Robert Gregg, the city's black community displayed a certain optimism. "It is ironic," he wrote, "that as thousands of black Southerners began to make their way to their 'Promised Land,' people already residing there felt that the newcomers signified the end to all promise."[77] Taking this into consideration, it is easy to see that pre-migration Philadelphia differed significantly from, say, Chicago of the same era. Absent was a voice like Abbott's, encouraging oppressed southerners to join him in the prosperous North.

Despite the fact that the extant population did not exactly throw out the welcome mat, the migrants began arriving in droves in 1916, drawn by the promise of employment at the Pennsylvania Railroad, Westinghouse, Franklin Sugar Company, Midvale Steel, Eddystone Munitions, and other local companies.[78] While these companies hired many of the migrants who were concentrated in North and West Philadelphia, the result of the same pressures that created urban ecosystems in the other cities, the majority found work in the service industry. Writes Gregg, "The new black communities were situated in areas providing little skilled employment because of early attempts to relocate industry outside urban centers; and when skilled jobs were available, black people were excluded by the unions." Consequently, as in other cities, most African Americans found work in "service occupations in the hotels, restaurants, and inns of the adjacent white communities" and as domestics.[79]

But the migrants did find work, leading, as Lanctot notes, to "unprecedented business opportunities resulting in the development of the Hotel Dale, Dunbar Theater, and the Brown and Stevens Bank."[80] They also patronized Bolden's baseball business, becoming ticket-buying Hilldale fans. Although the connections among the businesses fueling Philadelphia's African American ecosystem were not as direct as the links in Chicago and Kansas City, the entrepreneurial empire of financier E. C. Brown demonstrates some of the ways in which Philadelphia various ventures were interrelated.

On the front page of the October 6, 1923, *Pittsburgh Courier*, W. Rollo Wilson, a sports columnist for both the *Courier* and the *Philadelphia Tribune* who would later play an instrumental part in organized Negro baseball's second wave, trumpeted with unbridled enthusiasm that "staid" Philadelphia "has an organization which is shortly destined to be ranked as a 'national institution.' We speak with some degree of authority for its financial power is being used in all parts of the country to help the worthy responsible citizens who may call upon its resources. Southern farmers, northern business men, realty operators, theatrical enterprises—all are clients of the banking house of Brown and Stevens." Brown's backstory, Wilson continued with just a touch of exaggeration, "reads like one of Oliver Optic's books. It "is a tale which might well be told by fond mothers to the children on their knees."[81] But rather than reading like the life of one of the now forgotten nineteenth-century children's story writer and magazine publisher's heroes, Brown's tale sounds much like that of many other entrepreneurs in the African American ecosystem. Brown, the majority partner, had been involved in other ventures in Virginia before partnering with Andrew F. Stevens to open the private bank in March 1924. On the surface, the business appeared to be an unmitigated success, but in reality, it was highly speculative. According to Abram Lincoln Harris,

> The partners not only borrowed large sums on their personal notes. They used the bank's funds to finance concerns in which they were interested either as promoters or owners. . . .
> . . . There were no fewer than twelve of these subsidiary concerns to which the bank had made large advances or in which its funds had been invested. . . . The Dunbar Amusement Corporation was formed to construct a theater on the southwest corner of Broad and Lombard Streets in Philadelphia; the Payton Apartments Corporation was organized to purchase and operate apartments for Negroes in New York City; the Hillman Real Estate Company conducted business similar to that of the Payton Apartments and was also located in New York. The Elite Amusement Corporation was organized to supply Negro Theaters with vaudeville.[82]

Indeed, Brown's theatrical ventures, which included New York's Lafayette and Brooklyn's Putnam, were advertised as far west as Chicago in the pages of the *Defender.* Brown was also deeply involved in the NNBL, running unsuccessfully for the organization's presidency in 1920.

Like the Binga Bank several years later, the Brown and Stevens Bank failed as a consequence of financial irregularities. Certainly in the 1920s, the banking industry operated in an unregulated Wild West atmosphere, but financial enterprises owned by black entrepreneurs seemed particularly vulnerable. Harris describes Brown as "at heart . . . a buccaneer with little regard for sound principles of finance and banking."[83] This seeming disregard of what are now recognized as sound business practices appears to be a recurring theme in the African American ecosystems of this period as well as in mainstream business, though perhaps to a lesser extent. This phenomenon was also evident in the black entertainment industry, of which baseball played an integral role.

Brown and Stevens's entrepreneurial tendrils extended throughout Philadelphia's black leisure industries. The partners owned and operated black Philadelphia's premier showplace, the palatial Dunbar Theater, until it and their other theatrical enterprises fell victim to mismanagement—specifically, Brown and Stevens's illegal use of the bank's holdings to finance these ventures.[84] In August 1921, the two men sold the Dunbar Amusement Company to John T. Gibson, whose addition of the theater to his expanding empire cemented his position at the center of black Philadelphia's business world.[85] Gibson's most successful enterprise was Philadelphia's New Standard Theater, a rare black-owned outlet on the TOBA circuit.[86] The Dunbar, in contrast, never made money, even after the new owner changed its name to the Gibson, presumably to disassociate it from the public scandal of the collapse of the Brown and Stevens Bank. Gibson nonetheless was the city's most prominent black theater owner, receiving extensive coverage in the national black press. By any gauge, Gibson was very powerful.

As both a race man and an entertainment mogul, Gibson had his fingers in many pies. It seems almost inevitable that one would be black baseball. According to Lanctot, the Madison Stars, financed in part by Gibson, entered Philadelphia's sporting scene in 1920, complete with their own ballpark and Rube Foster's imprimatur. Foster's disdain for Bolden, whose control of Philadelphia's baseball scene roughly paralleled Gibson's control of the city's theaters, would have encouraged Foster's endorsement of Gibson's enterprise. But like so many other black ball clubs of the era and like the Dunbar Theater, the Madison Stars faltered, becoming what Lanctot refers to as a "developmental club" for Hilldale.[87]

Bolden was also a race man, but as Lanctot puts it, he was "a businessman first and a 'race man' second," a position he shared, at least in some respects, with Gibson.[88] Just as Gibson did business with the white TOBA administrators, Bolden regularly booked dates with white semiprofessional teams, hired white umpires for the ECL, and served as the only African American on the board of governors of the Philadelphia Baseball Association, which included sixty-five semiprofessional teams, most of them white.[89] On the surface, both Bolden and Gibson appear to have followed the pattern of black entrepreneurs in the entertainment business engaging financially with whites, a relationship often seen as incursion. But a closer look shows that the Philadelphia business owners were moving against the grain. Rather than functioning as black faces for white interests, they each represented a black face among a sea of white faces. To be sure, TOBA's control of the black vaudeville circuit constituted a form of incursion. Nevertheless, as race men working both sides of the color line, they represented a different kind of African American entrepreneur. On one hand, as black men operating black businesses for black consumers, they displayed Washingtonian tendencies when they "cast down their buckets" in the African American ecosystem. On the other, they also represented what might be interpreted as an economic iteration of Du Bois's notion of the Talented Tenth, his long-held contention that a core constituency of highly educated, "broad-minded, upright men," ready, willing, and able to work as equals with whites, could lead the race closer toward full political as well as economic emancipation.[90] Indeed, Bolden seemed to channel Du Bois, in the *Baltimore Afro-American*, writing, "The Eastern Colored League is composed of colored and white owners, the co-operative efforts alone of this group should warrant immunity from the citation of the race question. Close analysis will prove that only where the color-line fades and co-operation instituted are our business advances gratified. Segregation in any form, including self-imposed, is not the solution."[91]

Though Bolden's rhetoric in this passage reflects that of Du Bois, Bolden also indirectly identifies a problem that beset Negro baseball from its very beginnings and continued to do so throughout its run: the ubiquitousness of white booking agents. The contentious relationship between Negro League owners and booking agents may be traced all the way back to Brooklyn's Nat Strong and his involvement with semiprofessional baseball. In fact, Strong was the same white ECL owner referenced in the article. A first-generation American who according to various accounts was either of Russian-Jewish or Irish-Welsh descent,[92] Strong cut his teeth in the sporting goods business.[93] His connection to black baseball stretched all the way back to the late nineteenth century as part owner of the Brooklyn Royal Giants, who were managed by Sol White. In fact, one ad for Strong's booking agency, which he co-owned with H. Walter Schlichter, appeared in White's landmark *The History of Colored Baseball*.[94]

By the time the NNL played its first season, Strong's place in the business was both central and increasingly controversial, and by 1921, the black press had already begun to argue for the need, as a headline in the *Afro-American* blared, "to break Nat Strong." In answer to the question, "Who is Strong?" the article explained,

Nat Strong, white, is said to dominate the baseball activities among colored players in the East. With his hands on one hundred and fifty amusement places and parks he is said to be able to negotiate terms that block their advance and keep them in a state of stagnation.

This complete tie-up of the colored baseball men's hands, players say, "enables the Hebrew to exact a heavy toll from every game played by any group operated in his territory."[95]

Beyond labeling Strong as "white," the practice of racial identification being as common in the black press as it was in the mainstream, is the fact that he was represented as the source of all that was wrong in what was colloquially known as "colored" baseball, ratcheting up the vitriol by identifying him as "Hebrew." That Strong was perceived as Jewish was particularly important in the wake of the Red Summer of 1919, when the air was full of fear of "foreign" elements—communists, anarchists, Catholics, or members of what was increasingly seen as an "international Jewish banking conspiracy." This is a clear example of what social psychologist W. I. Thomas refers to as "the definition of the situation": If something is perceived to be true, it is true in its consequences.[96]

The *Afro-American*'s use of the language of lynching, specifically, the "tie-up" of the hands of "colored" men, along with mention of a "heavy toll" placed on owners, references, perhaps unintentionally, Shakespeare's Shylock exacting his "pound of flesh" in *The Merchant of Venice*. The relationship between team interests and promotional interests thus was broken from the outset. The editorial goes on to explain "how the system works: ten percent of each club's receipts to the 'boss,' sixty-five per cent to the club owners, and never more than twenty-five percent to the players. No matter how big the general receipts, the colored clubs are not given more than $500 for any game." Despite the inflated anti-Semitic rhetoric and the recurrence of incendiary nineteenth-century race language—the use of *boss* in this context was tantamount to a direct challenge to Strong— the anonymous author is accurate to some extent in describing booking agents' exploitative business practices. More significantly, the article's content underscores the extent to which the business of black baseball, however reluctantly, relied on the use of intermediaries, many of whom were (or were believed to be) Jews.

Both part of the African American ecosystem and outside it, Jewish promoters mediated between the insular economic world that marked African America and the mainstream economy, of which Jews were also neither wholly a part nor wholly outside. Ivan Light and Steven J. Gold refer to this role as that of the ethnic middleman. "Middleman minorities," they contend, "were marginal trading peoples, residing in diasporas, who continued this commercial livelihood into the modern age, despite the presumably adverse competitive climate created by modern capitalism." Jewish merchants provide the "star illustration" of this phenomenon.[97] Strong was Light and Gold's quintessential middleman, but he chose to neither work nor play in the middle ground. Whatever the truth of charges that he enriched himself at the expense of others, he unquestionably forged important instrumental alliances with black baseball men, especially with Bolden and with Harlem's multifaceted Alex Pompez.

New York

From the Great Migration on, Harlem was the largest black enclave in the United States. New York's African American ecosystem was synonymous with jazz, poetry, and the seemingly boundless energy of the Harlem Renaissance. But to look at Harlem solely in this fashion is overly simplistic and neglects its central place among the many urban centers undergoing similar development. The popular impression of Harlem in the first decades of the twentieth century is of a playground where white hipsters and thrill seekers partied alongside their black brethren in places like the Cotton Club, which is often cited as the preeminent Harlem nightclub. This Lenox Avenue establishment was founded in 1923, having previously been the Club DeLuxe, owned by heavyweight champion Jack Johnson before it was taken over by Irish American gangster Owney Madden. Although it employed black workers both onstage and off, it did not play a significant part in the local black economy because it excluded black patrons. In this it was not alone. Even institutions as intimately associated with black life in Harlem as the Hotel Theresa and the Apollo Theater were not open to African Americans until the early 1940s.

Harlem owed its position as a black enclave to Payton, the African American real estate speculator who built his empire by finding black residents willing to pay exorbitant rents for housing originally built for but never occupied by white, middle-class renters. In so doing, Payton anchored a new community by effectively eroding restrictive covenants aimed at keeping out African Americans. Several years before the migration began in earnest, a significant number of New York's black residents were displaced when the Midtown Tenderloin district was destroyed to make way for Pennsylvania Station. Without other options, they moved uptown to Harlem.[98]

As Payton's Afro-American Real Estate Company was failing in 1907, two of his protégés, John E. Nail and Henry C. Parker, formed their own real estate venture. Nail and Parker not only served as rental agents but also helped secure mortgages for black Harlem residents and owned and managed properties. Furthermore, Nail and Parker represented the churches that were Harlem's largest property owners, including St. Philip's Protestant Episcopal Church, then the city's biggest black church.[99] This is significant in that Harlem's black churches were its largest property owners, and they gave their business to black realtors to manage. The church's 1910 relocation to Harlem from downtown signaled that the Upper Manhattan neighborhood was poised to become the center of the city's black metropolis.[100]

Prior to the Great Migration, New York City was hardly a storied African American Mecca. In fact, in 1900, before the dislocation of the Tenderloin's residents, the census counted 38,616 Negro Manhattanites, with another 18,367 African Americans living in Brooklyn, which had only been incorporated into New York City three years earlier but was nonetheless the location of the city's black baseball scene in the first decades of the twentieth century. Even taking Brooklyn's residents into account, New York's nascent African American ecosystem was smaller than that of Philadelphia. By 1920, however, Manhattan alone had 115,133 black residents, most of them concentrated in Harlem's two square miles; a decade later, that number had nearly doubled again, reaching 224,670.[101]

Not all of Harlem's new black residents over these three decades migrated from the U.S. South. Immigrants from the West Indies made significant contributions to both Harlem's formal and informal economies as well as to the political and economic rhetoric of the period. Spanish-speaking arrivals came from Puerto Rico and other islands, though they did so in much smaller numbers than in the 1940s and subsequent years. In this regard, black New York was far more diverse and complex than the other emerging African American ecosystems that hosted Negro League teams.

This diversity played an important role in the development of Harlem's economy, introducing a chorus of new voices and interests. Nevertheless, the structures of Harlem's economy were built on the foundations laid by older entrepreneurs, including Payton, Nail, and Parker. Nail in particular exemplified what sociologist E. Franklin Frazier identified as a member of an emerging black bourgeoisie that could be found in every develop-ing black metropolis.[102] Like Philadelphia's Gibson, Nail had economic, political, and social interests that brought him into contact with mov-ers and shakers in virtually every sphere of Harlem life. He was person-ally involved with raising money to build the Rosenwald-funded Harlem branch of the YMCA, which opened in 1919 and was annexed to a grander facility in 1933. As the locus of community activities, the first Harlem Y served at various times as home to such Harlem Renaissance luminar-ies as Langston Hughes, Claude McKay, and Richard Wright. Nail was an active member of the NNBL and of the National Urban League, and the black press not only provided extensive coverage of his business and philanthropic activities but also prominently chronicled his activities in the society pages. In 1926, for example, the *Afro-American* noted that he addressed a meeting of the Urban League at New York's Town Hall on West 43rd Street: "A distinguished audience of both races" filled the facility "at the opening of the $350,000 campaign to assure the running expenses of the New York, Brooklyn and national Urban league for three years." Other speakers included Charles S. Johnson, the author of *The Messenger's* profile of black life in Illinois; Eugene Kinkle Jones, the Urban League's first executive secretary; poet Countee Cullen; and Lloyd Garrison, the organization's treasurer and the great-grandson of noted abolitionist Wil-liam Lloyd Garrison. "The climax of the evening," the piece contended, "came, however, when a letter from Casper Holstein, the donor of the $1,000 awards in OPPORTUNITY's recent literary Prize Contest was read, in which there was a check for $500."[103]

The *Pittsburgh Courier* also followed Nail's movements, observing earlier in 1926 that he, along with Holstein and a "committee of fifteen of Harlem's foremost citizens," had the pleasure of entertaining Chicago alderman Louis Anderson.[104] Nail seems to have interacted quite a bit with Holstein, who is identified in the *Afro-American* only as a "colored man" and in the *Courier* as "a philanthropist." Left unsaid, however, was the fact that Holstein ran the numbers rackets in New York.[105] The connections between Nail and Holstein and those among the real estate business, the National Urban League, and the rackets show not that the business of urban black America was somehow undermined by the involvement of racketeers but rather that Harlem's formal and informal economies, like those in the other cities that hosted black baseball, were inextricable parts of the same web. Nail's economic and social activities played an integral role in Harlem's economic activity.

Nail's influence in the Harlem ecosystem further extended into the entertainment business. Along with W. E. B. Du Bois and several other important figures, Nail served on the board of directors of Black Swan Records, founded in 1921 by Herbert "Harry" Pace, who was initially a partner in the sheet music business with W. C. Handy and later one of the principals in the merger that created Supreme Liberty Life. Black Swan was in essence the first and for some time the only black-owned label to record what were then termed race records—music performed by black artists and marketed to a predominantly though not entirely black audience. Although the company began by issuing novelty recordings, it soon employed Fletcher Henderson as its in-house piano player and arranger as well as Ethel Waters, whose presence added a touch of class to the musical undertakings while virtually single-handedly putting Black Swan at the center of the industry. Pace also sent Waters out on tour with a publicity machine that included Lester Walton, the first columnist of color to write for a mainstream New York City daily, the *New York World*.[106]

Pace's 1922 deal with John Fletcher, a white businessman, to purchase a bankrupt record pressing plant caused some consternation among participants in the African American entertainment world who perceived the deal as an incursion into this unique, all-black business.[107] However, it can also be seen as another example of the pattern that recurred throughout the story of urban, black entrepreneurship, with white economic involvement helping to further the black concern's success. The label went bankrupt, however, and Pace sold the Black Swan catalog to Paramount, a struggling rural Wisconsin label whose legacy often obscures that of Black Swan.[108] Nevertheless, while Pace would keep his hand firmly in the African American ecosystem through his long involvement in the insurance industry, this partnership with Fletcher can certainly be viewed as another example of white incursion.

In addition to his stint with Black Swan's Ethel Waters tour, which certainly afforded him a bird's-eye view of such developments, Walton covered the state of race business in his column for the *New York World*. In a piece reprinted in the *Pittsburgh Courier* on September 16, 1924, Walton wrote, "A question being generally discussed among local Negroes is: 'If an outlet for racial egoism must be had, is not Harlem a more ideal setting than somewhere in Africa or in a prescribed section of the United States exclusively occupied by Negroes?'"[109] The "outlet for racial egoism" to which Walton referred was the "negro empire on the dark continent" proposed by Marcus Garvey and his Universal Negro Improvement

Association (UNIA). No discussion of Harlem's ecosystem or the economy of black America writ large during and immediately after this period can avoid Garvey's reach. Even black baseball, which did not count any self-professed Garveyites among its entrepreneurs, was at least indirectly affected by Garvey's call for black economic self-determinism.

Garvey was a Jamaican immigrant who started out as a vocal proponent of Booker T. Washington's adamant assertion that the only way forward for the race was economic independence. But unlike Washington, Garvey's sense of economic independence came wrapped in the fiery rhetoric of separatism that placed him at the center of Harlem's political world. Garvey was a polarizing figure, resolute and opinionated. His rhetoric ruffled many feathers, including those of Du Bois, who never approved of Garvey's rhetoric or tactics, and those of A. Philip Randolph and Chandler Owen, publishers of *The Messenger*, who initially allied themselves with Garvey's crusade.[110]

The grandiosity of his overall plan to reverse the diaspora, proclaiming the first Back to Africa movement, fell outside the mainstream conversation about black progress through economic advancement. For a short period, however, Garvey's entrepreneurial activities placed him and his organization in the same category as businessmen such as Nail, Pace, and Holstein. In fact, Holstein supported the UNIA financially and wrote occasional pieces for the *Negro World*, the movement's official publication.[111] Although Garvey was ultimately discredited, a victim of powerful adversaries in the black communities, J. Edgar Hoover, economic irregularities, and the inability to strike a balance between rhetoric and reality, his message of independence through financial prosperity continued to resonate throughout Harlem's ecosystem.

While Garvey's influence on Negro League baseball was at best tangential, Holstein was an ardent fan of the sport. In 1926, already waxing nostalgic about the game's halcyon past when the Lincoln Giants and Cuban Stars could fill Yankee Stadium, the *New York Amsterdam News* reminisced about the "good old days" when "the entire old guard used to turn out in full force." But who led the old guard? Brooklyn Royal Giants owner John Connors, nightclub impresario Barron Wilkins, and Casper Holstein.[112] Connors and Wilkins would have had close connections to New York's rackets, perhaps claiming racketeers as financial patrons and/or participating in the rackets themselves. As the big man in New York's numbers rackets, Holstein would have joined Connors and Wilkins to watch the Cuban Stars. Moreover, Holstein could count Stars owner Alejandro "Alex" Pompez as a professional colleague and a friendly competitor.

Pompez, a Cuban American from Florida, operated in a section of Harlem with a concentration of ethnic Afro-Cubans who had also migrated north. Along with Bolden, Pompez was one of the few black baseball entrepreneurs to develop a rapport with Strong. Acting as a mentor of sorts, Strong actually gave Pompez his start in the business, hiring him and teaching him the details of the promotion business and the many other subtleties of black baseball's marketplace.[113]

As an American of Cuban descent, Pompez, like Strong, was an outsider. But as an Afro-Cuban and an increasingly successful businessman, cigar store owner, and renowned numbers operator, Pompez also functioned as an insider, able to use his skills as a booking agent without incurring the wrath of black baseball's other owners. In the words of historian Adrian Burgos Jr., "Pompez relied on his cultural background and the skills he had acquired working for Strong to secure bookings. From its inception he envisioned his baseball operation as one that cultivated the Americas, Spanish- and English-speaking, as its main market, one from which he could both acquire talent and attract consumers. That he himself was bilingual and multicultural made such an approach both manageable and successful; it would distinguish him from the other Negro-league owners and lead to his longevity in black baseball."[114]

According to Burgos, Pompez's arrival in New York coincided with the rise not only of black ball but also of the rackets: "The two enterprises were cottage industries for black Harlem and would become inextricably linked, as numbers money would largely underwrite the two longest-lasting Negro-league franchises to play in New York City."[115] Pompez's link to Holstein was solidified by the fact that they, along with "Madame" Stephanie St. Clair and Ellsworth "Bumpy" Johnson, were protégés of Dominique, the man who appears to have introduced the local iteration of the numbers game to New York in 1913.[116] Pompez was eventually forced to abandon the rackets and subsequently devoted all his entrepreneurial efforts to baseball, but during the ECL's run in the 1920s and after the league's dissolution in the 1930s, he continued to play in both fields.

As Pompez's narrative demonstrates, segregated professional sport, like other mainstream business ventures, often relied on the informal economy for operating capital. Despite the wide range of differences among the African American ecosystems that generated the first two Negro Leagues in the 1920s, those ecosystems seem conjoined by numbers or policy racketeers. So ingrained in the industry was capitalization from the rackets that the Negro National League was often called the Bankers' League, referring not to African America's few formal financial institutions like those operated by Chicago's Binga or Philadelphia's Brown and Stevens but rather to the type of informal financial institution run by Pompez, Henry Teenan Jones, Felix Payne, and St. Louis Stars' owner Richard Kent.[117]

But while Pompez and many other racketeers were successful baseball men, parlaying profits into their franchises, even the large funds generated by gambling on numbers and policy could not entirely solve black baseball's problem of operating capital and the impending economic collapse of the late 1920s, and that problem continued to plague black baseball from its first decades until its demise after World War II.

The Demise of the Original Leagues

Despite the ongoing conflict between Foster and Bolden as well as the ire incurred by Strong's perpetual presence, Negro League baseball appeared to be a permanent fixture of the African American ecosystem, an expanding response to the Major Leagues' exclusion of nonwhite players and general disregard for fans of color. The year 1924 even saw the institution of what was billed as the Colored World Series, a ten-game contest in which Wilkinson's Kansas City Monarchs defeated Bolden's Hilldale Club five games to four with one tie.[118] Games were played not only in Philadelphia and Kansas City but also in Chicago and Baltimore, allowing a wider fan base to experience what was promoted as a championship. Similar postseason championship series were also staged between the ECL and NNL winners for the next three seasons.

While publicly, the circuits appeared to be thriving, privately, this was not the case. These series were neither a financial success nor a public relations coup. As Lanctot explained, the events "attracted only modest attendance, failing to maintain the interest of fans over a prolonged period."[119] Indeed, the inability to generate a critical mass of fan interest for the championship exposed a major flaw in the business—its lack of organization. The random yet unavoidable challenges that inevitably arose with such a sizable enterprise quickly grew into major catastrophes.

The first blow was C. I. Taylor's death in 1922, which left his widow, Olivia, and one of his brothers, Ben, to manage the team. The ABCs had previously been a model of stability but soon became embroiled in an intense family conflict that spilled over into day-to-day team operations, resulting in a schism and Ben Taylor's departure for Washington, D.C., with the team's better players. Those players who remained in Indianapolis balked at the prospect of playing for a woman.[120] This fracture was compounded in the mid-1920s by player raids from the ECL, a practice that came to haunt the entire industry. Given that black organized baseball was built around many of the same tested principles on which white Major League Baseball operated, the participants in these first two Negro Leagues failed to act on the precept that a cooperative venture requires cooperation. And cooperation was something that was in short supply.[121]

Perhaps even more devastating than the loss of the well-respected Taylor was Rube Foster's abrupt departure from the league and from public life in general. In 1926, Foster was institutionalized for what the *Defender* described as "a nervous breakdown brought on by worries over baseball."[122] In Robert Peterson's landmark oral history of black baseball, *Only the Ball Was White*, Foster's son, Earl, recalled, "What his trouble was I don't know, but he was off and he never did get back to normal. . . . He wasn't dangerous or anything like that, but he couldn't be at home."[123] Rube Foster died four years later.

Although Foster was a controversial figure, he nevertheless functioned as the glue that held the NNL together. Chicago sports columnist Al Monroe suggested at the time that Foster might have been motivated primarily by the desire to extend his booking agency's power throughout the Midwest to mirror Nat Strong's eastern operation.[124] In contrast, the far more idealistic account in contemporary coverage of the 1920 Kansas City meeting portrayed Foster as seeking solely to provide a professional league for the race. Whatever his motivations, Foster played a central position in the business of black baseball, exemplifying a sort of forthright and emboldened ingenuity. Like those who started journalistic, insurance, and banking ventures or who entered other areas of the entertainment industry, regardless of outcome, baseball entrepreneurs found a hole in the mainstream economy and set about exploiting it.

Although Foster's absence and the death of Taylor were among the primary causes for the demise of this first iteration of organized black baseball, other events and conditions certainly contributed to its collapse. The Detroit Stars suffered a crushing blow when a catastrophic fire broke out in Mack Park on July 7, 1929, causing panic, some serious injuries, and more significantly the loss of a major Negro League venue. The *Defender* reported that an attempt to dry the field following a rainstorm had led to the disaster: "John Roesink, white, president of the Mack Ave. Exhibition company, which operates the park, is said to have telephoned for forty gallons of gasoline, but the oil station refused to deliver the same because there was no container at the park. Harold Speed, white, who handles the concessions at the park, and another man went for two five-gallon cans of gasoline. Some was poured over and around first base, while the second was emptied around second. When the first was ignited someone in the west end yelled 'Fire.'" While the *Defender* did not explicitly blame Roesink and Speed for the catastrophe, the fact that the race of each was duly noted goes beyond the *Defender's* usual practice of identifying by color those who were not part of the paper's primary demographic.[125] Although the article continues, "Notwithstanding what may have been the cause," thereby appearing to shift some of the culpability from the venue owner and the concessionaire, it is clear that the *Defender's* coverage places the lion's share of the blame on Roesink and Speed. That the fire was ruled to be accidental remained unimportant. That the fans blamed Roesink was the point, a point that seemed to linger, affecting the team's bottom line.[126]

The following season, patrons stayed away from games at the new Roesink-owned venue, Hamtramck Stadium. After Roesink told sportswriter Russell Cowan that he would not advertise in the black press because "I don't want to have 'nothing' to do with no 'shine newspapers,'" fans expressed their disdain for the owner by voting with their feet—and their money. According to a writer for the Associated Negro Press, "Since it has been learned that Roesink owns both the ball club and the park now known as Roesink's Stadium, Negroes here are planning a boycott for the remainder of the season. Roesink owned the old 'Mack Park,' which long condemned, was destroyed by fire and a host of people were injured while twenty were killed last summer." Accuracy seems to have been of little importance to the ANP writer here, as there were no fatalities resulting from the disaster.[127] Rather, calling attention to the horrors of white incursion, which was nothing new for the black press, was the point of this particular call to arms. The black press's response to the disaster and use of racial rhetoric bore much of the blame for the franchise's failure. Despite the fact that Roesink constructed a new ballpark, attendance dropped precipitously. Without a consumer base, the business struggled.

The failure of the ECL and NNL ultimately resulted from the endemic use of questionable business practices. Most notably, the teams lost sight of fans' needs. Detroiters were not alone in deserting their team. Journalist Raymond Drake asserted in 1929, "Negro baseball as conducted today is doomed." He continued, "Baseball, it seemed, was due to become a big business. It did for a few brief seasons—and then dropped back into the same old rut, the leagues developing into more of a booking agency instead of making progress and furnishing better ball for the fans who support the game. The fan on the other hand, decided to bear with them in the hope of seeing the leagues take on new life and build to the heights promised at the time of the organization. The fans waited long for the change. No change has arrived. The fans have become disgusted with the tactics employed by members of organized baseball and now it seems that they are ready for the showdown."[128] The reasons Drake gives for the dwindling fan base are, on the one hand, particular to baseball. But on the other, the essential problem he cites, failure to deliver on the promise of a professionally run organization, a problem that plagued other sectors of the African American ecosystem.

Both inside and outside of the entertainment industry, the lack of consistently good service was often cited as the primary cause for the failure of black business ventures. On September 7, 1929, the *Pittsburgh Courier* asserted, "Three of the chief complaints made against the majority of Negro businesses and investigators of the National Negro Business League are: Lack of proper service to customers, failure to keep books and failure to re-invest a sufficient percentage of the annual profits. As a result, businesses that could be flourishing are losing customers, failing to attract new ones and unaware of the exact status of their affairs." A particular concern raised by the columnist was the issue of lax attention paid to the customer base: "It is the more regrettable, because there is no excuse for poor service." It concluded: "Competition is growing increasingly stiffer in every line, and white capital is increasingly entering what has heretofore been known as strictly Negro fields. If we are to survive this competition, we must give as good service as the white business, reinvest more of our profits in our businesses and keep complete and up-to-date records of sales, expenditures and other transactions."[129]

The sentiment expressed in this column was repeated consistently in the black press. Not only were black businesses excoriated for failing to provide decent service, failure to provide value for the dollar was an equally pressing issue. If Negro businesses did not provide goods and services of equal value to those provided by white competitors, entrepreneurs should not be surprised if consumers of color took their business elsewhere.

Given the date of the *Courier* column, September 7, 1929, the fact that businesses were beset by failure, regardless of color, appears to be eerily prophetic, at least at first blush. On October 24, after having reached its peak four days earlier, the stock market crashed, leading to the panic that marked Black Thursday a mere five days later. Although this chain of events is generally cited as the onset of the Great Depression, the mainstream economy was showing signs of stress years earlier. According to economist John Kenneth Galbraith, the collapse of a Florida land speculation bubble, the widespread assumption "that God had intended the American middle class to be rich," and the soaring New York Stock Exchange indicated impending trouble.[130] "In the summer of 1927," writes Galbraith, "Henry Ford rang down the curtain on the immortal Model T and closed his plant to prepare for Model A. The Federal Reserve index of industrial production receded, presumably as a result of the Ford shutdown, and there was general talk of depression."[131]

For the African American ecosystem, the handwriting was on the wall. According to Juliet E. K. Walker, although the 1920s in many ways constituted the first golden age of black business, "black business remained on the periphery, a shadow economy, its profits eclipsed by the financial giants of the age."[132] And these businesses were built on a foundation that was at best shaky. Even when the economy soared, many black businesses had trouble staying afloat. On January 21, 1928, the *Pittsburgh Courier* opined that "any business failure is bad, but a failure in Negro business is the worst of all." Moreover, "business is largely maintained by confidence of the public, and the confidence of the Negro public in Negro business is not very strong."[133] Even though Philadelphia's Brown and Stevens Bank had failed as a consequence of financial mismanagement—what the *New York Amsterdam News*'s Kelly Miller described as "downright rascality"—its demise called attention to already waning Negro consumer confidence.[134]

As is virtually always the case in any economic downturn, the last hired were the first fired, and many African American workers found themselves unemployed. The Negro Leagues and other race enterprises depended on those hard-earned dollars, so Negro League baseball as constituted in the 1920s was doomed to failure. The ECL folded in 1928, though it was reconstituted as the American Negro League for just one final season before disappearing forever. Perhaps more telling was the collapse of the original organized Negro League, the NNL, which limped along until 1931.

But neither black baseball—nor black business, for that matter—went completely extinct. Wilkinson's Kansas City Monarchs weathered the

NNL's demise thanks to their owner's acumen gained through decades of experience in the baseball business. The Monarchs operated as an independent team, barnstorming the country and playing wherever they could get a game to generate money to continue operations. Other independent and semipro black teams, while hardly thriving, continued with business as usual in the many places that featured a critical mass of consumers. But all in all, the business of black baseball, much like other businesses found throughout African America—and all of America, for that matter—faded from view.

In spite of the economic collapse, one sector of the African American ecosystem—the backbone of the informal economy—continued to thrive: the numbers and policy rackets. Promising huge payoffs on paltry investments, its entrepreneurs flourished while its patrons dreamed of making a buck when so few were. Consequently, the racketeers, infusing much-needed capital into communities that were in such dire need, helped to revive and rebuild the business of black baseball during the height of the Great Depression.

3

The Depression, Black Business, and Black Baseball Revisited, 1930–1939

Introduction

On Thursday, October 29, 1929, after several months of volatility, the stock market plummeted. The popular assumption remains that the crash signaled the beginning of the Great Depression, which gripped America until the end of the 1930s. The reality is a little more complicated. As John Kenneth Galbraith notes, the stock market was "but a mirror" of "an image of the underlying or *fundamental* economic situation." In fact, Galbraith notes, "In June the indexes of industrial and of factory production both reached a peak and turned down. By October, the Federal Reserve index of industrial production stood at 117 as compared with 126 four months earlier. Steel production declined from June on; in October freight car loading fell. Home building, a most mercurial industry, had been falling for several years, and it slumped still farther in 1929. Finally, down came the stock market."[1]

Discussing the severity of the economic crisis, Galbraith continues, "The singular feature of the great crash of 1929 was that the worst continued to worsen. What looked one day like the end proved on the next day to have been only the beginning. Nothing could have been more ingeniously designed to maximize the suffering, and also to insure that as few as possible escaped the common misfortune."[2] Although, as Galbraith argues, the regular fluctuations of any business cycle meant that there was no reason to believe that a serious depression was in the offing until the speculative bubble burst on Black Thursday, thereby giving the collapse a

great deal of agency for the crisis, for the urban African American ecosystems that developed during the Great Migration's first wave, hard times
were becoming a fact of life well before the fall.[3] While misfortune was
common, it was more common for some than for others. As the jobs of
the booming 1920s began to evaporate, necessity forced white workers to
take the sorts of low-wage jobs they had previously rejected. "During a
labor surplus," observe Daniel Roland Fusfield and Timothy Mason Gates,
"black workers were not essential. Thus, employers frequently met their
reduced labor needs by downgrading white workers to jobs that had previously been held by blacks, while black workers were dispensed with."
African Americans found themselves pushed out not only of employment
in manufacturing but also of jobs in the service industries, where they had
commonly worked as domestics, waiters, cooks, and janitors. There they
were frequently replaced by whites.[4] Indeed, by 1933, the unemployment
rate for black males in thirteen large American cities stood at 52 percent,
more than twice the 25 percent rate for all workers in those cities.[5] With
the evaporation of jobs, black migration slowed considerably.[6] But for
those who had already come north, returning to the South was politically,
socially, and economically not an option.

This is not to suggest that all economic enterprises in the African American ecosystem were doomed to failure during the 1930s. Small, local businesses providing essential services, such as beauty parlors, barbershops, and
funeral homes, still had a modicum of success. So, too, did the entertainment industry, though in a very limited sense. Of Chicago, sociologists St.
Clair Drake and Horace R. Cayton note, "during the periods when the lower
class has had regular employment—the First World War, the Fat Years,
and the [post–World War II] period—it has been more inclined to spend
money for commercial recreation than for voluntary organizations. Even
during the Depression years when funds for recreation were very limited,
the neighborhood movie-houses, the cheaper taverns, and the pool-rooms
continued to do a flourishing business. . . . The crowds that frequented
Bronzeville's commercial dance halls, its wrestling and boxing matches, and
the city's baseball games were evidence that the lower class was able to gar-
ner enough from the relief, the WPA, and odd jobs to have a good time."[7] In
spite of the continued popularity of baseball among Bronzeville's residents
as well as those in other African American ecosystems, the original organized Negro Leagues were unable to weather the economic storm.

But in 1933, at the height of the Great Depression, the Negro National
League was reborn. Like so many other African American business

ventures, black baseball owed its resurgence to gambling, particularly the numbers and policy rackets. With money so scarce, the poor continued to lay down wagers in hopes of hitting it big. Explains Ivan Light, "Numbers gamblers view the game as a rational economic activity and characteristically refer to their numbers bets as 'investments.' Most gamblers understand their numbers best as a means of personal savings." From bettors' point of view, numbers and policy gambling offer a means to convert loose change into larger amounts: "The methodical style of numbers gambling also indicates that bettors have adopted a long-range perspective, suggesting a rational savings strategy."[8] The promise of an infusion of cash in return for a series of individual tiny wagers certainly appealed to poor urban dwellers, both black and white, and racketeers flourished among the working classes. And in black neighborhoods, numbers bankers, as they were known, provided the capital to reignite Negro League baseball along with other sectors of the entertainment industry.

As the proprietors of numbers and policy games, these entrepreneurs became race heroes. Like the ward bosses who administered political machines, numbers and policy bankers provided a series of services to their communities. "In the 1930s and 1940s," writes Juliet E. K. Walker, "black policy kings were regarded as heroes in the black community not only for their ability to generate wealth, but also for their substantial philanthropic contributions to black institutions and organizations as well as their political connections, often used to secure patronage jobs for blacks."[9] As Drake and Cayton observed, "All the Negroes involved in the game become legendary figures who 'never let a man starve,' who were 'honest,' 'big hearted,' 'kind' gamblers."[10]

The rackets themselves provided local employment for runners (those who collected bets from drops) and writers (those who wrote out betting slips). So well conceived were the rackets as a business enterprise that in 1938, as the depression waned, the writers for one Chicago policy wheel actually struck for better conditions, objecting to working a midnight drawing.[11] The rackets also supported any number of constituent businesses—retail establishments that served as drops as well as a cottage industry of various subsidiary enterprises.[12] Black newspapers from the 1930s were filled with ads for publications such as *Aunt Sally's Policy Player's Dream Book*, *Stella's Lucky Dream Book*, and *Number Hit Forecast and Guide* as well as the *Sargon Dream Book* and the *Mysterious Master Key Dream Book*, featuring the "Master Key System." Professor Nol Ram's *Lucky Special Black Cat Dream Book* promised to reveal valuable information on how to "Hit like the Brown Bomber."[13] Ishmael the Mighty, master of the Mysteries of the Occult, offered to send an "individually divined number," determined "according to the ancient and mysterious sciences of Kabalism and Numerology," to those willing to send him a dollar, warning subscribers, "Don't Tell Your Banker."[14] As the name suggests, dream books promised to translate dream imagery into gigs on which the dreamer could wager. Other diviners offering personalized services, lucky talismans, ointments, and other betting aids also advertised in black newspapers. Not only did such businesses support the writers, publishers, and printers of these books, but ads in the *Pittsburgh Courier, Chicago Defender, Philadelphia Tribune*, and other papers brought in much-needed revenue.

Enter Pittsburgh

For organized racketeers of all ethnicities in all areas of the informal economy, crime was not an end but rather a means of social and economic mobility. According to Light and Gold, "When they have matured out of youthful recklessness, many successful racketeers prefer legitimate business to illegal business. Indeed, for those most successful in organized crime, the usual way out of the rackets is not through police suppression, the legend of Elliott Ness notwithstanding, but rather through the slow, inter-generational transfer of assets from illegal business to legal business."[15] For some bankers in the African American ecosystem, the legitimate business of choice was baseball. Such was the case with Pittsburgh's Gus Greenlee, though baseball was not his only—or even his first—foray into the formal economy.

Greenlee, a migrant from North Carolina, was something of an economic Renaissance man despite his rural upbringing. He got his start in loosely organized crime as a bootlegger, partnering with Joe Tito, who along with his brothers purchased Western Pennsylvania's Latrobe Brewery in 1932 in advance of the presumed repeal of the Volstead Act. Initially known as "Gasoline Gus" based on his propensity to sell his wares out of the trunk of his taxicab, Greenlee would emerge as a darling of the black press, which regularly referred to him as "Genial Gus." Earlier in his career, however, a yet-to-be-so-genial Greenlee was not above hijacking beer trucks to add to his inventory.[16]

Greenlee and his partner, William "Woogie" Harris, were credited with introducing the rackets to western Pennsylvania in 1926.[17] He reputedly learned the ins and outs of running a numbers bank in Harlem, where he was tutored by his future colleague in black baseball, Alex Pompez. Pompez may also initially have bankrolled the Pittsburgh racketeer's numbers operation.[18] Perhaps because of his connection to Pompez, Greenlee was also occasionally referred to as the "Caliph of Little Harlem" a not-so-subtle reference to Pittsburgh's Hill District, Greenlee's bailiwick.[19]

Like several earlier black baseball entrepreneurs, most notably Chicago's Henry Teenan Jones, Greenlee also got into the cabaret business, turning his bootlegging operation into the Paramount Inn, a black and tan, which is a nightclub with an open-door policy regarding race. Greenlee and one of his partners in the cabaret venture, William F. Cleveland, also organized the eponymous Greenlee and Cleveland Booking Agency to supply "the demand for orchestras and entertainers to exclusive clientele."[20] Capitalizing on a new medium, radio, the commercial side of which was initially launched in Pittsburgh in 1921, in 1926 Greenlee produced *Pickering's Broadcast Studio*, an hour-long weekly program on WJAS that featured the stylings of the Paramount's house band, Lloyd Scott and His Famous Orchestra.[21] He also owned a Chinese American restaurant; a café, the Green Boot; a hotel; a pool hall; and the Belmont Inn, an ice cream parlor billed as "the Coolest Spot in Town."[22] In each of these ventures, Greenlee seems to have had a different partner.

Greenlee also played a prominent role in local politics. In 1929, his efforts on behalf of the Third Ward Republican organization, which included endorsing Charles A. Kline for mayor and Samuel L. Price for alderman, earned Greenlee an honorary poem in the *Courier*. While not a literary effort of the highest caliber, it appears to say something important about the way Greenlee worked:

> O, heed Gus Greenlee's message,
>   He's a friend so warm and true;
> Co-operation is the only means
>   Will ever pull us through.
> . . . .
> For every vote that you cast,
>   In every single place
> It means "appointment" to you when
>   It's fostered for your race.
> O would black Pittsburgh wake and see
>   and for their welfare think,

A nail hole in a battleship
  Will make the vessel sink.[23]

The poem also mentions Price's foe in the race for alderman, John J. Verona, the incumbent, in a less flattering light. In at least one instance, Greenlee became a pawn in a political feud when what the poem called his "reputed lottery" was raided by constables acting on Verona's orders.[24] To be sure, the occasional raid and arrest was an occupational hazard for numbers racketeers, even one like Greenlee who had such a strong foothold in the formal economy as well. Rather, this incident, Greenlee's involvement in local politics, and his multiple partnerships with a wide range of entrepreneurs on both sides of the legal divide indicated the tightly woven nature of the strands of Pittsburgh's African American ecosystem and Greenlee's importance to that ecosystem.

Many similarities appear between Greenlee's Pittsburgh and the other black enclaves built during the Great Migration. But the Iron City also differed in significant ways. Unlike the residents of other urban black enclaves, Pittsburgh's African Americans were divided by geography. Allegheny County's hilly terrain prevented blacks from becoming concentrated in a single neighborhood. While, at first glance, concentrating an ethnic or racial population into a single area does not seem to be particularly propitious, it has its benefits to the residents. Wide dispersal of a population robs it of its political power. For this reason, Pittsburgh's African American community lacked the voice in civic affairs that was available to residents of Bronzeville, Harlem, or the area surrounding 18th and Vine in Kansas City.[25] And while all of African America was negatively impacted by the depression, black communities in Pittsburgh and the surrounding counties were ahead of the curve in terms of hard times. Both black and white migrants had originally been drawn to the area to work in the steel and coal industries. "Newly opened jobs at places like Jones and Laughlin Steel enlarged Pittsburgh's black population from twenty-five to fifty-five thousand, while hiring by Carnegie Steel plants in Aliquippa, Homestead, Rankin, Braddock, Duquesne, McKeesport, and Clairton raised the black population in those neighboring towns from five to twenty-three thousand," writes Laurence Glasco. But when demand for steel declined after World War I, so, too, did the good times for the region's most disadvantaged citizens.[26] The depression consequently began for western Pennsylvania's African American communities while black enclaves in other cities were still in what Walker identifies as their "golden age."[27]

Under these conditions, Pittsburgh seems an unlikely locus for the resurgence of black baseball. Yet even before Greenlee became involved, the presence of African American industrial and recreational leagues meant that area residents retained a strong interest in the sport. One of these leagues operated out of the Hill's Crawford Bathhouse, a prominent recreational facility constructed originally as a gathering place for African American youth, much like the country's black YMCAs.[28] By 1927, the Crawford recreational team, occasionally referred to as "Murderers' Row," like the New York Yankees team of the same year, played its games at nearby Washington Park and received regular coverage in the *Courier*'s sports pages.[29]

According to Pittsburgh baseball historian Rob Ruck, Greenlee added the Crawfords to his growing cache of formal businesses in 1930, having been offered the opportunity several times. Ruck maintains that Greenlee may have bought the team for a variety of reasons: "Greenlee was in the middle of a hotly contested campaign and wanted to outfit the Crawfords in uniforms bearing slogans aimed at getting voters to cast their ballots for James J. Coyne for county commissioner and Andrew Parks for district attorney." Moreover, "Greenlee's advisors figured the ball club would serve as an effective blind for money earned through the numbers racket, money that might otherwise attract the attention of federal tax investigators."[30] Initially, Greenlee recognized the fact that he had no knowledge of the sport, but he became increasingly committed to team ownership, going on a spending spree that ultimately produced "the best team that money could buy."[31]

Greenlee was preceded on Pittsburgh's black baseball scene by Cumberland "Cum" Posey, the son of an African American coal and shipping magnate and one of the men who helped to finance the fledgling *Pittsburgh Courier*.[32] In the 1920s, Posey refused the invitation by fellow Pennsylvanian, Ed Bolden, to affiliate Posey's Homestead Grays with the Eastern Colored League (ECL); Posey also ignored Rube Foster's veiled threats about what would happen if the Grays joined any organized circuit other than the Negro National League (NNL). Posey's steadfast insistence on remaining independent was as much about maintaining autonomy over his ball club as it was about the rash of player raids that beset the organized leagues, ultimately contributing to the failure of the Indianapolis ABCs.[33] By every conceivable measure, save for being two of Pittsburgh's preeminent race men, Posey and Greenlee seemed to be diametric opposites. Posey represented what black city residents commonly referred to as "Old Pittsburgh," the region's pre-migration black bourgeoisie.[34] Unlike the flamboyant Greenlee, Posey was reserved in appearance and public demeanor. And unlike Greenlee, for whom sports represented merely a portion of his financial holdings, Posey had designs on cornering black Pittsburgh's athletic marketplace. He was an accomplished athlete and a newspaper columnist and was a force in the rise of professional basketball, having been a star college player before venturing into franchise ownership when he formed the Monticello team and later the Leondi Big Five.[35]

Posey was not immune to the vagaries of depression-era economics, however, and relied on numbers money when the going got tough. Indeed, to help capitalize the Grays, Posey partnered with Pittsburgh's other numbers king, Rufus "Sonnyman" Jackson. Jackson, like Greenlee, had a hand in the lucrative entertainment business, controlling jukeboxes throughout the city.[36] The reality of the period was that revenue streams often ran dry, requiring infusions of cash from wherever they could be found, and most often they could be found in the informal economy.

As might be expected, the two magnates, Posey and Greenlee, developed a mutual disdain for one another that was expressed through a fierce on- and off-field rivalry. That rivalry and the two men's willingness to recognize where their individual interests lay helped reenergize black baseball. Writing about a 1933 exhibition doubleheader between the Crawfords and the Grays, John L. Clark opined, "Cum Posey and Gus Greenlee have stopped cussing each other long enough to bring their clubs together," though the games offered "no proof that the two owners like each other better." Clark goes on to cite the contests as indication that the magnates knew what the fans wanted and understood that protracted squabbling could hurt the bottom line.[37] While the rivalry certainly invigorated what had become a moribund sporting scene both in Pittsburgh and elsewhere, Greenlee's efforts, backed by his considerable wealth and influence, ultimately revived the business of black baseball.

Greenlee Field

Greenlee's central role in the revival of black baseball as a business venture is best exemplified by his decision to build his own ballpark in 1932. Far more ambitious than Bolden's Hilldale Park in Darby, near Philadelphia, which closed the same year, Greenlee Field was the centerpiece of Negro League venues with a capacity of approximately 7,500, more than three times the size of Hilldale.[38] Strictly speaking, Greenlee Field appears to have represented the kind of economic self-determinism advocated by Booker T. Washington. However, Greenlee departed from the Washingtonian model in that one of his partners in this project, which also included fellow numbers operator Woogie Harris, was Greenlee's mentor in the bootlegging business, Joe Tito.

As a numbers banker, Greenlee provided capital to a wide selection of Hill businesses in addition to his own, including several loans that helped keep the *Pittsburgh Courier* afloat. Nevertheless, he lacked the funds to finance his ballpark. Capital came in the form of the Bedford Land Company, which Tito and other white interests controlled. Even so, the venue was named Greenlee Field and the Crawfords were the face of the field. Yet the presence of white financial interests significantly undermined the race man's control. According to Clark, who at one point also served as Greenlee's press agent, "No colored person except Greenlee had the final say about anything at the field, and Greenlee's option was confined to baseball." Indeed, Greenlee Field played host to a number of other sporting events, including boxing matches and football games. Tito and his white cohort controlled the lucrative prizefight business, reaping most of the profits, even though Greenlee was also in the business of fight management. And while the venue bore the name of a black entrepreneur, it employed few people of color. Tito hired white ushers and concessionaires, among them his brother, who sold Latrobe beer, to make wealthy white patrons feel comfortable. In so doing, Tito took the race out of what looked like a race business. In the words of Clark, "When men and women of color made two or three trips to Greenlee Field and discovered even that small wages paid to the required help at the park could not be re-circulated among the colored people," Greenlee lost some of the Hill district's goodwill.[39]

Like Policy Sam Young and his white backer in Chicago, Greenlee's association with Tito, in both the informal economy of bootlegging and the numbers and the formal economy of sports management, exemplifies the reality of doing business in the African American ecosystem. In fact, Greenlee field would not have been built without the help of Tito and another partner, Dr. Joseph F. Toms, the owner of the land on which the park was built.[40]

The new park put Greenlee in an ideal position to initiate his baseball venture, the new NNL, which was formed in Chicago on January 10, 1933, with other planning meetings held over the following months. Included in the venture along with Greenlee's Crawfords and, despite the enmity between owners, Posey's Homestead Grays were the Chicago American Giants, and the Nashville Elite Giants. (A Cleveland team was planned, but never formed.)[41] In spite of Posey's visibility, Greenlee was anointed president. While, in its early years, the NNL, as a business venture, was at best fiscally shaky, the action of the Pittsburgh entrepreneurs sowed the seeds for the black baseball revival that was to come. Without the uneasy cooperation of Pittsburgh's squabbling antagonists, the new Negro Leagues could not have become a full-fledged business enterprise helping to fuel the African American ecosystem.

Gotham

Like his friend Greenlee, Alex Pompez was a major player both in the rackets and in baseball, running a numbers bank out of his East Harlem cigar store at the same time he owned and managed the Cuban Stars. For more than a decade, Pompez's numbers business was wholly his, an independently run enterprise owned and operated by an Afro-Cuban resident of what would become Spanish Harlem. Pompez also was a darling of the black press, which predictably emphasized his formal business rather than his informal numbers operations. Speaking to Pompez's positive reputation as well as his status as a Latin American, the *New York Amsterdam News*'s Romeo L. Dougherty routinely referred to him as "Señor Pompez", and the "good Señor."[42] Although he learned the a great deal about business from the much-reviled Nat Strong, Pompez parlayed his place in the Harlem ecosystem, fueled in part by his connection to his other mentor, numbers impresario Dominique, as well as by his sterling reputation, into what were generally considered a pair of horizontally integrated race businesses par excellence.

But Pompez's circumstances changed dramatically. While Greenlee relied in part on capitalization from outside African America, Pompez had the outside world thrust upon him when Dutch Schultz (née Arthur Flegenheimer) began muscling in on the Harlem rackets and made the good Señor an offer he tried but ultimately could not refuse. Pompez was coerced into joining Schultz's widespread numbers operation, receiving a salary of $250 a week and 40 percent of the bank.[43]

As Adrian Burgos Jr. notes, Pompez, though hardly happy with the situation, used his time as a Schultz operative to reorganize his ball club, formerly the Cuban Stars, under a new name, the New York Cubans, presumably to better position them as Harlem's primary entry in the emergent NNL.[44] Not above learning from his protégé, Pompez took a page from Greenlee's playbook, proposing to create what Dougherty called "a real baseball park." The renovation of the venue, Dyckman Oval, Dougherty contended, would give black baseball what it needed to succeed as a business in New York at a time when the organized black game had yet to make an impact. The city-owned park was located in the Inwood section of Manhattan, to the north of Washington Heights, just a short subway, bus, or cab ride from Harlem. In Dougherty's view, black baseball would not become economically viable until fans did not have to travel from Harlem, where most of them lived, to the hinterlands of the Bronx to attend games at Catholic Protectory Oval or to Dexter Park, on the outskirts of Queens in the Woodhaven neighborhood on the Brooklyn border. The fact that Dexter Park was owned and overseen by Strong also did not endear the venue to Harlem's consumer base.

And as work commenced on the Dyckman Oval renovations in February 1935, Pompez opened baseball offices at 200 West 135th Street, between 7th and 8th Avenues, in the heart of Harlem. By physically separating his baseball business from his Schultz-controlled informal banking operations and hiring as his press agent a local celebrity, basketball star Frank "Strangler" Forbes, a former player with the Harlem Renaissance, whose home court was the nearby Renaissance Ballroom, Pompez professionalized his baseball operation and demonstrated that his Cubans were a local outfit with local roots, regardless of their exotic name.[45] Moreover, by centralizing his baseball business outside of Spanish Harlem, which was by every possible measure on the periphery of Harlem's main currents, Pompez gave notice that his team was to be Uptown's Negro League entry, the titular representative of the entire ecosystem. Indeed, these moves made Pompez a new type of race man for the age: multiethnic, resolute, and canny enough to recognize the potential market and move directly to it.

Though Pompez concentrated his formal professional efforts on baseball, he remained a numbers banker whose legal enterprises were capitalized by his illegal operations. Pompez remained tied to the Schultz organization to some degree even after Schultz's 1935 murder.[46] But in 1937, Pompez's business ventures, which included formal entry into the NNL in 1935 as well as his continued successful work in the rackets, ground to a halt when he was indicted by district attorney Thomas E. Dewey and fled the country, first to Cherbourg, France, via Canada, then to Mexico City.[47] He returned after making a deal in which he agreed to testify against James J. Hines, a powerful Tammany Hall machine politician with close ties to Schultz.[48] Pompez's involvement in the Hines trial and activity in the informal economy received considerable attention from the mainstream press, including the august *New York Times*, while his formal enterprises received almost none.

According to popular perception, this encounter with the law, the last and most serious of a history of encounters, led Pompez to extricate himself once and for all from the rackets. According to "Bankers Didn't Quit as Trial Went On!," which appeared in the *New York Amsterdam News* on October 15, 1938, however, "many numbers bankers who were snared in the net of District Attorney Dewey when he was a special prosecutor never relinquished their connections with the racket." The piece continued, "Pompez has been seen almost daily at his old Harlem haunts, talking with many of the boys who are still in the numbers racket. He keeps a 'stiff upper lip,' although it is rumored that he knows plenty which he will he not reveal even to Dewey . . . Pompez is simulating the role of a poverty stricken man. He appears on the streets not exactly in tatters but decidedly less debonair than before he took a 'run out powder' because of Dewey's heat."[49] If the *Amsterdam News* is correct, Pompez continued to profit from the rackets, even as he denied it. More significantly, it further emphasizes the undeniable influence of numbers money on black baseball.

Even as a race business, the rackets remained subject to white involvement. Greenlee's connection to Tito was voluntary and pragmatic. Tito operated mostly in the background while Greenlee represented himself as a race man through and through. Tito's influence on what appeared at face value to be a black-owned business did not really become an issue with consumers until Greenlee faced more serious financial problems. Pompez, in contrast, was literally strong-armed into doing business with white mobsters until the Dewey investigation severed Pompez's connection to the Schultz combine, at which point Pompez's business quietly returned to black ownership. However, the Schultz machine had no financial bearing on the operation of Pompez's baseball undertakings. Unlike Tito, who had a stake in Greenlee's sporting empire, Pompez's white partner in the rackets had no economic stake in the baseball business.

Like Pittsburgh, Harlem had two competing black baseball teams, though neither really played in the neighborhood. But unlike the Grays and the Crawfords, the Cubans and their ostensible competition, the New York Black Yankees, shared a thin market dominated by Strong. The teams faced competition not only from a wide variety of professional sports, race and otherwise, but also from a panoply of entertainment enterprises that demanded a portion of the extremely limited discretionary resources of an already impoverished consumer base.

The Black Yankees represented a threat to the existing baseball establishment. The team, like the Cubans, the Crawfords, and the Grays, was capitalized with numbers money, in this case from the bank of James "Soldier Boy" Semler. Semler, like Pompez, had learned the baseball business from Strong and reputedly inherited the team after the booking agent's sudden death in January 1935. Strong's level of involvement in the Black Yankees engendered much speculation in the black press, which seemed unclear about whether he owned a piece of the team or just handled its promotion. But a December 22, 1934, ad in the *New York Amsterdam News* offering "Greetings from NAT STRONG AND THE NEW YORK BLACK YANKEES" leaves little doubt that Strong was unafraid to attach his name—and by extension his money—to the team.[50]

Following Strong's death, which shook the NNL establishment despite its members' efforts to distance themselves from the booking agent's legacy, Semler, a league outcast, unambiguously announced his intentions.[51] According to a February 16, 1935, *New York Amsterdam News* article, "Yanks Defy New League,"

> Although thousands of baseball fans were wondering just what would happen to the Black Yankees with the passing of Nat C. Strong, Jimmie Semler, who emphatically states that he is the owner of the New York team in the face of many who are saying that he is only the "front" man, went on record the other day in defying the National Association of Negro Baseball Clubs to do anything that would break up his outfit.
>
> Semler says that he is not losing one night's sleep over the baseball situation, and insists that he will be able to run independently next season without losing any money. "I stand ready to meet the best teams in the League next summer, for the boys are going to play independent ball anyhow, and I do not see why they should not consider a team guaranteed to help them bring in the money.
>
> "I am using my right as a citizen of this country who has been guaranteed the protection of all its laws in maintaining a team outside of any organization. As I see it, I have more to gain at this time, and I will continue to operate as I have done in the past. I will not have any trouble finding places to play, and when the time comes it will be easy to see why the League will find more to gain by playing a team which I feel will be able to cope with the best in the association.

"Right here and now I challenge the winner of next season's best team and winner in the League series. I want to do something for the Scottsboro boys and I will let the first game be a benefit after expenses have been taken out. I am still carrying on at the old stand and your Black Yankees will be bigger and better this year. Let us carry on!"[52]

Despite such grand rhetoric, Semler's Black Yankees were never terribly successful either as a business or as a ball club. And although Semler had a reputation for violence, none of his ventures, formal or informal, were terribly successful.[53] Nevertheless, Semler attempted to gain admission to the NNL in 1935, garnering some support from the black press, particularly Romeo Dougherty of the *New York Amsterdam News*, though the league power structure rebuffed the efforts. The ensuing raids on his players did not escape his notice, and he filed suit against the owners of the two local teams that were most responsible for the raids—Pompez and Abe Manley, owner of the Brooklyn Eagles. But following negotiations, Semler dropped the suit, and his Black Yankees, whom the *Chicago Defender* frequently called the "stormy petrels of Negro baseball," joined the league in 1936.[54]

As Semler's and Pompez's experiences illustrate, the difficulty of doing business as a numbers operator or sports magnate in New York may well have had a pronounced negative effect on the capitalization of the city's black ball clubs. And these two men were not the only entrepreneurs—or consumers, for that matter—who found it difficult to operate in Harlem's ecosystem during the Great Depression. Renowned Harlem nightspots such as the West Indian–owned Renaissance Casino, with its famed ballroom, and the Savoy Ballroom, owned and operated by Moe Gale, known to the musicians he managed as the "Great White Father of Harlem," were not immune.[55] Nor were bootlegger Connie Immerman's Connie's Inn, which also followed the pattern of participation by white racketeers in the African American ecosystem, and Smalls Paradise, owned by Harlem's Edwin Smalls and featuring elaborate floor shows and dancing waiters.[56] All of these venues rose to prominence in Harlem's social and economic life during the high times of the 1920s and weathered the economic storms of the 1930s in no small part because they did not depend solely on black Harlemites for patronage. As was also true in Chicago's Black Belt, even during tough times, many residents were willing—if not eager—to spend whatever money they had on hand on entertainment. This was also true of Harlem's population. Nevertheless, much like Chicago, but on a far larger scale, Harlem's famous nightspots drew patrons from outside the community. All of these establishments were black and tans. Although the black and tan may be seen as a cultural phenomenon most closely associated with the Harlem Renaissance, the increasing visibility of jazz as dance music during the 1920s, the growing popularity of swing, and the clubs' open door policies as they pertained to the color line offered Harlem's ecosystem a huge advantage during the 1930s. Green trumped both black and white.

The mainstream press encouraged patronage of black and tan clubs, a phenomenon not lost on the editors of the *New York Amsterdam News*. On November 29, 1929, when economic limitations were far more pronounced Uptown than in the rest of New York City, the Harlem paper reprinted without editorial comment a piece from the *Brooklyn Daily Eagle* titled "As Seen Under the Caption of the Inky Way," that lauded the benefits of a trip to Harlem: "For Harlem is a fleeting glimpse into another world. There are no such people as populate Harlem elsewhere. There is no such place as Harlem anywhere else. And no writer—with due apologies to the famed scribes who have sought to perpetuate true Harlemania between the covers of their books—has ever actually caught it. You can learn about Harlem from Vachel Lindsay's epic 'Congo'—or you can learn about it from experience. The latter way is more fun." The article concluded with the fairly positive though no less patronizing assessment: "These people live and work in Harlem, happily cognizant that the thousands of gay, white celebrants and night owls who have almost completely deserted the downtown and midtown night clubs for the gayer atmosphere of Harlem's haunts, come there merely to see how life is really lived by a race that, happily, was born to live it!"[57] It would seem that the Harlem paper reproduced the *Eagle* article not to critique the tone of the piece, the Vachel Lindsay reference notwithstanding, but rather to indicate that the Brooklyn press saw Harlem as a place to party and, by extension, to spend money.

Harlem residents did not always welcome white patronage of local businesses. In "Harlem Sketch Book," a regular column in the *New York Amsterdam News*, Theophilus Lewis addressed the problem of hailing a taxi after a night on the town:

> Chauffeurs of the taxicabs that line up in front of Smalls' [*sic*] Paradise in the sinful hours do not like to take colored fares. A colored rider practically always means a short haul and a small tip. On the other hand, an ofay party may mean a trip to the far flung end of the Bronx or a spin to Greenwich Village, with an hour's parking in Central Park on the meter, plus a fat gratuity.

As their motive is purely economic, the taxi men's reluctance to take colored
fares is easy to understand and almost as easy to excuse. But some of them
carry their efforts to avoid colored passengers to unreasonable extremes and
become unpardonably abusive when a colored rider insists on being served.[58]

The target of Lewis's disdain is not the "ofay" club-goers—the people who
followed the *Eagle*'s advice and went Uptown to see for themselves—but
rather the taxi drivers, who not only refused fares based on color but did
so in an offensive manner.

Still, near the end of 1938, the *New York Amsterdam News* bemoaned
the fact that absence of white patrons meant the demise of many black
nightspots: "The direct result of the closing laws and other restrictions on
Harlem bars and nightclubs has been the discouraging of white pleasure-
seekers from coming uptown. Many clubs have closed down. Others are
struggling along with skeleton crews of workers and shows. Bartenders,
waiters, porters, and cooks are walking the streets because there is nothing to do in their line of work."[59] So, as difficult as it may have been to
secure a cab outside of Smalls, the white patrons who provided fares to
the drivers were essential to certain sectors of the African American ecosystem. This phenomenon can be further traced through the economic
realities facing black baseball.

One reason why Negro League baseball may have had limited appeal
in Harlem is that fans of the sport, regardless of color, had other options.
Harlemites had easy access to three Major League stadiums where, unlike
Forbes Field in Pittsburgh with its Jim Crow seating, fans were welcome
in the stands if not on the field of play. The Polo Grounds, located at the
bottom of Coogan's Bluff, lay on the border between Harlem and Washington Heights, while Yankee Stadium was just across the East River in the
Bronx and Ebbets Field was a relatively short and direct subway ride away.
Public transportation made all these ballparks easily accessible and open
to black baseball fans. While certainly not "race friendly" by any stretch
of the imagination, these popular facilities did not discriminate when it
came to paying patrons. The Yankees, Giants, and Dodgers may not have
depended on black patronage, but they were not inclined to turn away
dollars, regardless of origins. In contrast, the Black Yankees, the Cubans,
and Manley's Brooklyn Eagles could not survive without mixed patronage. According to Dougherty, "But for the support of white people here[,]
Negro baseball would certainly be in the dumps." He continued, "Dyckman Oval held a splendid crowd the opening day, but it is doubtful if

Señor Pompez has any reason to throw his hat in the air and whoop with joy, for even the night games are fully dependent upon the white fans for their support."[60] Contrary to common assumptions, the race sport did not have the luxury of leaning on a purely black fan base, although the Negro League establishment did not acknowledge the businesses' dependence on white fans. Both black and white operators of black and tan nightspots, however, understood this dependence all too well.

In this way, New York City was unique, though its African American ecosystem bore some similarities to those of other cities during the Depression, but the effects of the economy on the business of black baseball were fundamentally different in each location. Newark, New Jersey, for example, had a significantly smaller ecosystem and enjoyed close proximity to the contested territory of the New York City teams, but the professional black game enjoyed a more loyal race fan base across the river.

Newark

Black baseball in New York City was hardly a going concern when the NNL expanded into Brooklyn and northern New Jersey in the mid-1930s. Prior to Semler's entry into the league in 1936, the Black Yankees staged occasional contests at Yankee Stadium, always booked and promoted by Nat Strong. In fact, there was no permanent professional race baseball presence in the New York marketplace not somehow affiliated with Strong. Unlike Pittsburgh or Kansas City, where the Monarchs continued to operate successfully in spite of the collapse of both the original NNL and the world economy, the economics of black baseball in the New York marketplace were dicey even under the best of circumstances. Still, as the northern city with the largest African American economy, the greater New York metropolitan area appeared able to support one or more NNL franchises.

Recognizing the opportunity for expansion into a potentially lucrative market, the league admitted Abe and Effa Manley's Brooklyn Eagles at the 1934 league meetings, a year before the Black Yankees were admitted, entering into what appeared to be a mutually beneficial arrangement for the Eagles and the Major League Brooklyn Dodgers' ownership to rent Ebbets Field as their home park. Manley, like so many other Negro League entrepreneurs, was yet another numbers operator. But it was his wife, Effa, two decades his junior, who was the more baseball savvy of the two. Unlike

Olivia Taylor, who unexpectedly found herself running the Indianapolis ABCs following her husband's death, Effa Manley actively grasped the reins of what would become a first-rate ball club. The Eagles' entry into the NNL seemed to constitute a direct challenge to Strong's hegemony over New York's black baseball market. But the black baseball business in Brooklyn was not as vital—or as necessary—as the NNL originally imagined, and the franchise simply did not draw the crowds required to operate a profitable business. Furthermore, Strong's death prior to the 1935 season rendered the need to wrest power from him moot.[61]

Such was not the case in Newark, which, according to Frank Tucker's "Jersey Sports" column in the *Baltimore Afro-American*, had by November 1935 "earned the reputation of being one of the best drawing towns in the league."[62] In the fall of that year, the NNL's existing New Jersey franchise, the Newark Dodgers, owned by Charles Tyler, proprietor of a local hangout, the Chicken Shack, in Avenel, New Jersey, was facing financial difficulty. Although Tyler's team had its fair share of fans, he could not sustain the franchise. Tucker laid the blame for Tyler's economic misfortunes at the feet of the league, which scheduled games in Newark at odd times rather than when the public expected them to be played, citing the team's prior owner, Elizabeth, New Jersey resident, Kirkpatrick Marrow, as his source.[63]

Whether the NNL was culpable for Tyler's misfortunes is subject to speculation. What is beyond speculation is that the Newark owner owed Abe Manley about five hundred dollars, but rather than pay off the debt in cash, Tyler cleared it by turning over his financially floundering franchise to Manley instead.[64] The Manleys saw the opportunities Newark offered and merged their stagnant Brooklyn club with the Newark Dodgers and moved across the Hudson in time for the 1936 season. The Manleys retained the name, Eagles, regardless of the name's associations with the original club and the Brooklyn newspaper.

The new Eagles played home games in Ruppert Stadium, which the Manleys rented from and shared with the minor league Newark Bears. Prior to becoming involved with the organized Negro circuit, Abe Manley had some limited experience with semiprofessional black baseball in Camden, New Jersey, where he got his start in the rackets before expanding into Newark, giving him a unique perspective on the African American economies in both North and South Jersey.[65] Abe Manley's rackets may have capitalized the Eagles, but Effa Manley was the driving force behind the organization's on-field and financial success.

Before their team relocated to New Jersey, however, the Manleys had already established themselves as members of Harlem's bourgeoisie. Effa Manley was more visible presence than her husband in Harlem's social, political, and to a certain extent economic circles. Fashionable and elegant, she regularly appeared in the society pages of the local black press, while Abe Manley kept a far lower profile. For a woman operating in Harlem's male-dominated ecosystem, numbers banker Madame Stephanie St. Claire notwithstanding, it was essential that Effa Manley project just the right public facade. It may have been acceptable for a man in the same milieu, such as Alex Pompez, who could be seen walking around in shabby clothes to give the impression of relative poverty, following his brush with Dewey. But it would not do for a woman of Effa Manley's social status, particularly because, unlike the majority of Harlem's successful female business entrepreneurs, she was not engaged in the beauty business.

In addition to her social activities, Effa Manley was a fixture in the community's political life and a forceful social activist, focusing on issues of color and access. In 1934, she and Lucille Randolph, the wife of A. Philip Randolph, joined with other female members of Harlem's black bourgeoisie to form the Citizens League for Fair Play. The Citizens League objected to the fact that Harlem's premier retailers, among them Blumstein's department store, the largest establishment on the neighborhood's primary commercial thoroughfare, West 125th Street, served an overwhelmingly African American clientele but employed few black workers and relegated them to menial positions. The Citizens' League, essentially an outgrowth of the Harlem Housewives League, organized pickets against Blumstein's and other white-owned retailers. The resulting actions were collectively labeled as the "Don't Buy Where You Can't Work" campaign. Based on a similar action in Chicago's Bronzeville, organized in 1929 by A. C. O'Neal, the editor of the radical black newspaper, *The Whip*, the original campaign was referred to as "Spend Your Money Where You Can Work."[66] Effa Manley played an instrumental role in negotiating a settlement with Blumstein's, a family-owned business. The retailer hired fifteen African American sales clerks, albeit light-skinned women, and promised to hire twenty more.[67] Blumstein's capitulation also led other local white merchants to hire black employees.

Although Blumstein's appeared to have lost its struggle with the Citizens' League, the store was really the victor. The owners placated members of the community by hiring a selection of its most attractive young women, thereby engendering goodwill on the part of the mainstream of its consumer base. The store's apparent willingness to evolve into what was perceived as a more race-friendly commercial venture was looked upon favorably by the socially progressive *New York Age*. Unlike its competitor, the *New York Amsterdam News* did not actively support the pickets in deference to the fact that the retailer was one of the paper's primary advertisers, but the *Age* did not count on advertising revenue from Blumstein's. For this reason, the *Age* did not have a vested interest in supporting the store, though in effect, this is what happened. Its support of the settlement, while unencumbered by financial considerations, allowed Blumstein's to solidify its place in the community. In turn, the retailer improved its own bottom line by appearing to move with the times during a period of harsh economic circumstances, as it cashed in on the patronage of race consumers.[68]

Some of the rhetoric of "Don't Buy Where You Can't Work" is summed up in a headline for a clothing store advertisement, appearing in the *American and West Indian News*, touting the establishment's owners as "American Negroes competing against Jews in the Haberdashery World." Much of the tension in the "Don't Buy Where You Can't Work" campaign resulted from the fact that many of Harlem's retailers were Jewish. Consequently, the language of the movement and of the larger community frequently conflated *white* and *Jewish*. These tensions between the Citizens' League for Fair Play and 125th Street's white merchants, Jewish and otherwise, resembled the uneasy relationship between the NNL owners and booking agents, particularly as it pertained to the color line.[69]

Though white involvement as well as incursion into black business, including that of the NNL, was always present, it was not necessarily a given. The seeds for the "Don't Buy" protests as well as other attempts to organize both individuals and entrepreneurs of color to support economic progress through self-sufficiency were sown by the efforts of the Colored Merchants Association (CMA), a cooperative of African American grocers established in the 1920s and strongly influenced by the National Negro Business League (NNBL). According to a short spring 1930 piece in the *New York Times*, not generally known at the time for its coverage of African American business affairs, "The Colored Merchants' Association was founded to provide a system of cooperative buying, selling and advertising and to obtain the benefits of larger capital. It has grown rapidly and now steps into the class of a large business." With only one black-owned grocery store for every nineteen hundred Americans of color, Robert R. Moton, who had succeeded Booker T. Washington at the helm of the

Tuskegee Normal and Industrial Institute and was president of the NNBL, called for the development of a race-owned grocery chain. According to Moton, "Stronger and better Negro business enterprises will build a larger customer group, give employment to Negroes and enable them to get out of the lap of philanthropy. The Negro will be put on his feet as a producing and contributing citizen."[70]

Announced with a great splash in the pages of the *New York Amsterdam News* and the *New York Age*, CMA model stores opened in Harlem beginning in April 1930.[71] Indeed, the opening of the Harlem store generated national coverage from the black press. The *Pittsburgh Courier* noted,

> Millions of Negroes in the United States are asking what the race can do to be saved. . . . One thing, however, is certain and known to all. Unless you have money in this or any other country you cannot amount to much. The group without a solid economic foundation will never amount to anything or solve any of its problems no matter where it may be. Money and property represent power. The more power an individual or group possesses the less oppression and restriction is suffered.
>
> Negroes will never acquire the power necessary to ease pressure upon them until more of them get on the receiving side of the counter. In brief, our group will always be more or less of a slave group until it begins to sell as well as buy, and it cannot increase its buying power until it sells more.[72]

But, as with black baseball, what worked in a more limited marketplace with fewer options did not necessarily work in the larger African American ecosystem of the North in general and New York City in particular. Despite a barrage of press coverage linking the success of the stores to the betterment of the race and touting the CMA's line of black-produced flours as a way of linking race progress to donuts, toilet soap, and mayonnaise, the effort failed as a result of poor sales.[73] In fact, CMA stores failed throughout the country, but perhaps none so visibly as in the big city with the highest concentration of black residents. But unlike the NNL's Brooklyn franchise, which abandoned the city proper for the greener fields of Newark when it failed to draw, the CMA was not as flexible. In reality, it is only possible to extend the analogy so far. Nevertheless, the essential difference between Harlem's CMA grocery and the Newark Eagles, strictly in business terms, is rooted in both the nature and the financial underpinnings of the respective enterprises. While CMA grocery stores depended solely on support from the community, the Eagles and other black baseball franchises often relied on alternative sources of funding from the numbers and policy rackets when the box office could not keep pace. Moreover, the comparisons further underscore the extent to which the rackets coursed through the bloodstream of the African American ecosystem.

Reinvigorating Chicago

During his tenure as president of the NNL, Gus Greenlee not only presided over what was at the time black baseball's premier venue but also unveiled a promotion that served the reorganized Negro Leagues well throughout the rest of their history: the East-West Classic, an annual all-star game. This event, introduced in 1933 by the fledgling NNL in its first year of operation, represented Greenlee's hand in the revival and renewal of professional black baseball. Greenlee invested $2,500, hardly a trifling sum at the height of the Depression, even for a successful numbers racketeer. Greenlee's stake allowed the league to secure the rental of Chicago's Comiskey Park, further underscoring his commitment to the overall venture as a mechanism to publicize the revival and renewal of professional black baseball.[74]

A member of Greenlee's organization, journalist Roy Sparrow of the Hearst-published *Pittsburgh Sun-Telegraph*, who also served as the team's traveling secretary, may have conceived of the idea for the East-West Classic in conjunction with the *Pittsburgh Courier*'s Bill Nunn.[75] Some evidence also shows that *Chicago Tribune* sports editor Arch Ward, the father of the Major League All-Star Game, initially held two months earlier at the same venue, may have been involved in creating the Classic as well.[76]

Although published reports put attendance at the 1933 Classic at between fifteen and twenty thousand, a respectable gate, the game's real impact was not financial; rather, it was a public relations gold mine. Sparrow handled the promotional effort. Ward's *Tribune* also dedicated an uncharacteristically large number of column inches to the East-West game. Although it was not unheard of, mainstream publications rarely covered race team sports to this extent, indicating that Ward was directly involved in promoting the game.

The Major League All-Star Game, which provided a model for the Negro League's version of the event, similarly served as a promotional tool to boost fan interest during the heart of the depression.[77] Paralleling the strategy used by the Major Leagues, the organizers of the East-West

Classic placed ballots for player selection in the pages of black newspapers, providing readers with a sense of agency. In this way, the East-West game served as a cross-promotion. On one hand, the press spread the word about the game, publicizing black baseball in general; on the other, circulation increased as fans had incentive to purchase the *Chicago Defender,* the *Philadelphia Tribune,* the *New York Age,* and as many as fifty-two other black papers to acquire ballots and to keep tabs on the voting.[78] Ward's *Tribune* and other mainstream newspapers also reported on the voting, an indication that they may have benefited from such coverage.[79]

Ward and the *Tribune's* involvement in publicizing the Negro League game fits the pattern of white involvement in the economics of black baseball, demonstrating yet again that such participation was not always exploitative. Rather than functioning as a sort of incursion, the *Tribune's* interest in the Classic offered benefits for all parties involved. As fans traveled to Chicago to attend the exhibition, they became consumers in Bronzeville's formal service economy, patronizing hotels, rooming houses, bars, and restaurants as well as in some of its less formal establishments. In effect, the promotion functioned as baseball's version of a black and tan, since the businesses around Comiskey Park profited from the game-day traffic on a date when the park would otherwise have remained dark. By the mid-1940s, attendance at the East-West Classic rivaled that of the Major League All-Star Game.

The growing popularity of the East-West Classic also brought black baseball in Chicago back into focus. As in other original league cities, when the organized, professional game faltered, independent and semi-professional teams continued to operate. The lack of a formal structure for the first NNL led to shifting ownership, a phenomenon that affected even Rube Foster's former team following his departure from the baseball landscape. John M. Schorling, a white sports entrepreneur and the son-in-law of White Sox owner Charles Comiskey, took control of the original Chicago American Giants and assumed ownership of the old wooden ballpark where the White Sox had most recently played, renamed it Schorling Park, and made it the American Giants' home field.[80] Schorling subsequently sold the team to a group of white businessmen headed by florist William A. Trimble, who was reputed to have close connections to white Chicago's informal economy.[81]

In 1932, Robert A. Cole and a business associate, Horace Greeley Hall, purchased the team from Trimble, with Cole placing his personal stamp on the club by renaming it Cole's American Giants. Cole was already a force in Bronzeville's ecosystem and was involved with the gambling rackets, but his participation in the formal economy of the black metropolis was far more extensive and more diversified than that of virtually any other black baseball magnate. Baseball comprised but a small part of his of his business holdings and was financed primarily by his ownership of the Metropolitan Funeral Systems Association (MFSA) rather than by gambling, though gambling had provided his original stake to buy the company and in emergencies could be relied on to make up any financial shortfalls. After the MFSA became a serious player in Bronzeville's economy, Cole, not a long-standing member of Chicago's black bourgeoisie but rather a migrant from rural Tennessee, became one of Bronzeville's most important businessmen, yet he also remained something of an outsider. A former Pullman porter, Cole personified the ideal of the elusive American Dream to his fellow migrants. In this regard, Cole followed in the footsteps of the founders of the Bronzeville community, Mushmouth Johnson and Teenan Jones among them. According to Suzanne E. Smith, Cole's reputation as both a successful gambler and a bold businessman afforded him the ability to operate effectively in both Bronzeville's formal and informal economies.[82]

The MFSA initially sought to provide people with affordable burial insurance and later offered life insurance to Bronzeville residents. In 1927, Cole purchased the MFSA, a conglomeration of black insurance companies that Cole had helped to found during the flush times when migrants were still pouring into the area.[83] This gambler turned magnate, who owned the American Giants until 1935, and Hall, an MFSA executive, who assumed control thereafter, were unique among black baseball's owners. Cole built a legitimate business empire surpassed only by Chicago's other black insurance giant, Supreme Liberty Life, at a time when most businesses were storefront operations that "sprang up in houses, basements and old buildings."[84] And Hall was an important day-to-day administrator for the company.

In addition to the insurance company, Cole founded Metropolitan Funeral Parlors, America's most lucrative black funeral home chain.[85] Like the business of segregated baseball, the funeral business was one of the few economic arenas available to entrepreneurs of color. But while most funeral home owners were involved in the African American ecosystem on the local level, Cole's funeral business represented a move into a regional and national marketplace. Moreover, by connecting burial insurance with the funeral industry, Cole created a sophisticated vertically integrated business model.

The MFSA weathered the storm of the depression through a number of sound business decisions, diversifying its holdings in sensible ways. When still more money was needed, Cole resorted to his considerable skill at poker and blackjack to keep the MFSA solvent.[86] According to Cole biographer Robert E. Weems Jr.,

> Besides using gambling winnings to keep the MFSA afloat during the early years of the Depression, Cole also used his unique source of extra capital to subsidize a variety of community improvement activities. Among the projects funded by Cole and the MFSA during the 1930s were building a recording studio for Jack L. Cooper's pioneering "All Negro Radio Hour" [and] publication of the *Bronzeman* magazine, a precursor of *Ebony* and *Jet*. . . .
>
> The Metropolitan Funeral System Association's involvement with activities outside the realm of insurance reflected Cole's desire to use the company as a means to undertake a broader "racial mission."[87]

Cole also pursued much more innovative and far-reaching forms of involvement in the entertainment industry than those explored by black baseball's other owners. Cole was a pioneer in black radio, especially with his support of broadcaster and fellow black entrepreneur Jack L. Cooper. According to Adam Green,

> The "timeshare" agreement with [radio station] WSBC, where broadcast slots were purchased for a flat fee, left location of sponsors and advertisers to the broadcaster. Here Cooper proved most adept, convincing local businesses in furniture, clothing, food, and other trades to solicit black customers through his radio programs. Nor were Cooper's ties confined to white businesses. Black-owned Metropolitan Funeral System Association built him a studio in the early 1930s in exchange for four regular plugs. . . . Seeking to consolidate these gains, Cooper started what was probably the first official black advertising agency in 1937 to cultivate retail clients: the Jack L. Cooper Advertising Company. The arrangement represented another idea of black community through radio—not only that of cultural audience or virtual public, but also validated consumer market. Cooper would not secure national advertisers until the late 1940s, around when they became commonplace throughout black radio.[88]

Cole's entrepreneurial ventures, including but not limited to his American Giants, also served to illustrate how closely woven the strands of Chicago's African American ecosystem were. As a mortgage lender engaged in formal banking activities, the MFSA also had a stake in many other Bronzeville businesses of varying sizes. For example, in 1938, the association made a three-thousand-dollar loan to Robert Abbott, publisher of the *Defender*.[89]

Like Greenlee and Pompez, Cole also got into the ballpark business, but rather than build or significantly reconstruct a new facility, Cole headed up a group of local race men who leased Schorling Park in 1932.[90] After he renovated and renamed the facility Cole Park, however, the city of Chicago seized it following its inaugural season and sought to convert it into a dog track.[91] But this never happened as a consequence of political opposition to dog racing, and Cole's outfit reacquired the facility for his team in 1934.[92]

But in 1935, Cole's American Giants dropped out of the NNL, the result of both a conflict between Cole and Greenlee and the difficulty of scheduling league games against the New York–area Cubans and Eagles and other eastern teams.[93] Neil Lanctot argues that Greenlee's dispute with Cole derived from the perception that the Chicago entrepreneur's diverse business ventures meant that his attentions were spread too thinly to sustain a league franchise. As far as Greenlee was concerned, Cole Field had fallen into disrepair, preventing league from staging promotions there.[94] The ouster of the Chicago club from the league, however ironically, may be seen to presage the difficulties that large conglomerates encountered in running Major League franchises in the second half of the twentieth century. Cole differed from other Negro League owners in that his attention was not centered on running his sporting enterprise. Although his team drew and played well, Cole did not have the focus needed to effectively manage a Negro League franchise.

The Giants did not remain independent for long. Hall assumed sole ownership of the team and reverted to using the name the Chicago American Giants. Along with the Kansas City Monarchs, the Detroit Stars, the Birmingham Black Barons, and the short-lived Indianapolis Athletics and Cincinnati Tigers, the Giants formed a second organized Negro circuit, the Negro American League (NAL) in October 1936. The new league chose Hall as its temporary chair before settling on a well-respected Chicago alderman, Major Robert R. Jackson, as its first president.

By all measures, Major Jackson was a race man extraordinaire. A Chicagoan born and bred, Jackson represented another local iteration of the American Dream writ large, rising from manual laborer to community leader. Wrote the *Pittsburgh Courier* in 1935, "He shined shoes, sold papers, saved his money and studied at night, and this formula of rugged individualism, lifted him to the pinnacle of success as a civic leader and public office holder."[95] Jackson solidified his place within the community when he spearheaded a move to ban D. W. Griffith's controversial film, *Birth of a Nation*, from being screened in Illinois. Following a stint in the state legislature, Jackson followed Oscar De Priest, the first African American elected to Congress in the twentieth century, as alderman. Jackson, whose political activities were chronicled in *The Crisis*, was an active member of the National Association for the Advancement of Colored People (NAACP) and owned a piece of the Lincoln Giants.[96] Jackson's ascension to the leadership of the NAL may be seen as an attempt to imbue the new circuit with a sense of respectability, legitimacy, and professionalism that was essential to its early success.

The level of professionalism that Jackson brought to the NAL appears to have represented an attempt to change Negro League baseball's business culture. For example, he mandated that the league purchase balls before the season to assure consistency on the field of play, drawing them closer to Major League practices. He also instituted the use of "duplicate roll" tickets throughout the league to better track of the gate at each game.[97] As a businessman and NAACP member as well as an elected official of color operating within the mainstream, Jackson was a race leader very much in the mold of the type suggested by W. E. B. Du Bois. Jackson's attempts to professionalize Negro League baseball by looking to examples of successful Major League practices reinforces this notion. At the same time, as a rugged individual who represented the race through hard work and attention to detail rather than through formal education, he embodied Booker T. Washington's ideal of the man who betters the lot of his people through economic achievement within the community. Thus, Jackson injected the Washingtonian ideal of self-determination into the Du Boisian model, functioning as a coalescence of the two.

Joining Jackson in league leadership were Dr. J. B. Martin of Memphis, who later became the NAL's president, and Frank A. "Fay" Young, the dean of Negro sportswriters, as vice president and secretary, respectively. Monarchs owner J. L. Wilkinson, the only holdover from Rube Foster's original NNL to join the new circuit, served as the NAL's treasurer, an obvious choice in light of his wealth of experience in both the game and the business and his financial and promotional acumen.

Barnstorming with the Monarchs

That Wilkinson clearly understood what it took to keep his baseball outfit going in the face of economic uncertainty is evidenced by the fact that his Monarchs thrived during the depression. A baseball entrepreneur with a history of barnstorming that extended back to the first decade of the twentieth century, Wilkinson returned to his roots. Using techniques honed by his experiences with a Bloomer Girl club and his All-Nations Team, he helped preserve black baseball by moving both inside and outside the African American ecosystem, taking a major step forward while at the same time drawing on proven past experiences.[98] As the original white owner in the first NNL, Wilkinson was in the unique position of being a full participant in a race business who could simultaneously engage comfortably in professional relationships with controversial yet necessary Jewish booking agents, particularly Chicago's Abe Saperstein.

Wilkinson's greatest contribution to the business of black baseball during the 1930s was the introduction of night games, an innovation that the Major Leagues soon adopted. At a time when his contemporaries were struggling to keep their clubs solvent, Wilkinson's creative use of existing technology kept the Monarchs on the road as the busiest barnstorming act in baseball. As Jules Tygiel explains, "In 1929 owner Wilkinson had commissioned an Omaha, Nebraska, company to design a portable lighting system for night games. The equipment, consisting of a 250-horsepower motor and a 100-kilowatt generator, which illuminated lights atop telescoping poles fifty feet above the field, took about two hours to assemble. To pay for the innovation, Wilkinson mortgaged everything he owned and took in Kansas City businessman Tom Baird as a partner. But the gamble paid off. The novelty of night baseball allowed the Monarchs to play two and three games a day and made them the most popular touring club in the nation."[99]

Praise for Wilkinson's traveling light system appeared not only in the pages of the black press but also in small-town papers throughout the Midwest; in Canada; in Nuevo Laredo, Mexico; and in parts of Texas, where the team first used the system during spring training. Kansas's *Hutchinson News* devoted half a column to an article about the lighting system, noting that the game was to start at "9:15 o'clock to allow business men and their employees to attend." The article eclipses a neighboring piece describing the upcoming Major League World Series between what amounted to the hometown St. Louis Cardinals and the Philadelphia Athletics and describes the system in minute detail, including a reference to the "marine type 6-cylinder gas engine, which is cooled by a specially built radiator." Exclaimed the author, "This light plant has attracted the attention of city officials in many cities who are interested in power plants for their cities."[100] Not only did Wilkinson's light system have implications for baseball, but it had civic implications as well. That the *Hutchinson News* paid scant attention to issues of race cannot be overlooked. The word *Negro* appears just twice in this article, both in relation to the unqualified excellence of the Monarchs. But the paper's overt giddiness about the possibilities of the technology comes blaring through. And articles such as this one can be found in similar such small-town mainstream papers.

As barnstormers, neither Wilkinson nor his players were strangers to the world of novelty baseball. Night baseball certainly opened an entirely new market for the club by offering those with jobs and the discretionary income to afford admission—typically fifty cents—an opportunity to attend ball games that were previously unavailable to them. By extension, it allowed the Monarchs and their opponents to collect a decent gate at a time when paying crowds were difficult to generate. Moreover, the novelty of night baseball was itself a major drawing card.

In addition to fairly regular games with the House of David, a white barnstorming team associated with a religious cult from Benton Harbor, Michigan, the Monarchs staged contests, both day and night, often on the same date, with the Cuban House of David. Formerly the Havana Red Sox, the Cuban House of David, operated by Syd Pollock, who capitalized on the popularity of the original bearded nine and who would come to play a much larger role in the business of black baseball, was one of a growing number of black comedy teams that also served as the Monarchs' opponents. Another such novelty team was Saperstein's Zulu Cannibal Giants. Although routinely pilloried in the press, Saperstein's team had a following, and not just among white fans, in spite of the fact that their act was no doubt offensive to race leaders and others in the African American community—then as now. This, however, was a reality of unaffiliated, Depression-era black baseball, that in spite of its controversial content, it sold tickets at a time when tickets were hard to sell. What this further suggests is that baseball on the periphery was moving in the same direction as other elements of the American entertainment industry, resorting to whatever was necessary to keep afloat during difficult financial times. And while this period marked the waning days of vaudeville—essentially another form of barnstorming—it also witnessed the birth and expansion of the next generation of African American traveling entertainment, the Chitlin' Circuits of music and comedy. Indeed, Wilkinson's portable lighting system revolutionized the entertainment world as much as it did sports, as demonstrated by the adoption of night baseball by the Major Leagues starting in 1935.

The Problem of the Black-Owned Venues

Wilkinson's use of the time-tested methods of showmanship coupled with new innovations enabled the Monarchs to remain solvent. Wilkinson kept his team on the road, even as many other remaining owners struggled, including those who maintained control of their own venues, either through long-term rental arrangements or, in very rare cases, through ballpark ownership, generally financed through profits from the normally depression-proof rackets. Thus, even Greenlee and Pompez, in spite of their circumstances, were themselves not immune to the vagaries of economic life in African America or the problems of keeping an NNL franchise afloat. As a consequence of his legal problems, Pompez was unable to field a team in 1937 or 1938.[101] Semler's Black Yankees, having entered the NNL a year earlier, played at Dyckman Oval in the absence of Pompez's Cubans during the 1937 season, but the team's presence was not enough to keep the venue that Pompez had leased from the city in the NNL's hands, and it was demolished at the end of season. The New York metropolitan area was left with only one stable Negro League venue, Newark's Ruppert Stadium, the Eagles' home park.

After the loss of the Manhattan facility, the Black Yankees played on Randall's Island, located in the East River between Harlem and the South Bronx, during the 1938 season. Despite rhetoric to the contrary in the *New York Amsterdam News* and elsewhere—"Harlem's Representatives in the Negro National League Now Boast of Best Home Grounds," which looks suspiciously as if it were placed by Semler—the new venue was far from ideal from an economic standpoint.[102] At least one advertisement for the Black Yankees included in small print the rather Byzantine directions for reaching Randall's Island via bus, subway, and/or trolley, with connections to a ferry, and including transit pricing. Additional promotions, like a swing contest between amateur bands, appear to have been necessary to draw fans, and the *Chicago Defender* pointed directly to the inconvenience of travel, describing the new venue as "almost a total loss to successful baseball promotion."[103] In 1939, with the economy beginning to rebound, both Pompez and Semler returned to the less-than-ideal arrangement of renting Yankee Stadium for their teams' games.[104]

Dyckman Oval was not the only race-controlled venue capitalized by numbers money to fail. Although it was administered by the prime mover behind the new NNL, Greenlee Field, too, ran into financial trouble in 1938. Long under attack from the black press and community members for too much white involvement as well as its inadequate grandstand seating and lack of cover, Greenlee's eponymous ballpark sunk into a sea of red ink. Failing to convince Joe Tito and the Bedford Land Company to make the necessary improvements, and sensitive to the criticism leveled against him, Greenlee bought out his partners and assumed the debt. Faced with the effects of a crackdown on numbers operations in Pittsburgh and a big hit that forced large payouts to bettors, Greenlee's bank became less profitable and could not provide the capital to solve these financial difficulties.[105] Taking a page from mainstream organized baseball, Greenlee attempted to sell season tickets, a practice not yet associated with black baseball. Greenlee also tried to sell common stock locally. According to the *Pittsburgh Courier*'s John L. Clark, "At that time there were 15 or 20 race men in the position to invest from $1,000 to $5,000 and still not draw heavily on their reserve. Not a single individual could be induced to join the corporation and as a result, the sale of common stock fell through." Clark then launched into a scathing indictment of those "race men" who had failed to come to Greenlee's aid: "Well the story is over now. The people who were to be accommodated and probably benefitted, turned their backs on one of their own kind. This turnabout was not staged when Greenlee was dreaming of his field, but after he had shown that he meant business. He had invested a small fortune, and induced others to go along with the idea. Greenlee field was a reality, with some beautiful history behind it when the SOS was sent out in 1935. But the people of Greenlee's race preferred to see the venture fail." Clark concluded,

> Nobody will be justified in rejoicing, whether enemies or friends to any members of the corporation. Not even the housing authority agents, or any other representatives who had any part in the squeeze deal that caused every stockholder to finish up empty handed. Regardless of what mistakes were made, or who made them, a purer racial interest should have been manifested to keep Greenlee Field out of the list of failures. And since there was no individual, or

group of individuals, blessed with that foresight, that courage to be a part of the thing and correct the faults, it is safe to say that Pittsburgh is no place to attempt big things for Negroes.

Greenlee Field joins the list of banks, industries and other enterprises which should not be again attempted in this city for the next 100 years.[106]

Without actually addressing anyone in particular, Clark appears to include the owners of the rival Homestead Grays, Cum Posey and his brother, Seward (often See), not to mention Greenlee's fellow racketeer, Rufus Jackson, in this withering indictment. Clark implicitly reminded his readers that unlike Greenlee's Crawfords, the Homestead Grays played not in a race venue but rather in solely white-owned and -operated Forbes Field, where fans and players of color were subject to segregated arrangements.[107]

By 1940, Pittsburgh's African American ecosystem, once so full of promise as a locus for the business of black baseball, supported a franchise in name only. Posey's franchise began to play its home games in the nation's capital at Griffith Stadium and became known as the Washington Homestead Grays, presaging the practice of renaming embraced by the Los Angeles Angels of Anaheim in 2005. Greenlee, for his part, refocused his sporting efforts to the management and promotion of boxing. Greenlee Field was demolished, and the land was used as the site of one of urban America's first public housing projects.[108] These changing fortunes effectively marked the end of what had been a successful if wholly unpredictable decade in Pittsburgh's otherwise depressed economy.

However ironically, at the same time that black baseball ceased to be economically viable in Pittsburgh, the Negro Leagues were poised on the verge of a renaissance. With the Monarchs, the American Giants, and the other teams in the fledgling NAL, black baseball was back in business, complete with what seemed to be a well-conceived two-league organizational structure—at least on the surface. As the Great Depression came to a close and the industrial war machine stirred the national economy, a second wave of rural migrants streamed into the urban Black Belts of the North, Midwest, and West, creating a renewed market for organized Negro League baseball.

4

The Second Wave and the Business of Black Baseball, 1939–1946

Introduction

In late 1939 and 1940, the American war machine geared up, providing new economic opportunities for the hard-strapped, depression-weary country. Black Americans were among those to reap a limited portion of the benefits. Although African Americans faced discriminatory hiring practices in the war industries, people again began to flow into urban centers at a steady pace, creating the second wave of the Great Migration. Observes Isabel Wilkerson, "What started as a little-noticed march of the impatient would become a flood of the discontented during World War II, and by the tail end of the Migration, a virtual rite of passage for young southerners."[1] Historian James Patterson notes,

> Thanks in part to the rapid mechanization of cotton production in the early 1940s, which ultimately threw millions of farm laborers out of work, and in part to the opening of industrial employment in the North during the war-time boom, roughly a million blacks (along with even more whites) moved from the South during the 1940s. Another 1.5 million Negroes left the South in the 1950s. This was a massive migration in so short a time—one of the most significant demographic shifts in American history—and it was often agonizingly stressful. The black novelist Ralph Ellison wrote in 1952 of the hordes of blacks who "shot up from the South into the busy city like wild jacks-in-the-box broken loose from our springs—so sudden that our gait becomes like that of deep-sea divers suffering from the bends."[2]

The new migrants further broadened the Negro Leagues' market. By 1944, 1.5 million African Americans had found work in war-related occupations, with much of this employment in cities with Negro League franchises—Chicago, Newark, Philadelphia, Baltimore, and Cleveland. The leagues boomed and remained major players in the entertainment industry, with franchises not only in cities with long histories of black baseball, organized and otherwise (Kansas City and New York, for example), but also in Birmingham, Memphis, Pittsburgh, and St. Louis.[3] The exception was Indianapolis. The Indianapolis (sometimes Cincinnati) Clowns were for the most part a barnstorming enterprise, owned and operated by former vaudeville promoter Syd Pollock out of his Tarrytown, New York, offices. Like the northern cities that drew migrants, the southern urban centers that supported organized league teams offered employment opportunities in the war industries that attracted workers from rural areas.

Just how many new migrants arrived in northern cities during this period is unclear. Accurate census data depend on full and accurate reporting, which was neither always desirable nor always possible for new urban dwellers of color. As Wilkerson explains, "The numbers put forward by the census are believed by some historians to be an underestimate. Unknown numbers of migrants who could pass for white melted into the white population once they left [the South] and would not have been counted in the Migration. Colored men fearful of being extradited back to the South over purported debts or disputes would have been wary of census takers. And overcrowded tenements with four or five families packed into kitchenettes or day workers rotating their use of a bed would have been hard to accurately account for in the best of circumstances."[4]

As was true during the Great Migration's first wave, Chicago was the destination of choice, at least initially, for a large proportion of the new migrants. And as was also true of Chicago's African American economy before the war, the appearance of financial success was tied up with ideas of race consciousness.[5] The idea that salvation might be found in economic progress—both an expression of and an extension of Booker T. Washington's approach—took public form with the 1940 American Negro Exhibition, intended to showcase black economic strength. This first black World's Fair opened on July 4 at the Chicago Coliseum, on the Near South Side, and closed on September 2, running concurrently with the second season of the 1939–40 New York World's Fair, the theme of which was "The World of Tomorrow." The Chicago event functioned in the shadow of this mainstream effort, mirroring it in much the same way that black business, including the Negro Leagues, often mirrored mainstream ventures.

The American Negro Exhibition was the brainchild of Claude Barnett, founder of the successful Associated Negro Press, a wire service built on the model of the mainstream Associated Press. Joining Barnett was Truman Gibson Jr., son of the president of Supreme Liberty Life Insurance, a Bronzeville institution and the largest race business in America. Supreme Liberty Life had been founded by Truman Gibson Sr. and longtime race entrepreneur Harry Pace, whose previous venture had been the failed but nevertheless important Black Swan Records. According to Adam Green, the presence of the younger Gibson, who served as the executive director of Supreme Liberty Life, meant that the event had the backing of an extremely influential black-owned enterprise.[6] And as advertising in the black press indicates, it also had the backing of many others. Scores of articles and advertisements urged visitors from around the country to attend, while Chicagoans and other city dwellers saw high-end promotional material with monumental, faux-classical motifs that stylistically resembled not just those found in ads for the World's Fair but also, however ironically, in promotional material for the 1939 Berlin Olympics.

But despite the exhibition's Washingtonian focus on race pride and economic self-sufficiency, complete with the imprimatur of the National Negro Business League (NNBL), it also had white sponsors and backers. In Green's words, "Prominent Chicago whites, for whom the politics of color had been a point of tension since the horrific race riot of 1919, assisted at several junctures. The $75,000 legislative grant signaled the state government's interest. . . . Financial help came from the Rosenwald Fund, the local philanthropic organization administered by well-known negrophile Edwin Embree."[7] In this regard, the exhibition, which also featured Chicago sociologist E. Franklin Frazier sitting in a booth and essentially serving as an exhibit, much in the way that Sitting Bull was exhibited at the 1893 Chicago Columbian Exhibition, followed in the mode of white participation that had always been present in the urban African American ecosystem. But in this case, the white businessmen and philanthropists rather than the black entrepreneurs receded into the shadows without divesting themselves of their economic say in the event. This was a pattern that would continue to reproduce itself in the years to come.

Though white participation in the exhibition was essentially philanthropic, if not a little paternalistic, it lacked the taint of exploitation that was often thought to be at the root of black ventures involving white backers. In this case, the Washingtonian model of race elevation through economics informed the language of the black press and community leaders. But while the rhetoric of economic self-sufficiency may have reigned supreme among those serving as the voices of the various constituencies, it did not filter down to consumers in terms of real dollars spent and the attitudes of those who spent them. Not only was the exhibition itself a financial failure, when it came to the simple exchange of dollars for products, race pride often proved no match for the calculus of consumerism.[8] "Over and over," write St. Clair Drake and Horace Cayton, "Negroes in Bronzeville reveal a conflict between the economic imperative of 'making ends meet,' and the social demands of 'race pride.' They insist that Negro merchants can't give equivalent goods and services for the same price" and that "colored housewives charge that the quality and stock in Negro stores is poor."[9]

The tensions created between the politics of race consumerism and the realities and constraints of being a consumer resonated in this way throughout the African American ecosystem and extended to businesses run by proprietors of color. According to Ivan Light and Steven J. Gold, "Depending on the common tool kit of business skills and techniques, most ethnic entrepreneurs rely on the same market for supplies, capital, labor, and consumers; sell the same type of goods and services, use comparable business practices. Accordingly, businesses run by co-ethnics are similar, and, as such, prone to fierce competition. Without the ability to control competition, ethnic business can become antagonistic."[10] Such antagonisms, interracial and coethnic alike, played out repeatedly in black business circles, whether on the street level in grocery stores and dry goods emporiums or on organizational and administrative levels. These key issues taking shape within broader black business circles played out in Negro League offices and annual meetings, simultaneously leading to the height of the leagues' economic potency and setting the course for its decline in the postwar period.

Black Baseball's Ethnic Middlemen

For the black baseball establishment, dealing with white booking agents and occasionally owners had generally been considered a necessary evil of doing business, Kansas City's J. L. Wilkinson and T. Y. Baird notwithstanding. But with Negro League baseball again becoming an economic force in the early 1940s, racial antagonism among owners and operators came to the fore, reaching new levels of vitriol. Such profoundly personal venom is clearly evident in an August 1, 1941, letter from Newark Eagles owner Effa Manley to Seward "See" Posey, business manager and booking agent for the Homestead Grays. A dispute had arisen with the ubiquitous Eddie Gottlieb over a scheduled date at Yankee Stadium, prompting Effa Manley, rarely at a loss for words, to offer a revealing glimpse of the emerging battle lines: "With us divided and fighting each other, we are playing right into the hands of these smart men who see the possibility our baseball offers, and are trying hard to eat it all up. If they are not stopped now, there won't be any stopping them. . . . [B]ut I really believe if the Poseys [Seward and his brother, Cumberland] and Sonnyman [Rufus Jackson] make up their minds to, and the Eagles join them, they can stop Gottlieb, Wilkinson, [William] Leuschner, [Abe] Saperstein and all the other Jews who want to join where Negro baseball is concerned."[11] Although not all of the men Manley named were Jewish, she equated *white* with *Jewish*, embracing the anti-Semitic rhetoric of the period and arguing that the sport's African Americans needed to work together to combat the perceived Jewish power grab.

Both part of the black ethnic economy and outside it, Jewish promoters and booking agents, some of whom were also owners, may be defined as ethnic middlemen, mediating between the insular African American ecosystem and the mainstream economy, of which they also were neither wholly a part nor wholly outside. Gottlieb, for example, not only owned a piece of the Negro American League (NAL) Philadelphia Stars but also controlled access to various venues throughout the Northeast, including Philadelphia's Shibe Park and New York's Yankee Stadium, receiving 5–10 percent of the gate for each promotion he brokered. Gottlieb's role as a middleman was hardly unique; other ethnic middlemen served as brokers in various economic sectors. But in the case of Negro League baseball, most middlemen were Jews.

Jewish entrepreneurs were certainly no strangers to African American ecosystem, where they had a large presence in retail. Such establishments as Blumstein's department store in Harlem, the subject of the "Don't Buy Where You Can't Work" campaign, made Jewish business owners a visible and at times problematic presence in black communities. Indeed, that visibility lay at the root of what often proved to be very public conflict. That such antagonisms informed relations between Jews and African Americans is unsurprising, given the number of times the two ethnic groups had competing interests. But Jews' whiteness, or near-whiteness, as defined by the dominant Anglo-Saxon, Protestant culture, provided business interests with a certain measure of flexibility to operate more freely in both the mainstream white economy and the black ecosystem. Precisely this ability to traverse both the black and white worlds gave rise to the notion of middlemen or, to be more precise, ethnic middlemen. And this mediating role played by Jews or those presumed to be Jews in black baseball's economic structure is exemplified by Edward (née Isadore) Gottlieb.

Gottlieb got his start in the sports business as a player and manager for the semiprofessional baseball and basketball teams sponsored by the South Philadelphia Hebrew Association, popularly known as the SPHAs. The baseball club, often billed as the Philadelphia Hebrews, routinely competed against black nines, giving Gottlieb considerable experience in black athletics. His eventual control over so much of the apparatus of Negro League baseball in the Northeast, the center of operations for the Negro National League (NNL), made him what his fellow owners perceived as an economic threat to organized black baseball. Of course, Gottlieb was neither the first white man nor the first presumed Jew to wield such power over the enterprise. Nat Strong, for one, had been omnipresent in the NNL's first iteration. Gottlieb was, in fact, one of Strong's associates, sharing many of the veteran booking agent's business methods. And like Strong, Gottlieb had a working relationship with fellow Philadelphian Ed Bolden, co-owner of the Stars. Moreover, Gottlieb's relationship with the other owners, though fraught, was often mutually financially beneficial. Nevertheless, certain members of the Negro League establishment, most notably Effa Manley, as well as many members of the black press routinely leveled harsh criticisms at him.

Other Negro League entrepreneurs, in contrast, had cordial working relationships with Gottlieb, at least publicly. Posey, for example, writing with the *Courier*'s Wendell Smith, referred to Gottlieb as "honest in his dealing and a good baseball man." But Posey and Smith also damned their subject with faint praise by adding that Gottlieb "must come to realize that the Negro National League was not organized for his benefit."[12] Two years earlier, Posey had defended Gottlieb against criticism from the black press, noting that he and black baseball's other white owners had helped support the league financially when it was at its "lowest ebb."[13] These contrasting depictions of Gottlieb reflected his place as a middleman. On one hand, his predatory practices as a booking agent benefited his bottom line and constantly irritated the Manleys and other owners. On the other, Gottlieb clearly made essential contributions to the league's financial well-being, especially in the later days of the Depression.

Gottlieb's checkered reputation as a middleman dropped precipitously when his exclusionary practices regarding professional basketball took center stage. Gottlieb's involvement in black baseball coincided with his efforts to build a segregated professional basketball industry in the game's South Philadelphia hub. That infant sport was dominated by both Jewish players and Jewish interests, and Gottlieb's role did not go unnoticed in black economic and journalistic circles. The *Courier*'s Smith wrote caustically in January 1947, "One of the most conspicuous figures at the baseball meetings was our old friend, 'Brother Eddie' Gottlieb. It is more than ironical that a man who practices discrimination so avidly be a member of a meeting held to elect the president of the Negro National League. . . . He refuses to hire a Negro player on his basketball team, solely because it 'wouldn't work out.' In the summertime, however, he operates a Negro baseball team and makes thousands of dollars off the Negro public."[14] Smith's excoriation of "Brother Eddie" serves to highlight the often problematic if not contradictory nature of the middleman relationship with regard to race sport. As a preeminent Jewish middleman, Gottlieb was a force in black baseball, though he was also intimately involved in establishing yet another color line in American sport, albeit short-lived, as a founding father of American professional basketball.[15]

Along with Gottlieb and his sometime partner, William Leuschner, Abe Saperstein was another of the problematic Jewish middlemen. With broad interests in race sport that included publicity ventures as well as proprietorship, Saperstein is best known as the longtime owner and operator of basketball's Harlem Globetrotters, a team with no historical connection to New York that used the location as a shorthand for the color of its players. Saperstein owned both the basketball enterprise and an independent barnstorming baseball team of the same name; however, he did not own an organized Negro League franchise. Rather, the seat of his power was his Chicago-centered booking operation, which included boxing as well as baseball and basketball.

Saperstein entered race sport as both an athlete and a promoter. His considerable promotional expertise manifested in his role as the owner and operator of the Zulu Cannibal Giants, a novelty barnstorming team that he acquired in 1926. Saperstein's interest in organized Negro League baseball, however, resulted primarily from his control over access to Chicago's venues as well as his involvement in much of the publicity for league promotions in the Midwest. Saperstein, like Gottlieb (and previously Strong), was yet another thorn in the side of black baseball's entrepreneurs. His domination over Comiskey Park, home of black baseball's biggest promotion, the annual East-West Classic, was of particular concern. The anger Saperstein generated among the black press as well as the owners provided a road map of the extent to which his interests and the interest of black baseball's ruling class diverged. As Frank "Fay" Young wrote in the *Chicago Defender* in 1940, "Perhaps the Negro press, seemingly ignorant of the charges, would like to be informed that white Abe Saperstein, who wants to control the Negro American League booking and the publicity, is now letting out the word that none of the Negro sports writers can write anything on the East versus West baseball classic unless they get the information from him. Saperstein, who cannot tax the two leagues five-percent for booking the East vs. West game, now comes forth with the brazen statement that no news can be had in the daily press unless through his office which has all white help. Since it is a ball game played by two colored teams the fans are anxious to know why."[16]

Unlike the black owners and press, Saperstein had the ability to place coverage in the mainstream daily press, thereby reinforcing his middleman position. Perceived whiteness gave Saperstein access to—though not ownership of—outlets that remained unavailable to African Americans, a power that rankled Young. But more significant than Saperstein's access to the white press was the fact that the Negro Leagues paid him a great deal of money for using that access to their advantage. For the 1943 East-West Classic, for example, the NNL spent a $351.50 on signage, a sound truck, and ads in small black newspapers yet paid Saperstein $700.00 for his promotional expertise and connections.[17] For the perpetually cash-strapped Negro Leagues, this was no small investment. By generating income for himself and for the league while possessing neither the burden nor the benefit of an ownership stake and keeping his personal sport-related business alive, Saperstein was the epitome of the Jewish middleman.

Black Baseball's Impresario

Another prototypical middleman, at least at the start of his career, was Syd Pollock, owner of the resilient Indianapolis Clowns. Pollock, however, subsequently came to play a very different role in the Negro League narrative than the other ethnic middlemen. Like Saperstein, Gottlieb,

Leuschner, and Strong, Pollock began his career as a booking agent, but he never controlled important venues or exacted fees from his fellow owners for booking dates. Rather, his sole bailiwick was independent bookings in small towns. That Effa Manley did not include Pollock in her diatribe suggests that his role, at least at the time, may have been less threatening to the Negro League establishment than that of the other "Jews" whom she perceived as interlopers. Pollock received at least as much negative press as Saperstein and Gottlieb, but the criticism was of a very different nature.

Pollock got his start as a vaudeville manager and was the exclusive booking agent for the Maggie Riley Devil-Dogs, described by promotional materials as a "Male Semi-Pro team . . . with Baseball's $10,000 Female 'Wonder Girl.'"[18] More tellingly, he served as Northeast booking agent for Saperstein's Zulu Cannibal Giants, and the two men maintained a close working relationship until the late 1940s. And like Wilkinson before him, Pollock also had an ownership stake in several novelty teams, including the Cuban House of David and perhaps all or part of the Puerto Rican Clowns and the Borneo Cannibal Giants.[19]

Pollock's most profitable enterprise, however, was his ownership of the Ethiopian Clowns, a popular and talented barnstorming outfit. Given the team's name; the players' uniforms; which included war paint and grass skirts; and Pollock's practice of calling players by pseudo-African sobriquets such as Tarzan, Impo, Nyasses, Kalahari, and Wahoo, with its particularly suspect origins, it is not hard to see why they were forced to the periphery of the organized sport. The NAL banned league franchises from booking dates with the Clowns in 1940, and the NNL followed suit two years later.[20]

Although the Ethiopian Clowns played twice in the *Denver Post* Tournament, a well-regarded semiprofessional competition, placing third in 1939 and winning it all in 1941, critics led by Cum Posey and Wendell Smith accused the team of perpetuating negative stereotypes of African Americans with their signature physical comedy, pseudonyms, and traditional clown makeup.[21] Posey accused the Clowns of mocking Ethiopia, which at the time was fighting for independence from Italy, a cause wholly embraced by the black press. Indeed, Ethiopia had become a cause célèbre for the black press as early as 1935, following the Italian invasion, with sportswriters expressing their support via their coverage of the Joe Louis–Primo Carnera fight of the same year.[22] Mostly overlooked by the press, however, were the no less problematic connotations of *Ethiopian* dating back to minstrel shows. More than one hundred years before Emperor

Haile Selassie returned to Addis Ababa on May 5, 1941, so-called Ethiopian delineators—white, blackface performers such as Thomas "Daddy" Rice, the creator of the Jim Crow character—were constructing a form of blackness that played effectively on predominantly northern stages where actual African American culture was in short supply until the Great Migration.[23]

In 1944, Smith responded to Pollock and his team by railing, "If there were such a thing as a baseball fascist, we'd expect to find Syd Pollock on the list, because he did more than any other person in the sports world to belittle the plight of Ethiopia while it was being raped by Italy. Mr. Pollock carried on the ingenious idea of calling his club the 'Ethiopian Clowns.' He painted his players' faces in diverse colors, made them go into a song and dance on the playing field, and in general was a party to what might be termed a 'burlesque' campaign that belittled the tragedy of Ethiopia."[24]

As disconcerting as some of the Clowns' humor may have been, the team's primary—though not sole—audience was African American. The Clowns were unquestionably popular and made money, even when they were banned from competition with league teams. Performances by the Clowns, though haunted by the specter of minstrelsy, actually closely resembled classic vaudeville routines and reflected the whole range of American humor rather than relying entirely on perpetuating ethnic stereotypes. Much of American humor—stand-up comedy, improvisation, or sketch comedy—is indebted to the minstrel show in general and specifically to the same routines that informed the Clowns' performances. As is the case with much if not all of vaudeville's contested ethnic humor, the Clowns' routines subtly reclaimed some of the more dehumanizing elements of minstrelsy by restoring humanity to previously dehumanized characters.[25] This strategy seemed to play well with the team's target audiences, which appeared eager to shell out their hard-earned pay in spite of the disapproval from the black baseball establishment and from African American journalists. In short, the Clowns played good baseball, and audiences thought that their routines were funny, and they voted their approval with their pocketbooks.

In addition to the requisite pregame spectacles of pepper and shadow ball, routines perfected by earlier novelty teams, both black and white, Clowns games featured Richard King, who performed under the stage name of King Tut, and his diminutive partner, Spec Bebop. According to Donn Rogosin, "Tut's character was the pompous overdrawn hick in fancy clothes; his uniform sometimes consisted of tuxedo and top hat. He would play dice against himself, lose his coat, and then, stripped down to polka-dotted underwear, win it all back. Bebop would enter the stands, sit on women's laps, and have his picture taken."[26] Characteristic of their humor was the "Dentist Sketch," in which Bebop was the unwilling patient/victim of the incompetent tonsorial artist, Tut, who pretended first to pull several of Bebop's teeth and then to blast out the rest with a firecracker, leaving the field full of dried corn kernels, to fans' delight.[27]

While calling Pollock a fascist may be hyperbole, Smith was not wrong in claiming that the outfit's humor also contained elements of burlesque; however, these, too, appealed to fans. A fairly typical routine that the players called the "Saturday Night Whore" featured

> Tut in drag, wearing lipstick, tight dress, wig and heels[. He] sashayed and tripped through foul territory toward home plate. As he moved, he adjusted the straps holding up his low-cut neckline, checked that his pocketbook was safely closed, checked that the seams in his stockings were straight and powdered his nose with a puff three times normal size, replenishing it in a small bucket. Great clouds of white rose as Tut patted his face. Then, delicately lifting each arm, he slapped gobs of powder onto each armpit. The grass beneath him whitened hard like a January blizzard. He opened his purse, took out a mirror, and checked the face then armpits in the mirror, satisfied. Finally, he lifted the hem of his dress high, revealing lace panties, and daintily applied powder into each shoe. One of the Clowns players approached Tut from the dugout, and offered his arm, which Tut graciously accepted, and the player escorted Tut, still sashaying and tripping, off the field.[28]

Given Pollock's background in vaudeville, it is not surprising that the "Saturday Night Whore" resembles the comedy of Tut's contemporary, Milton Berle, who began his career on the vaudeville stage and brought his drag act to television in 1956, while the Clowns were still on the road. Tut in drag also seems to be a direct ancestor to Flip Wilson's "Geraldine" and any number of characters played by Martin Lawrence and Tyler Perry. Despite their popularity, however, the Clowns' appeal as a comedy act was never as widespread or as lucrative as Berle's, Wilson's, or Perry's, and even in the 1940s, when the audience for black baseball was at its peak, the segregated sport never garnered the attention of its white, Major League counterpart. Nevertheless, the earning power of Pollock's mixture of sport and traveling circus was nothing short of a barnstorming bonanza within the limited terms of the industry.

Moreover, criticism of the Clowns in the black press was far from unanimous. E. B. Rea, sports columnist for the *Baltimore Afro-American*, opposed the leagues' ban on contests against the Clowns, declaring it "about as funny as the Clowns themselves." Rea accused the leagues of being afraid of competition from Pollock's competent, versatile outfit and compared the Clowns' act not to minstrelsy but rather to that of white novelty teams: "I wouldn't consider the Clowns' style of play a 'detriment to colored league baseball,' as the powers-that-be so aptly play it, any more than I would the House of David as a humiliating act against the white American and the National League."[29]

Given the Clowns' popularity and the support of at least some black sports scribes, the leagues eventually relented, largely for financial reasons. After agreeing to lose the makeup, drop *Ethiopian* from their name, and tone down but not eliminate their antics, the Clowns were admitted into the NAL in 1943, although according to future Hall of Famer Buck Leonard, "players didn't like it so much. . . . [W]e didn't want the Clowns in the league, but they were such a good draw, everyone else wanted them."[30] Nevertheless, as official NAL representatives, the Clowns necessarily became part of the larger business institution that was black baseball, representing first Cincinnati and later Indianapolis. But they rarely played in either of those cities, instead continuing to barnstorm around the country. They played a full schedule of preseason games against semiprofessional and professional African American teams in the South, providing entertainment by African Americans for African Americans as well as for white fans, who were always part of the Clowns' consumer base. By extension, the team supported other African American businesses, necessarily patronizing black-owned enterprises while on the road in a country still under the yoke of Jim Crow. Thus, what the Clowns ultimately brought to the business of black baseball moved far beyond the diamond and well into the African American ecosystem.

Advertising and Promotion

No matter how much audiences loved the Clowns, they would not have done as well as they did at the box office without an extremely creative approach to advertising and promotion, which are the keys to any successful commercial enterprise. Given the fly-by-night nature of independent, barnstorming baseball, regardless of its ethnic base, publicity through print media and via word of mouth was absolutely essential, a matter that Pollock recognized better than the rest of his competitors. And while official league games were booked in advance and their schedules were generally available to fans, extra dates were often scheduled with little advance notice. Ensuring a healthy gate, therefore, depended upon getting the word out.

Like every other black baseball team, Pollock's "aggregation," as he routinely called the Clowns in team publicity, depended first and foremost on placards and posters in the windows of bars, restaurants, barbershops, beauty parlors, and other businesses in the African American ecosystem. Pollock's placards regularly publicized his enterprise with flashy display type declaring them to be the "Number One Show Team in Baseball History" or "America's Greatest Negro Attraction," using the owner's signature hyperbolic language. Smaller copy declared, "Combine Jesse Owens and Houdini, Multiply by Nine, and You Have An Idea of the Speed, Pepper and Downright Slugging Ability of the Ethiopian Clowns."[31] Graphics were similarly showy, generally including visual images of the team's clowns rather than of its ballplayers. In many cases, placing ads in the windows of local businesses benefited both the Clowns' and the businesses, drawing people to the ballpark as well as into the businesses, especially bars and restaurants that also offered entertainment.

Although radio was ubiquitous by the 1940s, print culture remained dominant, black baseball advertised in newspapers, though not as often or as thoroughly as might be expected, particularly in light of the large circulations of some African American weeklies. In 1945, the *Pittsburgh Courier* had a national circulation of 277,000, the *Baltimore Afro-American* had 235,000, and the *Chicago Defender*, still significant but no longer the most important of the weeklies, maintained a respectable circulation of 100,000, a number that nearly doubled over the next two years, in no small part as a result of the steady influx of migrants pouring into Chicago.[32] These numbers are impressive by any standards, particularly for a publication catering to a specialized demographic. But in spite of these healthy figures, Negro League display advertising remained surprisingly scant, in part as a consequence of the way in which the black papers both promoted and covered the Negro Leagues. Although the black weeklies dedicated a relatively large number of column inches to sports, they relied almost exclusively on press releases and other material provided by the teams. Indeed, the cost of carrying dedicated baseball beat writers, so common in the mainstream press, was beyond the budgetary restrictions of most black papers, which may account for the disconnect between franchises and the most logical place for the leagues to promote and publicize their businesses.[33] In addition, sports columnists including Fay Young and Wendell Smith frequently wrote about issues both on the field and in the clubhouse, sometimes not in an entirely flattering light.

Why did such widely read publications find themselves so strapped for cash that providing firsthand coverage by dedicated staff members proved difficult if not altogether out of the question? Moreover, why were Young, Smith, and other columnists who depended at least in part on race sport for both their livelihoods and their subject matter so free with their criticism? The answer is that newspaper budgets depend on advertising revenue. During the Great Depression, major retailers and national companies supported mainstream newspapers but virtually ignored the potential of targeting consumers of color. Other than the alcoholic beverage industry, which recognized—in large part as a result of racist assumptions—that African Americans were potential consumers, large advertisers were slow to contribute to the bottom lines of the black weeklies. The majority of advertising in the black press, in contrast, was generated by small local businesses as well as manufacturers and distributors of "ethnic" beauty products such as hair straighteners and skin lighteners, patent medicines, and dream books.[34]

The dearth of national advertisers in the black press was not lost on race leaders, among them W. E. B. Du Bois. But while the black press regularly attempted to attract national campaigns with large advertising budgets, Du Bois praised the weeklies for their independence. In the second of a series of Associated Negro Press articles dealing with black journalism that appeared in the *Defender*, Du Bois wrote,

> The attitude of the white press is conditioned very largely upon the advertising revenues so much that it is more or less true as is so often charged that the great newspapers of the United States are no longer free expressions of opinion but rather express business which has such a large stake in the newspapers through advertising. . . . The Negro press on the other hand has comparatively small advertising revenue. The rule of advertising agencies is not to place advertising in Negro papers, since, as they argue, all Negroes read white newspapers in addition to their own weeklies and as both are published in English there is no need for additional advertising as in the case of the foreign language press.
>
> Thus even in the case of papers with circulation between two and three hundred thousand a week the advertising revenue from national advertisers

is practically nil. Consequently it depends to a much larger extent upon the demand and goodwill of its readers and is more sensitive to changes in public opinion.

Du Bois further lamented that the black press "has been tempted in the past to questionable advertising policies: giving publicity to fortune tellers, get-rich-quick schemes and projects obviously unfair if not illegal." But he praised the previously reviled beauty industry as a black-owned and -operated enterprise whose scope expanded to selling face powders, hair straighteners, and other formerly race-based beauty products to white consumers.[35]

To a great extent, Du Bois's stance on the black press's freedom from the influence of national advertising may be interpreted as rationalization. That the black press lacked large national advertisers at this point may have allowed the weeklies to remain critical of white business practices, particularly as those practices pertained to race issues. But the black press, like black baseball, was perpetually undercapitalized, and both were occasionally forced to seek alternative means of income.

As Adam Green contends, "While African-Americans had of course bought and sold retail goods throughout history, their collective status within the world of mainstream commerce to date had been one of invisibility and alienation. Up to World War II, it was customary for businesses, especially national businesses, not to advertise directly to blacks. This practice—the denial of what Roland Marchand calls 'consumer citizenship'—was an especially bitter arrangement during the interwar years. With modernization in retail and advertising, legitimacy as a consumer helped constitute the core of popular ideas of social identity and belonging within the United States."[36]

Marchand links politics with the marketplace, conceptualizing constituencies of consumer citizens, when he writes, "Representation in this theoretical consumer republic rested on the 'one man one vote principle,'" a system that disenfranchised Negroes as well as other lower-income Americans. He continues, "The high courts of national advertising were known to send down split decisions. In American metropolitan centers, insisted the Portland *Oregonian*, 'only half of the population falls in the Able-to-Buy class.' In the low-rent sections of the city, families were not markets (consumer citizens) 'in the ordinarily accepted sense of the word.' Their incomes were too low."[37]

On both the local and national levels, black baseball provided advertising revenue for the black press, even when mainstream corporate advertisers did not. But the Negro Leagues and independent teams had their own budgetary constraints. On occasion, large ads for black baseball events appeared in the *Courier* and other papers. For example, a quarter-page ad in the September 4, 1941, *New York Amsterdam News* publicized a "Stellar Attraction," a doubleheader between the Homestead Grays and the Newark Eagles at New York's Polo Grounds that was to benefit the Fight for Freedom Committee.[38] The annual East-West Classic also generated column inches and advertising revenue. But such events were exceptions rather than the rule. Most ads were one or two columns wide and one-sixteenth of a page high and generated neither substantial revenue for the publication nor substantial attention for the advertiser.

But as a master promoter, Pollock essentially bucked that trend. Large ads for appearances by the Clowns, both before and after they entered the league, were a regular feature in the black press as well as in small-town newspapers outside black metropolises. Pollock, as was his wont, generally used sensationalist language, positioning his club as a circus more than as a baseball team. Moreover, Pollock capitalized on the black press's structural inability to provide regular game coverage and consequent reliance on game accounts generated by the teams. While many of the other franchises provided straightforward accounts of the action on the field, Pollock manipulated the sports pages into serving as free promotional vehicles, printing what would come to be known in the advertising industry as advertorials, the print version of infomercials. On August 3, 1945, the *Atlanta Daily World* ran an item announcing, "The Cincinnati-Indianapolis Clowns of the Negro American League will present not one but two of the funniest comedians of baseball in their big fun-sideshow accompanying their appearance against the Atlanta Black Crackers. . . . One is the nationally-known King Tut, veteran Clown comic and long considered the outstanding fun-maker of Negro Baseball." This advertorial occupies more than an entire column and goes on to describe Tut's myriad skills as a baseball clown.[39] Masquerading as journalism, such Pollock-authored pieces appeared in the black press during and after the 1940s.

Although Pollock was the Negro Leagues' version of P. T. Barnum, who was generally considered to be the father of modern advertising and promotion, Pollock was certainly not the only league owner to take advantage of whatever advertising options were available. Over five dates in April

1941, for example, the Manleys spent a total of $44.55 on placards alone (equivalent to more than $500.00 in the early twenty-first century).[40] Effa Manley and other owners also routinely relied on game-day sound trucks as weapons in their promotional arsenal.[41]

Despite the fact that radio had become extremely popular, Negro League baseball received very little on-air coverage. Like large, mainstream print publications, radio had little interest in promoting African American sport.[42] Indeed, Saperstein's contacts in the white press and his ability to secure mainstream coverage of the East-West Classic solidified his position as publicity agent for the annual promotion, in spite of objections by Effa Manley and race journalists. Negro League owners, particularly Manley, made rare forays into radio promotion and publicity in the 1940s. Her place in the interconnected Harlem and Newark ecosystems gave the Eagles' owner and managing partner a broad range of contacts in business and the media. Perhaps her most important contact was Sherman L. Maxwell, known to his listeners as "Jocko," who was reputed to have been the first African American sportscaster.[43] In May 1940 correspondence, Maxwell thanked Manley for giving him complimentary season passes and promised in return to publicize the opening day gala on the radio.[44] Manley was engaging in the business practice later known as payola that generated a major scandal in popular music broadcasting in the 1950s. But in the world of Negro baseball, where mainstream publicity was hard to secure as well as maintain, it made a great deal of sense to reward a race man who could publicize the product. Furthermore, by publicizing the Eagles on Maxwell's broadcasts, Manley was attempting to expand the team's market beyond Newark to include New York City, exponentially multiplying the number of paying customers for her team and for the league as a whole. In 1942, Manley made it clear to Maxwell that coverage of the Eagles alone would not be adequate; rather, she sought national coverage for the entire league.[45] This goal, however, proved elusive.

For all of Manley's rhetoric of race pride and attempts to rid the Negro Leagues of "Jews" and other white interlopers, she was no stranger to crossing the color line, especially when doing so helped the bottom line. Jerome Kessler, a Jewish publicity agent, handled the Eagles' promotional efforts until he entered the military to serve in World War II. Oliver "Butts" Brown, a journalist with the *New Jersey Herald News* and later Kessler's temporary (and less than competent) replacement as Manley's publicity agent, wrote to the owner on April 4, 1940, to take her to task for working exclusively with a white agent:

In past years you have offered the explanation for employing a white public-ity man to the fact that a Negro could not get the releases in the white daily papers. There may be some justification in this position but when put under careful investigation it sort of pales into insignificance.

In the first place, 98 per cent of your attendance at games at Ruppert Sta-dium is colored. Suppose the Negro papers took the same position as white and said they wouldn't print anything released by a white press agent, what would happen? After all, yours is a colored enterprise, chiefly supported by Negroes and the benefits should go to members of that race.[46]

On the surface, Brown's criticism of Manley's failure to use a public-ity agent of color seems valid. The Negro Leagues did, after all, position themselves as a race business, dedicated to both entertaining and some-how enriching the African American ecosystem. And it was Manley her-self who admonished her fellow owners to rid black baseball "Jewish" interlopers. But Manley also understood that she was running a business that depended above all on publicity to stay solvent. If Kessler was the best agent around, then it made sense to employ him, regardless of color or religious affiliation. After Brown took over, Manley became frustrated when the editor of the *Kansas City Call* asked her to provide information about the Eagles: "Isn't it a shame a paper has to write and ask for informa-tion[?] The fact is Butts is a very poor publicity man. He does not know the first thing about publicity for a ballclub."[47] Thus, when it came to run-ning her business, race consciousness had to take a backseat to the team's well-being.

If, as Brown suggested, 98 percent of the Eagles' audience was "col-ored," Manley was hoping to change that demographic. Attracting white fans would increase the Eagles' gate. Newark had a much smaller black business presence than neighboring New York City or nearby Philadel-phia. Relying entirely on race sponsorship for the team might have put the undertaking in more financial peril than was otherwise necessary. The Eagles consequently entered into an agreement with the Newark outlet for Adler Shoes, a national company best known for its elevator shoes, to print the team's programs. Adler also sponsored the printing of schedules for the Newark Bears, the Eagles' co-tenant at Ruppert Sta-dium.[48] Like her employment of Kessler, the deal with Adler reflected Manley's pragmatism, which contradicted her race-inspired rhetoric. But such compromises were part and parcel of doing business effectively in the Negro Leagues.

Manley, Pollock, and their ilk also worked diligently to offer the best possible product to their consumers. Negro League baseball featured a host of extremely talented players, some of whom would go on to make their marks in the Major Leagues. Purely from a baseball standpoint, Josh Gibson, Oscar Charleston, James "Cool Papa" Bell, and George "Mule" Suttles were star attractions and could be counted on to draw fans based strictly on talent. But in terms of promotional value, none of these stars shined as brightly for as long—and made so much money for both himself and his employers—as did Leroy "Satchel" Paige.

Paige, like Pollock, had a little P. T. Barnum in him and took great pains to demonstrate it at nearly every stop in his storied career. As close to an iconic American figure in the typically marginalized Negro Leagues as ever existed, Paige's ability to generate excitement that translated into ticket sales put him in a promotional class heads above the rest, making him the most important human resource in all of black baseball. His promotional as well as baseball skills allowed him to cash in on his celebrity at a time when even the best players in the segregated game struggled financially. According to Donald Spivey, that Paige was so well aware of his status became both a blessing and a curse to the Negro League's owners. While other ballplayers were typically contractually tied to a single team, Paige marketed himself as a commodity, playing for as many as forty different clubs throughout his career and occasionally appearing on the mound for only a few innings at a time before heading off to pitch for another club. He also headed up barnstorming teams that traveled with and played against Major League stars, many of whom were as anxious as he was to capitalize on their celebrity—and his. In Spivey's words, Paige "was increasingly becoming more his own person and demanding a larger share of black baseball's economic pie. Paige had become not only the major gate attraction at the East-West All-Star Game by the mid-1930s; he also had become the biggest draw in all of Negro League baseball. He entertained the fans by shuffling to the mound, doing tricks with the ball, performing wildly exaggerated windups and other crowd-pleasing antics. But when the ball left his hand, it was all business. He showboated and boasted on the mound and backed it up with sterling pitching. Spectators adored him." Spivey continues, "Paige sold his baseball skills to the highest bidder. He understood that baseball was a business and that his growing superstar status had cash value."[49]

As an individual who understood his own value, Paige reportedly earned as much as forty thousand dollars a year prior to desegregation, making him one of the most highly paid athletes of any race in any sport at the time.[50] But for all his drawing power and promotional guile, Paige was a near-constant irritant to those who employed him. Though officially under contract to the Kansas City Monarchs, he regularly moonlighted with other teams in nonleague promotions. In a sense, his availability and responsibilities always remained in question. Paige was particularly skilled at playing both sides against the middle, creating a great deal of demand for his services and conflict among those who wished to secure them. In spite of the fact that he was difficult to control—or to be more precise, that he assumed agency over his own commodification—his tremendous appeal always seemed to place him in the middle of some high-profile baseball attraction, leading more than one journalist to wonder aloud whether he was running black ball.[51] In 1941, Ric Roberts of the *Afro-American* called Paige simply "the finest box-office attraction ever developed by Negro League baseball thanks to a cordial colored and white press." That season was "a high water mark for Paige, and for the managers in both leagues. Wilkerson [sic] has been kind enough to struggling owners, to allow his costliest property to jaunt about the country . . . attracting unprecedented thousands and filling up coffers with good old American legal tender."[52] In this way, Paige and Pollock shared the understanding that showmanship could be transformed into dollars and led the way in using promotions for both individual good and the good of segregated baseball as a whole.

Wartime Challenges

All the promotions initiated by Paige and Pollock, Effa Manley's forays into radio, and even the argument over publicity for the East-West Classic would have had little or no impact had there not been a consumer base with disposable income to spend on entertainment. As Drake and Cayton observe, entertainment was one of the first nonnecessities on which the residents of the black metropolis spent their incomes, even during the depression. But as employment increased and the African American eco-system grew incrementally during the 1940s, so did the purchasing power of its inhabitants. Unemployment among African Americans dropped precipitously during 1942 and 1943. "Race Employment Biggest in History: Discrimination Felt to Be at All-Time 'Low,'" trumpeted a headline in the November 28, 1942, issue of the *Pittsburgh Courier*; less than four months later, the paper announced that "statistics secured from 23 leading industries in Baltimore, Md, show that from May to September, 1942, there was a 33 per cent increase in the employment of Negroes."[53]

Many of the newly employed were hired by mainstream businesses previously unwilling to employ people of color. "Firms which never before hired colored persons," noted the Associated Negro Press, "are now coming 'into the fold' at the rate of fifteen per week."[54] Pepsi, previously segregated, was particularly aggressive in opening up its race employment practices, with its new hires including Herman T. Smith, identified in the *Defender* as a "well-known race promotion [*sic*] and former newspaper man," to a prominent sales post.[55] Such actions signaled that at least one national business was on the verge of enfranchising a whole new demographic of consumer citizens. This increased hiring of African Americans resulted not only from wartime labor shortages but also from official and unofficial quotas imposed by the armed forces on the number of African Americans who could serve. In 1943, for example, African Americans comprised roughly 10 percent of the population but only 5.9 percent of the members of the armed forces.[56]

With the Major Leagues depleted by the departure of players to serve in the war and the pockets of Negro Leagues fans newly filled, black baseball anticipated a boom; wartime travel restrictions, however, hindered the fiscal health of the sport as well as every other sector of the entertainment industry, color notwithstanding. Rationing of rubber and gasoline had a major impact on the way in which the business approached a broadening marketplace. The Office of Defense Transportation (ODT) restricted civilian use of buses, not only because of the resources necessary for their operation but because the military required all available vehicles.[57] Nevertheless, attendance at Negro League games reached an all-time high during this period, especially in the Northeast, where the relative proximity of teams made the difficulty of travel less onerous. Crowds at Newark Eagles' home games as well as Yankee Stadium promotions, for example, consistently topped sixteen thousand and not infrequently numbered as many as twenty-five thousand paying fans.[58]

Of course, the Negro Leagues were not the only business enterprises negatively affected by World War II travel restrictions, nor were they the only elements of the African American ecosystem to find a way to operate under trying circumstances. For traveling musicians, both in big bands that played major venues and acts in the Chitlin' Circuit that performed in small clubs and juke joints, wartime restrictions made operations difficult. Big bands that headlined major venues also generally had the financial resources to travel by train, especially in the North and Midwest, where theaters and large nightclubs were generally located along rail lines and where performers of color could find accommodations, crowded though they might be. Benny Carter, the popular and versatile bandleader, for instance, personally expressed his intentions to take to the rails, given the ban on charter buses. So, too, did Lionel Hampton and his band.[59] For musicians on the Chitlin' Circuit who performed in small clubs and juke joints, however, wartime restrictions made operations difficult. Similarly, the economics of Negro League baseball made train travel cost-prohibitive, at the very least.[60]

In September 1942, a group headed by bandleader Cab Calloway, National Association for the Advancement of Colored People executive secretary Walter White, and Columbia Records impresario John Hammond argued before the ODT that the music industry should be granted an exemption from the wartime travel restrictions. Citing "insurmountable difficulties" given the serious impediments to travel, particularly in the South, the ODT awarded music industry officials five buses for use in the southern tier. The exemption was granted with the understanding that musicians in their own way were vital to the war effort.[61]

Negro League owners, too, appealed the ODT's ruling, arguing that bus travel was necessary, especially in the South, to keep the business alive. Calvin Griffith, owner of the Major League Washington Senators, backed the effort because he relied on income gained from renting his park to black baseball teams. In 1943, the NAL received an exemption for bus travel in the South, and the NNL received a similar exemption the following year, but those exemptions were never as sweeping as those enjoyed by the music industry.[62] Black baseball simply lacked the mass appeal beyond the narrow confines of the African American ecosystem that black music achieved.

Among the music industry entrepreneurs to whom the ODT granted the use of a bus were Denver Ferguson and his younger brother, Sea. The Ferguson operation closely resembled that of many of black baseball's owners. Like Greenlee, Pompez, and Abe Manley, Denver Ferguson capitalized his formal business, the management of musicians, with money from his policy operation, which centered on Indiana Avenue in the heart of Indianapolis's African American business district. Ferguson, a migrant, developed his own version of the policy game known as Baseball Tickets, in which the betting sheet resembled a baseball scorecard, with gigs entered as hits, runs, and errors and the results based on the scores of black baseball games.[63] According to historian Preston Lauterbach, "Enthusiasm for the pastime ran high on the Avenue, as locals tracked the results of Cuban, Mexican, and Panamanian winter baseball with a zeal that matched their daily devotion to the major and Negro Leagues from spring to early fall."[64] But Ferguson's real impact came not from the policy rackets but from his creation of the Chitlin' Circuit itself, which he managed into a vertically integrated business. This model became increasingly important after the war, especially as the U.S. political and cultural climates continued to evolve.

Double V and Race Businesses

In July 1942, not needing to take advantage of the ODT exemption, Hampton and his band traveled by train to Miami Beach to perform for the troops, thereby "crashing the 'color ban' which has for years been established by an iron-clad law, which prohibited race entertainers to exhibit at the famous southern playground before whites," according to the *Courier*.[65] In this case, the performance presaged the slow process of desegregation that was to come in all areas of the entertainment industry. More important, however, was the rhetoric framing the marketing of the tour. Before the tour began, Hampton changed his outfit's name to the Double V Band, a reference to the *Courier*'s landmark publicity campaign, calling for "victory abroad against our enemies, and victory at home against segregation" and other forms of race-based discrimination.[66] For two years, the *Courier* published weekly articles emphasizing the necessity of success on both fronts, printed pins and banners, and encouraged activity that would publicize the campaign. According to journalist and historian Patrick Washburn, "The *Pittsburgh Courier* had a neat diagram, which was this Double V with an eagle in the middle, and people loved this kind of diagram. And you had women walking around with Double Vs on their dresses. You had a new hairstyle called the 'doubler' where black women would walk around and weave two—two Vs in their hair. You had Double V baseball games, Double V flag-waving ceremonies, Double V gardens. I mean it's just Double V this, Double V this, Double V this. And the *Pittsburgh Courier*, which was looking for circulation, played this to the hilt."[67]

Given his connection to the *Courier*, to which he regularly contributed as a columnist, it is hardly surprising that Cum Posey would trumpet the campaign, calling for "every team in Negro organized baseball to wear the 'Double V' on their uniforms. This symbol of victory abroad and at home is more vital to us than any athletic victory any of us might attain."[68] An important if unarticulated aspect of the Double V campaign was the simultaneous invigoration of race pride. Like the earlier "Don't Buy Where You Can't Work" campaign, in which Posey's colleague, Effa Manley had a leading role, and the Double Duty Dollar doctrine, Double V seemed, at least on the surface, to call for active support of race businesses. Indeed, several of the many letters to the editor published in the *Courier* in response to Double V suggested that Negro businesses should use the paper's emblem in promoting their efforts—"So much so," wrote Harlem resident Macon Thornhill, "that I think it will be a good idea for every Negro in business, or otherwise, to use the Emblem."[69] In this sense, Double V would serve the same purpose as the "Negro Owned" signs that appeared in store windows during periods of rioting from the 1930s well into the 1970s. Displaying the Double V connoted black proprietorship or at least solidarity with the race cause. Going even further, another letter called for the commodification of Double V into "a united national effort embracing the full co-operation of the Negro press, fraternities, churches, businesses, and all other organizations. Let us have millions of buttons to be sold to every Negro in America. Let us have stickers for our cars and placards for our homes."[70] The writer did not mention who would profit from the sale of such merchandise, but the language used equates patriotism, race pride, and profit. Support for Double V was functionally equivalent to supporting the *Courier*, which had originated the campaign and the logo.

By publicly endorsing his newspaper's campaign, Posey was essentially cross-promoting his product. On one hand, support for Double V, no matter who called for it, seems to have also supported the circulation of the *Courier*. After all, it was the *Courier*'s campaign and its emblem. On the other, while vocally advocating support for the campaign to his presumably increasing readership, Posey also advertised his product, proclaiming its patriotism. What better way to show off the Double V spirit than to take in a Sunday baseball doubleheader, participating in not only the "official" national pastime of baseball but also the unofficial one, profit through enterprise? And what better team to see than Posey's Homestead Grays, now headquartered in the nation's capital?

But Double V also had unintended consequences. By advocating an end to segregation at home, Posey was implicitly calling for an end to precisely the circumstances that had rendered black baseball a necessity. The many ancillary businesses that existed as a response to these conditions called further attention to the contradictory nature of the Double V project. As insidious as segregation most certainly was, it nonetheless provided a space for the birth and evolution of an African American ecosystem. A certain group of black entrepreneurs, among them Posey and his fellow owners, had a vested interest in the status quo. As E. Franklin Frazier observed in a 1947 article, "It is the Negro professional, the business man, and to a lesser extent, the white collar worker who profit from segregation. These groups in the Negro population enjoy certain advantages because they do not have to compete with whites."[71] Double V exposed the extent to which the voices of change clashed with the forces of the status quo, creating a contested terrain of operation for black businesses such as the Negro Leagues and the hotels, clubs, and restaurants that baseball executives, players, and fans patronized. Still, during and immediately after the war years, black baseball and the other segments of the race entertainment industry remained a necessity. The beginning of the gradual desegregation process may have been just over the horizon, but segregated facilities remained a reality.

The NNBL articulated the need to deal with this contested terrain in positive terms. Addressing the group's annual meeting in August 1942, league president Dr. J. E. Walker noted that "the school room must teach [business] theory to send forth merchants. If Negro youth are to explore New Frontiers for Negro business, the inspiration must be given by the schools. Everywhere we have a local branch, it should assume the leadership and guide our people along the economic path."[72] Taking a decidedly Du Boisian stance, NNBL leaders urged education of future African American entrepreneurs so that they did not need to "cast down their buckets" where they were, as league founder Booker T. Washington had advocated, but rather could compete in a postwar environment of the sort envisaged by the Double V campaign. In short, Walker demanded that black business owners learn to operate in a more democratic marketplace where the only color of any significance was green.

A Changing Political Landscape

Though wartime prosperity and the promise of a more democratic marketplace as advocated by Double V infused the rhetoric of progress for the race, the potential of economic stagnation in the early postwar environment was a definite reality. The possibility of massive job loss and with it the potential for a diminishing consumer base was not lost on either the black press or the Department of Labor. Citing a gain of approximately one million jobs between 1940 and 1944, the January 1945 issue of the *Monthly Labor Review*, an official publication of the Department of Labor, expressed concern about the potential for a severe decline in employment for African Americans in semiskilled positions in the industries most closely related to the war effort. The study, prepared by Seymour L. Wolfbein of the Occupational Outlook Division of the Bureau of Labor Statistics, reported that urban industrial employment had increased during the war years, while the number of those employed in agriculture decreased accordingly. In addition, Negroes had made substantial inroads in government employment.[73]

On the subject of employment prospects for African Americans after the war, however, the study expressed concern, noting that "the Negro has made his greatest employment gains in those occupations (especially semiskilled factory jobs) which will suffer the severest cutbacks during the postwar period." Wolfbein continued,

> The Negro gains have taken place in congested production areas where considerable readjustment of the labor force will be necessary. In general, the Negro has been able to get his war job in areas where a substantial proportion of the labor force was also engaged in war work. . . . These cities, of course, will experience considerable labor turnover in the immediate postwar period.
>
> . . . [I]n those occupations and industries in which the Negro has made his greatest employment advances, he was generally among the last to be hired. Therefore under seniority rules, he is more likely to be laid off than the average worker in these occupations.
>
> The war has given many Negroes their first opportunity to demonstrate the ability to perform basic factory operations in a semiskilled and skilled capacity. The consolidation of the Negro's gains in the postwar period (and this is true, of course, for a sizable, proportion of other workers as well) is dependent in large measure upon the volume of employment that then prevails.[74]

The potential for mass unemployment among participants in the African American ecosystem was so great that the *Pittsburgh Courier* cited the report's findings.[75] The *Courier's* editors clearly wanted to broadcast their concerns and create a sense of awareness among their readers. The

Double V campaign could not be considered a success if it resulted in substantial declines in African American employment.

But what would have amounted to an economic catastrophe never manifested as predicted. A 1947 follow-up study by Wolfbein noted that no significant drop in employment had occurred. Though black workers continued to experience higher unemployment rates than their white counterparts, a higher percentage of black laborers were employed in manual labor and service, and black labor collectively remained less potent, wartime economic gains persisted. According to Wolfbein, "Reconversion of industry to peacetime activities brought no major downgrading in the occupational composition of the Negro worker. This is especially significant in view of the concentration of wartime employment advances of Negroes in those occupations, industries, and areas in which the postwar readjustment was most severe. Essentially, the maintenance of high labor demand during the transition period enabled these workers to hold on to many of their wartime gains. Both the war and postwar experience emphasize the importance of full employment to the position of the Negro in the labor force."[76] Considerable income disparities between African American and white workers persisted, with those gaps greater in the South than in the urban Northeast and Midwest. However, the inequalities had narrowed considerably, enough to alter the discussion of what was next on the agenda.[77]

Among the possible reasons for the continued success of African Americans in the workplace was the fact that a number of states passed antidiscrimination laws as the war ended. The first—and, from the point of view of Negro League baseball, most important—of these emergent measures came when New York State adopted a measure guaranteeing equal employment opportunities across racial boundaries. On March 23, 1945, New York governor Thomas E. Dewey, who as state prosecutor had hounded Cuban Stars owner Alex Pompez for his participation in the numbers rackets, used twenty-three pens to sign Chapter 118 of the Laws of 1945, the Ives-Quinn Anti-Discrimination Act (sometimes Quinn-Ives), setting up a permanent state commission to eliminate biased employment practices.[78]

According to the *New York Times*, the new law "was likened to the Declaration of Independence, the Bill of Rights and the Emancipation Proclamation, since it is intended as an implementation of the statement in the Declaration of Independence that 'all men were created equal.'" The many pens were to be distributed as souvenirs to the bill's sponsors, most notably New York State Assembly leader Irving M. Ives, a Republican, and Elmer F. Quinn, the Democratic Senate minority leader.[79] In contrast to the *Times*'s approving tone, the *Wall Street Journal*, not surprisingly, expressed doubts about the new law on the grounds that "a penal statute is not the remedy for the evil at which this law is aimed." But even the more conservative paper conceded that the bill's passage afforded Dewey the opportunity to make strides in stopping job discrimination.[80]

According to an article distributed by the National Negro Press Association, during the first year following the passage of Ives-Quinn, the New York commission received "370 complaints and initiated 107 of its own." Furthermore, "a breakdown of the complaints showed that 207 were based on color, eighty-nine on creed, sixty on national origin and fourteen miscellaneous."[81] The *New York Times*, covering the same report, quoted the state commission as exclaiming, "This law soundly carries forward the mandate in the Declaration of Independence which, after declaring that all men are endowed with the rights of life, liberty, and the pursuit of happiness, states: 'To secure these rights governments are instituted among men.'"[82]

Although the majority of the 207 color-based cases that came before the New York commission were resolved through legal enforcement, the case most closely associated with the passage of Ives-Quinn, and certainly the case most closely associated with baseball as both a business and an institution, concerned Brooklyn Dodgers president Branch Rickey. On October 23, 1945, Rickey signed Kansas City Monarchs shortstop Jack Roosevelt Robinson to play for the Montreal Royals, the white baseball club's farm team. The signing was nothing short of a watershed moment. It changed the culture of Major League Baseball while having a demonstrable impact on the business of the Negro Leagues. And its implications for the broader African American ecosystem reverberated for many years. Once the color line in white organized baseball was breached, the meaning of race pride through purchase power and consumer citizenship gained new significance as African America prepared for Robinson's progression into the white game.

5

Desegregating Baseball and Its Economic Implications, 1946–1948

Introduction

When Jackie Robinson officially desegregated the Major Leagues in 1947, the black baseball establishment had yet to fully digest the implications of his signing. Robinson's first appearance at Ebbets Field on April 15 served as a bellwether of what was to come and reverberated throughout the African American ecosystem over the next few years. As Negro League fans began to reinvent themselves as Major League fans, Negro League baseball, a central node in a broader ethnic economy created by the unprecedented demographic shifts of the first half of the twentieth century, was pushed into the shadows by mainstream business interests looking to expand.

Negro League owners were collectively slow to react as their traditional fan base shifted toward the slowly integrating Major League product—first the Brooklyn Dodgers, then the Cleveland Indians and the St. Louis Browns, and ultimately other franchises. Against the backdrop of African American soldiers returning from the war with increased expectations for civil liberties and improving economic opportunities, desegregated baseball appeared to be a harbinger of black progress. But "progress" in the abstract ran headlong into the reality of the accounting ledgers of black businesses. While parts of the country watched the first televised World Series in 1947, complete with Jackie Robinson in a Dodger uniform, introducing if not naturalizing the image of a black man in a white sport, many African American businesses, dependent in part on the patronage generated by Negro League baseball, found their livelihoods threatened by the hegemony of white business practices.

Despite the immediate effects of the 1945 Ives-Quinn Anti-Discrimination Act, which led directly to Dodger president Branch Rickey's decision to sign Robinson, Negro League owners did not appear to have a plan in place to deal with the effects of desegregation on their businesses. A 1946 study conducted by New York's City College Social Research Laboratory brought the potential impact of Robinson's entry into the Major Leagues to the fore. The study proposed that the public image of an athlete of color competing side by side with white athletes would have a propitious economic effect for the African American community as well as positive sociopolitical implications: "Negro stars might well prove to be lucrative drawing cards, as witness the huge crowds which turned out at the Yale Bowl last fall to see the Yale football team with its brilliant Negro athlete, Levi Jackson."[1]

As the front offices of the first handful of Major League teams mined the Negro Leagues for cheap yet effective labor, Negro League owners were caught between the likelihood of economic ruin and the material significance of broader social progress. Owners knew that their enterprises could not survive for long without their fan base, which inevitably would be stripped away along with their star attractions. Black baseball's entrepreneurs also knew that preventing players from crossing a fading color line was not a viable option, at least politically. Many Negro League owners had long positioned themselves as vocal advocates for civil rights through such community projects as "Don't Buy Where You Can't Work." Now they found themselves in a fight for their fiscal lives as they attempted to secure compensation from white baseball for the appropriation of their most valuable human resources. Although the Negro National League (NNL) and Negro American League (NAL) had attempted to model their administrative structures on the Major Leagues, they were in reality constantly changing conglomerations of owners whose interests were more often than not at odds with one another. Long before the color line was breached, there was no love lost among these entrepreneurs. Major League owners certainly were not immune to interpersonal conflicts, but because the Major Leagues were overseen by what amounted to a powerful executive branch in the form of the league presidents and the commissioner, internecine conflict did not interfere substantially with the way the business was run. But in contrast to and in spite of what at times appeared to be extraordinary gains during the war years, the NNL and the

NAL remained bastions of individual interests and resultant infighting. The weakness of their executive branches consequently left them open for exploitation.

The desegregation of the Major Leagues did not emerge in a vacuum. While the legal gains of Ives-Quinn were certainly contributing factors, changes in the American landscape contributed to the weakening of the color line and the broad connotations of the segregated dollar. Returning black soldiers had fought in segregated units but were nevertheless convinced that their contributions to the victory would lead to a new push to dismantle the color line on the home front. New social awareness if not radicalization became a more permanent and prominent feature of black life, contributing to the rapidly changing nature of the African American ecosystem. Returning war veterans brought a new social awareness to communities empowered by the rhetoric of Double V, but African Americans had already exhibited social awareness and pushed toward equality. So why did these basic changes in American life occur at this specific juncture, and what factors led to this particular breach of the color line? More significantly, what implications did desegregation carry for the African American ecosystem, constructed as it was around the notion of the segregated dollar?

A Changing Landscape

If the returning soldiers had been the only segment of the population driving change, the larger picture would not in all likelihood have been altered so drastically. But urban African America, like the rest of the country, was a significantly different place at war's end than at the outset. The second wave of the Great Migration, though it began prior to the attack on Pearl Harbor, escalated throughout the war. Individuals fled the poverty and structural injustice of the South in favor of the potential for improved economic conditions in the North and West. The mechanization of agriculture in general and the cotton industry in particular effectively ended the plantation system. On October 2, 1944, on Howell Hopson's plantation near Clarksdale, Mississippi, engineers from the International Harvester Company publicly tested their picker and baler, which reduced the cost of producing a bale of cotton from $39.41 when processed by hand to $5.26 when processed mechanically.[2] Seemingly overnight, a population that had been tied to the land for generations found itself loosened from its traditional moorings. What ensued was that an entire population that had known only the difficult, brutal, and exploitative sharecropping life found that even it was no longer available to them. As a direct result, both black and white tenant farmers were compelled to look elsewhere in an increasingly crowded postwar labor market. But while white sharecroppers had other options in the southern economy, their black counterparts generally did not, creating the impetus for the last wave of the Great Migration.

The new migrants gravitated toward already established communities in the North and West where, not coincidentally, African American eco-systems had matured and race sport was a regular feature of everyday life. This final stage of the second wave swelled already crowded traditional black communities well past their bursting points. Indeed, as World War II began, 77 percent of black Americans still lived in the South, with 49 percent living and working in the agrarian belt. By the time the migration slowed to a trickle at the end of the 1960s, approximately 5 million people had flooded into northern and western cities, more than three times the 1.5 million who had migrated prior to this period.[3]

Complicated by postwar housing shortages and discriminatory housing practices, legal or otherwise, the majority of these new arrivals landed in already overcrowded black enclaves such as New York's Harlem, Chicago's Bronzeville, North Philadelphia, and Cleveland's Near East Side. Conflicts over housing as well as jobs occasionally resulted in limited inter- and intr-aracial violence. The memory of race riots in Harlem and Detroit in 1943 reignited tensions, that were compounded by a rising crime rate resulting from poverty and increased population density. These circumstances sug-gested that trouble loomed just over the horizon.[4]

In a South Side Chicago section of the Black Belt bounded by Cot-tage Grove Avenue on the east, State Street on the west, 47th Street on the north, and 55th Street on the south, the population density reached an estimated 90,000 people per square mile. *Chicago Defender* crowded conditions as "even worse than can be found in Bombay or in Hongkong before the outbreak of the second world war. . . . Restrictive covenants and discriminatory policy of building and loan agencies have combined to keep the Negro from expanding beyond the narrow geographical limits of the South Side belt. Even in public housing projects financed by taxpayers' money, Negro occupancy has been challenged with bricks, bats and bul-lets. . . . There seems to be no immediate relief in sight and as the situation becomes worse, the relations between the two races degenerate."[5]

Founded in 1939, the Chicago Housing Authority spent the next two years building a series of segregated housing projects, three for white residents and two for blacks, but the new projects did little to alleviate the problem. Chicago's black population, denied access to more desirable residential neighborhoods, spread from the traditional South Side Black Belt to the city's west side, which had long housed a small percentage of people of color. As the population expanded, so too did Chicago's African American economy. In an optimistic article in the *Defender*, Henry Brown described the growing neighborhood and its commercial sector: "Thousands have swelled the ranks of the newcomers until today the west side is populated by more than 65,000 Negroes. In some sections it bears the earmarks of a slum area, rickety old buildings which have stood since the world's fair of '93 and the old brown stone fronts that weathered the Chicago fire. Store front churches, dream book shops, taverns, mumble jumble junk dealers, resale shops, fish shacks and hamburger huts are part of the Lake street landscape."[6] Despite the fact that Brown's article is titled "A Glimmer of the Future," the commercial area he describes appears to be very much like that of the South Side's business district minus the large theaters, hotels, and other neighborhood landmarks such as Metropolitan Mutual's Parkway Ballroom.

Harlem was equally overcrowded, and New York's black population also expanded into what had been working-class white ethnic neighborhoods. By 1946, the city's African American population had spread into Brooklyn's formerly Jewish and Italian Bedford-Stuyvesant neighborhood, ushering in the beginning of a racial and ethnic shift that over the next decade came to define many of Brooklyn's working-class neighborhoods, including Flatbush and Brownsville.[7] Predictably, as black residents established themselves in communities, they faced open hostility from their neighbors.

Prior to these changing residential patterns, Brooklyn had also been home to a small African American community, a portion of which was solidly middle class and had helped to support the borough's Negro League teams, owned, at least in part, by Sol White and Nat Strong.[8] Immediately after the war, however, the African American presence grew exponentially, accompanied by an influx of Puerto Rican immigrants and soon followed by other people of color from elsewhere in the Caribbean.[9] Friction arose between Brooklyn's increasing black population and its established ethnic, non-Protestant working class as well as its middle class. White, ethnic Brooklyn rooted for Robinson and the other African American players who soon joined him on the diamond at Ebbets Field and helped propel the Dodgers to a string of National League pennants, but many of these die-hard fans also began to leave their "beloved" Brooklyn, only to be followed by the franchise itself after the 1957 season.[10]

The same year that Robinson broke into the Majors, William J. Levitt broke ground for a new housing development on what had been a Long Island potato farm. Levitt had grown up in Brooklyn's Bedford-Stuyvesant when it was a working-class Jewish enclave, but he and his family, like many other whites, fled when African Americans—in this case, an assistant district attorney and his family—moved onto the block. As such, the Levitts represented the first wave of what would come to be known as *white flight*, a pattern that would be reenacted time and time again in the decades to come.[11]

Levitt was no stranger to real estate. His father was a real estate developer, and young Levitt and his brother, Alfred, received a U.S. government contract to construct homes for 2,350 war industry laborers in Norfolk, Virginia. But the Levitts ran into trouble, unable to meet either budgetary restrictions or deadlines. Levitt then went on to serve in the military as a U.S. Navy Seabee, primarily involved in the construction of "instant" airfields with all manner of temporary structures. As David Halberstam explains, these experiences both before and during the war "provided [Levitt] with a magnificent laboratory in which to experiment with low-cost mass housing and analyze it with his peers—a chance he might never have had in civilian life." After the war, with these skills in hand, Levitt oversaw the largest construction of private housing in American history, becoming by every measure the father of modern suburbia.[12]

Among the first to move out to what became known as Levittown and the similar subdivisions that soon followed were segments of Brooklyn's white ethnic population, who made up a large percentage of Jackie Robinson's supporters. Moreover, as "fear of crime" became a euphemism for racial animus, the continuing flight of white ethnics was hastened both by public policy and unscrupulous but lucrative real estate practices.[13] As part of a depression-era attempt to help faltering real estate and insurance markets, banks introduced the practice known as redlining, in which the value of a whole neighborhood was assessed based on the quality of its housing stock and, more significantly, the homogeneity of its population. "Redlined" neighborhoods, as opposed to blue-lined and yellow-lined areas, were deemed the most risky, virtually guaranteeing that banks would not lend money to individuals purchasing homes there. The practice of blockbusting soon followed: real estate agents instilled fear of falling property values in response to redlining, encouraging longtime occupants to sell their homes, usually to African Americans, quickly. The agents enjoyed large profits in the process. Because neighborhoods were redlined once they had "gone black," the initial African American home-owners watched their property values plummet. In response, some homes were subdivided into kitchenette rentals or rooming houses, while oth-ers were abandoned or allowed to deteriorate, creating slum conditions.[14] This process replicated itself not just in Brooklyn and New York City but across the national urban landscape. The move toward suburbanization and these shifting demographics had unavoidable implications for estab-lished African American ecosystems.

The "New" New Negro

The majority of Levittown homeowners were returning veterans. In light of the dire postwar housing shortages and the incipient baby boom, white ethnics were encouraged to populate new suburban enclaves and were eager to do so. But for people of color who were eager to take advantage of new housing opportunities, the option was simply not available. As Levitt noted, "I have come to know that if we sell one house to a Negro family, then 90 or 95 percent of our white customers will not buy into the com-munity. That is their attitude, not ours. . . . As a company our position is simply this: We can solve a housing problem, or we can try to solve a racial problem but we cannot combine the two."[15] In fact, the newly returning black servicemen, who had protested the type of systematic segregation and discrimination characteristic of the new suburbs while in the military, were not only rebuffed privately by developers and new homeowners but rebuked publicly by no less a voice than secretary of war Henry Stimson, who opined, "What these foolish leaders of the colored race are seeking is at bottom, social equality."[16]

When black war veterans came home to urban segregated communi-ties populated by recent migrants, the result was a great deal of embitter-ment. "Just carve on my tombstone," one serviceman wrote, "here lies a black man killed fighting a yellow man for the protection of a white man."[17] Many soldiers and civilian workers shared the sentiment. Not all returning veterans resented their part in the war effort, but there was a general sense that such blatant discrimination was no longer tolerable. Many veterans of color were quite vocal about their refusal to return to the racial status quo, a situation highlighted by the discriminatory housing situation. Having traveled to Europe, Asia, and Africa and seen the ramifications of a social hierarchy steeped in racialized thought, veterans brought back to America a new sense of purpose to the fight for equality and became civically engaged. African Americans who served only in the United States, among them Jackie Robinson, also developed this sense of purpose. Robinson's career path showed possibilities to a new breed of politicized young black veterans and their families.

The daughter of sharecroppers in Cairo, Georgia, Robinson's mother joined the first wave of the Great Migration, though she moved to racially and economically mixed Pasadena, California, rather than one of the more common urban destinations. Like his older brother Mack, an Olympic track star who matriculated at the University of Oregon, Jackie Robinson attended a fully integrated college, UCLA, where he lettered in baseball as well as basketball, track, and football, the sport in which he made his athletic reputation. His ability to navigate the vicissitudes of the white world was informed in no small part by his experiences at UCLA. Two of his backfield mates on the Bruins football team, Woody Strode and Kenny Washington, played roles similar to Robinson's when they entered the National Football League in 1946.[18]

Financial difficulties and the war ended Robinson's formal education before he graduated from college. But as formative as his experiences at UCLA might have been, his time in the armed forces molded him into a bold force in the burgeoning postwar racial discourse. Vocal when it came to perceived slights, Second Lieutenant Robinson, who, with the help of heavyweight champion Joe Louis had already desegregated the officer training school at Fort Riley, Kansas, quickly established a reputation as a combative soldier unwilling to accept prevailing racial mores. Most glaring was his 1944 arrest and subsequent court-martial while stationed at Texas's Fort Hood, where he was involved in an altercation after refusing to move to the back of a bus when instructed to do so by the civilian driver on a military transport.[19] Robinson's military counsel, Captain William A. Cline, "managed to introduce enough into evidence to strongly suggest Robinson had been consistently confronted with a racially hostile environment. By separating facts from interpretations, Cline introduced the very real possibility that scarcely suppressed racial animosities may have provoked Assistant Provost Marshal Gerald Bear to overreact to Robinson's assertiveness, construing it as 'uppity' rather than [a] legitimate expression of righteous resentment."[20] Robinson was acquitted of the charges and given an honorable discharge after it had been determined that he could better serve his country in civilian life.

In many ways, Robinson's actions suggest that he and others of his generation were intent on bringing something new to the conversation concerning race and the role of African Americans in postwar America. Taking elements of Alain Locke's concept of the New Negro a step farther, Robinson's promotion of race pride, economic independence, and political engagement among African Americans translated theory into practice, making him an example of what might be defined as a "New" New Negro.[21] Robinson and his cohort, newly energized, were unwilling to subscribe to Booker T. Washington's notion of casting down their buckets where they were. They were no longer willing to live their economic and civic lives in the shadows. Rather, they sought to expand beyond the narrow confines of the color line into the mainstream of American life. Beginning with Robinson's initial meeting with Rickey, a moment that remains akin to a national myth, the signing put the white world on notice that a formal challenge to the status quo was coming.

In his 1968 profile of Robinson in *Ebony*, veteran sportswriter, editor, and columnist A. S. "Doc" Young described the initial meeting between Robinson and Rickey as fraught with obstacles, not the least of which was Rickey's concern that Robinson's unwillingness to quietly suffer racial indignities had the potential to derail the experiment. Indeed, Rickey required that Robinson agree to suppress his potentially aggressive responses to slights, real or perceived, for his first year in the Majors. According to Young, "This shocking move required, of course, some Booker T. Washington compromises with surface inequality for the sake of expediency."[22] While Robinson's apparent compromise may have appeared Washingtonian, by signing to play for a white franchise, he was, in actuality, rewriting portions of Washington's rules of engagement. By integrating his experiences and skill set into the white game, Robinson injected a heavy dose of W. E. B. Du Bois's insistence that the field of play be level, with no artificial boundary lines created by color.

Robinson leveled the playing field in terms of economics as well as of sport. Baseball is, after all, a business, and Robinson was well paid for his pioneering efforts, receiving compensation similar to that of his white counterparts and considerably more money than he ever would have earned in black baseball. According to Rickey biographer Lee Lowenfish, in addition to a respectable minor league salary of six hundred dollars a month, Robinson received a signing bonus of thirty-five hundred dollars, a "relatively high figure from Branch Rickey, a man who loathed the concept of bonuses for unproven talent."[23] In this regard, Robinson exemplified the New New Negro not because of his vocal opposition to discrimination but rather because of his willful crossing of the economic color line, his tacit unwillingness to cast down his proverbial bucket safely on the Negro League side of the divide. His fans, many them newly minted Dodgers supporters of color, expressed pride not in terms of the segregated dollar but essentially by buying, at least symbolically, where they could (now) work.

Robinson was not the only figure in the African American ecosystem who questioned the concept that the existing order was the key to genuine progress in the early postwar years. John H. Johnson, though not a military veteran, also challenged notions of progress by redefining race pride and the function of economic activity. A publishing magnate whose contributions to the industry at times bordered on the mythological, Johnson followed a career arc that further demonstrated the extent to which the postwar period was rife with change both within and without black entrepreneurial circles. Writes Derek T. Dingle, "Without the intervention of banks, the Small Business Administration, set- asides, or rich uncles, he built Chicago-based Johnson Publishing Company, Inc., into the largest self-made black business in the world. Even the rich and powerful dub him 'The Godfather' for steadily growing his vast enterprise for 57 years, through recessions, industrial revolutions, and personal tribulations."[24]

Johnson made his mark first with *Ebony*, which commenced publication in 1945, and later with *Jet*, founded in 1951. He had begun his career in publication in 1939 as editor of Supreme Liberty Life's in-house employee magazine, which was little more than a collection of articles from other places, culled and collated by Johnson. This experience led him to conceive of his first major publication, *Negro Digest*, which, like its namesake, *Reader's Digest*, printed condensed versions of stories from other sources. The articles in *Negro Digest* were not written exclusively by authors of color, and they did not necessarily deal specifically with race. Rather, the content focused on issues and ideas that would interest African American readers.

Ebony, which became Johnson's flagship publication, paralleled *Negro Digest* in that it was aimed at the race but was not necessarily a race publication in the strictest sense. As Adam Green explains, *Ebony* contained "features on exemplary individuals, as well as rising stars of sports, stage, and the arts, original ideas of the black public presence integral to our own racial lexicon today."[25] The magazine was modeled on the immensely popular *Life*, the first weekly to utilize photodocumentary to tell stories. Among the articles and profiles in *Ebony*'s first issue, which hit newsstands on November 1, 1945, was a piece on the Dodgers' signing of Jackie Robinson.[26] *Ebony* was an immediate success and by 1946 had eclipsed the *Pittsburgh Courier*, reaching more than three hundred thousand paid subscribers to become the most widely read black-owned publication worldwide.[27]

Johnson's operation, which also included a cosmetics venture founded to enlarge the publishing enterprise's revenue stream, constituted a new type of race business in that it was not capitalized informally by funds from the numbers or policy rackets. Instead, the initial investment came from a formal source, Supreme Liberty Life.[28] Johnson's association with the black insurance giant went back to his childhood, when company president Harry Pace, also the founder of Black Swan Records in the 1920s, gave Johnson a part-time job that allowed him to continue his education.[29]

While it is possible to argue that *Ebony* and Johnson's other periodicals were just another iteration of the traditional black press, predicated on the notion of keeping black dollars within the community, Johnson's approach represented a new trend in black business. A first-wave migrant from Arkansas, he had studied business at both the University of Chicago and Northwestern University, though he graduated from neither. These experiences gave him a firm grounding in economic theory and practice of a type generally unavailable to owners of small businesses in the African American business world. Rather than bank on the idea that African Americans would buy his magazines based entirely on the fact that they were published by a coethnic, he created a superior product that appealed to the evolving tastes of his public. Not only was *Ebony* modeled on *Life*, it looked like *Life*. It sold the image of African Americans as fully enfranchised consumer citizens. In this regard, Johnson Publishing differed from other race businesses not only by attempting to mirror the mainstream but by succeeding. Like Robinson, Johnson came to represent another clear example of the New New Negro.

Black Baseball's "Boardroom"

Faced with an eroding fan base, certain factions of Negro League ownership attempted to take a page out of Johnson's playbook, though perhaps not consciously so. Neither the NNL or the NAL power structure moved to emulate mainstream business practices, but Gus Greenlee, who had left black baseball when it became financially impractical for him to continue, did. Greenlee reconstituted his Pittsburgh Crawfords in the early 1940s, though they operated independent of league affiliation because the NNL rebuffed Greenlee's attempt to join. In response, he and several other independent owners formed the United States Baseball League (USL), a new enterprise that attracted a fair amount of attention as evidenced by the fact that reports announcing its 1944 creation were reprinted in most of the major black weeklies. Greenlee proclaimed, "We are going to operate this league on a pattern as close to the Major League as possible." The USL, he said, will "name a president and secretary who are in no way connected with any of the teams. . . . We want a real president . . . and will select a man whose character and reputation is above reproach: a man whom the entire public will respect."[30]

Greenlee's declaration was no doubt directed at the existing Negro Leagues, which had yet to appoint a neutral party to serve in a leadership capacity. Indeed, Thomas T. Wilson, president of the NNL, and John B. Martin, who held the same position with the NAL, were owners and consequently often found that their decision making received criticism from league rivals. Neither Wilson nor Martin was ever fully free to assert any significant level of authority without incurring charges that he was acting solely out of individual rather than collective interest, and these charges often contained more than a grain of truth.[31] And even when they did act in the league's interest, they lacked particularly strong leadership skills. This deficiency, coupled with the near-constant suspicion from some of the other owners, left the presidents ineffective and the league exposed from an administrative standpoint. As Cum Posey complained to Wendell Smith in the *Courier*, "Now we have a new problem confronting us . . . and that concerns Negro players going into white organized baseball. Martin and Wilson have been in a position to protect our interests for years but they haven't done it."[32] The problem, according to Posey, was not that the league presidents were too powerful but that they were inept and therefore subject to manipulation by some of the more aggressively self-interested owners, Eddie Gottlieb among them.

At a June 1943 joint meeting of the leagues, Newark Eagles owner Effa Manley called for the appointment of an independent commissioner who could make sound decisions and adjudicate disputes without the taint of any sort of conflict of interest.[33] Manley's plea for leadership was a response not to the potential threat posed by the USL but rather to the scourge of player jumping and poaching that had plagued both the NAL and NNL for some time. That neither league could devise a viable administrative structure headed up by a strong, leader with no existing financial interest in either league, demonstrated the extent to which the industry was effectively rudderless. At a time when they desperately needed strong governance to deal directly with threats from a rival black league and the even greater economic threat of impending encroachment by white baseball, the Negro Leagues failed to forge a coherent response.

The NNL and NAL's lack of a collective response to external pressures was foregrounded by Rickey's use of the USL as cover for what was essentially a raid on black baseball. More telling were Greenlee's apparent understanding that desegregation was inevitable and his recognition that the only way for black baseball to function as a race business in light of desegregation was as a preparatory circuit—a minor league that constituted an established and essential part of the machine that was mainstream organized baseball.[34]

Writing to Abe Manley, co-owner of the Eagles, just three months after the Robinson signing, Allen Johnson, owner of the NNL's St. Louis Stars, explained why he was deserting the established league for Greenlee's venture: "I believe the Negro owner is just about at the end of the rope as far as baseball is concerned. This will be his final year of activity, unless he takes every advantage of every offer that is being made now. This does not mean that there will not be some Negro teams, but I mean every Negro big league owner will have muffed the final chance to get into organized baseball." Johnson continued, "If the Negro owner does not perfect a league capable of being recognized, then in another year or two, white baseball men are going to step in, organize a Negro Loop, perfect it, apply for admission to the Minor league circuit of National Professional Baseball and every Negro club will be raided, and the owners who are now struggling on with the present Negro setup, will be left out in the cold and with no redress. . . . I am certain that any thinking businessman, regardless of baseball, can see this handwriting on the wall."[35] No longer an NNL owner and thus no longer directly affected by the recurring conflicts among Negro League owners as well as between the two leagues, Johnson recognized that the breach in the color line would inevitably widen, encouraging the white baseball establishment to further reach in and wrest their product away from black baseball's owners. In Johnson's estimation, failure to act would mean failure, period.

Almost four full months passed before the Negro League owners seriously addressed Johnson's concerns. Rufus "Sonnyman" Jackson, president and co-owner of the Homestead Grays, boldly proposed that the black ball clubs apply "for membership in the Major Leagues under the jurisdiction of Commissioner [A. B. 'Happy'] Chandler."[36] But the Negro League teams never received serious consideration for entry into the Major Leagues. In contrast, Johnson's proposal that the NAL and NNL agree to function as a minor league circuit was at least fiscally realistic, given that the Negro Leagues would soon be forced to sell talent to Major League owners for considerably less than the players were worth. By following Johnson's proposal and becoming part of the organized minor league system, black baseball theoretically could have positioned itself as a viable part of the larger institutional infrastructure of professional baseball. But this idea also did not come to fruition. More than racism, black baseball faced the problem that the industry was built on the shifting sands of Jim Crow in that it relied primarily on segregated consumption patterns.

Many of Johnson's concerns were articulated in other quarters. As Neil Lanctot notes, "To continue to exist and flourish, black baseball and other black institutions would increasingly have to prove their legitimacy outside of a purely segregated context. Black baseball would thus have to work with, rather than against, white professional leagues, and as journalist Cleveland Jackson warned, 'open opposition to Major League owners would spell disaster to the Negro circuits. They're operating on a wish and prayer and know it. The majors hold all the aces and know it.'"[37] Lanctot also observes that the events of 1947 underscored the structural problems that relying on race dollars presented for this segment of the African American ecosystem: "The year also exposed the essential weaknesses of black business when subjected to outside competition. For years, the leagues had been slow to make necessary improvements in administration and publicity, content with the knowledge that black baseball fans would continue to patronize their games. But the enterprise's still considerable deficiencies became strikingly more apparent when facing actual competition for the black consumer dollar from a better financed and run organization that provided the regular statistics and standings long craved by black fans."[38]

The problem of wider competition with regard to the segregated dollar was not lost on postwar observers. In fact, well before 1947, the issue of race pride through consumer practice revealed a growing disconnect between consumers and entrepreneurs. In *Black Metropolis*, sociologists

St. Clair Drake and Horace Cayton examine this conflict between race pride and consumer savvy. Faced with a choice of "buying black" or getting the most for their money in terms of both quantity and quality, the average Bronzeville housewife felt that colored merchants simply could not compete with their white counterparts.[39] In fact, for much of its history, the National Negro Business League (NNBL) addressed similar problems; it, too, found no lasting solutions, and the problem continued to burden the organization.

An American Dilemma

Social theorists also had concerns about the issue of white business competition with the African American ecosystem. In his landmark 1944 study, *An American Dilemma: The Negro Problem and Modern Democracy*, Nobel Prize winner Gunnar Myrdal shed considerable light on the problems both facing and posed by race businesses: "The weaknesses of Negro business chauvinism are apparent from consideration of the facts about existing Negro business. Insofar as Negro-owned business is inefficient compared to white-owned business, it cannot exist for a long time."[40]

Myrdal's conclusions were not drawn in a vacuum. The data and commentary gathered in *An American Dilemma* came from reports by African American leaders and social critics, among them writer James Weldon Johnson, a cofounder of the National Association for the Advancement of Colored People. For Johnson, the issue of the race dollar was particularly pressing. Focusing on the sustainability of race pride as an economic model, Johnson wrote, "Now, 'race pride' may be a pretty good business slogan, but it is a mighty shaky business foundation. A Negro American in business must give as excellent quality, as low a price, and as prompt and courteous service as any competitor, otherwise he runs a tremendous risk in counting on the patronage even of members of his own race. 'Race pride' may induce them once or twice to buy . . . a pair of shoes that cost more and wear out quicker, but it won't keep them doing it. The Negro businessmen who have succeeded have been those who have maintained as high quality, as low prices, and as good service as their competitors."[41]

John H. Johnson's publishing empire offered a prime illustration of a successful race business built on what Johnson identified as sound business practices. By proactively structuring a business that could withstand the collapse of a soon-to-be outdated economic model—that is, reliance on the segregated dollar—Johnson implemented proven business practices in his work with *Negro Digest*, *Ebony*, and *Jet*. Johnson struck an innovative chord, finding a creative and productive way to "cast down his bucket" by providing a high-quality product that was built to compete with mainstream publications long after the breaching of the color line enfranchised black consumers. In this sense, his company met the challenge set forth by James Weldon Johnson, however indirectly. By creating a product intended to appeal directly to the African American market despite the changing landscape, John H. Johnson embraced the sort of business practices championed by the NNBL and rooted in the vision of its founder, Booker T. Washington.

In contrast to Johnson's innovative publishing empire, Negro League baseball continued to operate as it had for the better part of three decades, hewing to the model established by Rube Foster in the 1920s. Black baseball's owners fostered their fair share of innovations in response to the prevailing economic climate, including night baseball. But notwithstanding any promotional innovations, the Negro League entrepreneurs continued to conduct business as usual. Any attempts to forge a cohesive response to the gradual erosion of their industry and its market share were undermined by the absence of strong and effective leadership and a collective unwillingness to move beyond Foster's original vision for the game. The sort of strong leadership needed to keep black baseball vital would have required innovations along the lines of those Johnson Publishing introduced into the ecosystem, including the development of a means for securing a steady flow of capital without relying heavily on the informal economy as well as the production of a highly competitive product. For baseball, such a product would have meant adhering to regular schedules, keeping league disputes behind closed doors, and ensuring customer satisfaction both within and outside of the ballpark. The addition of adequate concessions, for example, which were absent from many smaller Negro League venues, might have gone a long way toward keeping customers and their dollars in the industry, a shortcoming understood by players as well as fans.[42]

Ralph Bunche, an African American diplomat and another important contributor to Myrdal's study, contended that such changes might not have been enough to save black baseball, let alone the broader segregated ecosystem. Bunche, who in 1950 became the first person of color to receive the Nobel Peace Prize, regarded the efficacy of race business significantly differently from many of his contemporaries. Like James Weldon Johnson,

Bunche challenged Washington's position that progress could be achieved only through economic opportunity. Though he made no pretensions to being an economic theorist, Bunch posited that by itself, emulating mainstream business practices would not be enough to build, let alone sustain, a thriving economic milieu. In fact, he maintained that commerce alone could impair the race's ability to find enough common ground to construct a viable, vital response to the color line and all that it represented. "It would seem clear," he wrote, "that this hope for the salvation of the Negro within the existing ideological and physical framework, by the erection of a black business structure within the walls of white capitalism, is doomed to futility." He continued, "The apologists for the self-sufficiency ideology are in pursuit of a policy of pure expediency and opportunism through exploitation of the segregation incident to the racial dualism of America. They refuse to believe that it is impossible to wring much wealth out of the already poverty-stricken Negro ghettos of the nation. Moreover, it should be clear that Negro enterprise exists only on the sufferance of that dominant white business world which completely controls credit, basic industry and the state." Moreover,

> "big" Negro business is an economic will-'o-the-wisp. Negro business strikes its appeal for support on a racial note, viz: the race can progress only through economic unity. But the small, individually-owned Negro businesses have little chance to meet successfully the price competition of the large-capital, more efficient and often nationwide white business. The very poverty of the Negro consumer dictates that he must buy where buying is cheapest; and he can ill afford to invest in racial good-will while he has far too little for food. In this sense, Negro business looms as a parasitical growth on the Negro society, in that it exploits the chauvinistic protection of "race loyalty," thus further exploiting an already downtrodden group.[43]

Bunche's stance appears to be far more in keeping with that of Du Bois than that of Washington. The diplomat's contention that a reliance on the segregated dollar would impede rather than stimulate progress may certainly be applied to the business of black baseball. But even the most foresighted Negro League owners were clinging to the older business model. Sonnyman Jackson's fantastic dream of becoming a third Major League and the slightly more realistic notion of serving as an affiliated minor league loop remained rooted in Foster's original Washingtonian vision of black baseball as a race business. After all, a Negro league, affiliated or otherwise, was meant to be just that—an entertainment circuit whose success was predicated on the segregated dollar.

Bunche's admonition may also be applied to the Negro League product itself. League moguls' biggest concern was that if organized white baseball poached their most valuable resource—their players—black ball would not draw enough spectators to remain afloat. To this extent, the Negro Leagues shared similar concerns with the white game. Both were businesses, and the players, regardless of color, were labor and were treated as such.[44] Strictly in terms of the economic challenges facing a segregated black business, including issues related to questionable capitalization, problematic scheduling, and the challenge of conducting a race enterprise in an environment still very much committed to Jim Crow policies, the exploitation of marginalized Negro League labor was even more extreme than that found in the Major Leagues. As Bunche wrote, "The advocates of Negro business have little to say about the welfare of Negro workers engaged in such business, except to suggest that they do not suffer from a discriminatory policy of employment."[45]

Indeed, despite its hardships, life in the Negro Leagues was still life in professional baseball. It offered a select few players a degree of financial independence and celebrity. Yet the number of players who fled their existing teams for opportunity elsewhere, frequently abroad, suggests that players in the segregated sport were restless and discontented, perceiving themselves as at least at times mistreated by team owners and perceiving the industry in general as lacking stability. Black baseball's most marketable commodities had begun jumping to foreign leagues as far back as the late depression years, with the most celebrated such instance occurring in 1937, when Satchel Paige and Josh Gibson, among others, went to play for Rafael Trujillo's national team in the Dominican Republic.[46] Shortly thereafter, the leagues suffered further defections when Newark Eagles stars Ray Dandridge and Monte Irvin, along with Roy Campanella of the Baltimore Elite Giants and several other notable players, left to ply their trade in Mexico, which was significantly less dangerous than working under the watchful eye of the vengeful Dominican dictator.[47] At least for a brief time, the Mexican League posed a genuine threat to the hegemony of the Negro Leagues. Players who jumped to Mexico typically enthused about better pay, more comfortable living conditions, and perhaps most tellingly, the distinct absence of Jim Crow.[48]

As co-owner of the Newark Eagles, Effa Manley was particularly dismayed at the prospect of the loss of her most bankable talent to Mexico.

Manley expressed her concern to Irvin in a letter dated February 9, 1946, attempting to convince him to return to the Eagles rather than play in Mexico after his military service ended. In addition to citing his potential use of the GI Bill to return to school, she dangled the possibility that he could sign with a Major League team—scouts would be more likely to see him perform in Newark than in Mexico. Taking a less-than-subtle shot at Rickey, she implored, "This is one of the important reasons you should play in America this year, so you can be seen[,] for one thing. If the experiment with Negro's in the Majors is successful, all the teams will be ready to take you, and almost all of them pay better salaries than Brooklyn."[49] Although she couched her argument in terms that highlighted the benefits to Irvin, Manley also sought to retain control of her worker and thereby her product. Irvin and other Negro Leaguers were by no means representatives of what Bunche refers to as "an already downtrodden group." They, too, benefited from continued employment in the industry. But when business was good, Manley and her fellow owners enjoyed membership in what Bunche identified as the small middle class that banked on "the race conscious Negro masses" to grow business.[50]

Bunche was far from the only critic to take segregated business to task. In an article published just three months before Robinson's 1947 Brooklyn debut, Chicago School sociologist E. Franklin Frazier examined what he maintained was entrepreneurs of color's personal stake in preserving vestiges of segregation. Like Myrdal, James Weldon Johnson, and Bunche, Frazier took on the issue of segregated business's role in the African American ecosystem: "The segregated community, which is essentially a pathological phenomenon in American life, has given certain Negroes a vested interest in segregation—involving more than dollars and cents considerations."[51]

Prior to the mid-1940s, black baseball and other race businesses filled an important niche. Conditions in the urban communities formed as a result of the various waves of the Great Migration created a demand for entertainment. But as the Major Leagues began to cross the color line, race institutions could no longer bank on such narrow consumer loyalty alone, and the increasingly entrenched economic system and the livelihoods of the individual entrepreneurs became imperiled. On these points, Frazier noted caustically, "As a rule Negro businesses are not willing to compete with businesses generally; they expect the Negro public to support them because of 'race pride.' Colored people are told that Negro enterprises are rendering a service to the 'race.' In fact, however, the majority of Negro businesses are operated by the owners themselves, and therefore provide few, if any, jobs for Negro workers. Moreover, patrons of these enterprises have to pay high prices for inferior goods and services."[52]

Unlike the small businesses referenced by Frazier, black baseball provided a substantial number of jobs and paid fair wages, though certainly not in keeping with those of the highest level of organized baseball. And at least when there were no other options for spectators, the Negro Leagues provided a decent product at a fair price. But as Major League Baseball became a possible destination for some black ballplayers and consequently more appealing to black fans, race pride underwent a redefinition. Evidence of this ongoing redefinition may be found in the number of column inches the black press devoted to the Negro Leagues. Where Negro League coverage, spotty and inconsistent though it was, had previously taken center stage, articles about "how our guys are doing" in the Major Leagues came to dominate the sports pages. Black baseball's moguls could not simply urge patrons to "buy black" when fans could be proud of their coethnics' performance in a wider, more visible sphere. From the standpoint of the increasingly enfranchised consumer, black baseball's entrepreneurs were no longer "rendering a service" worth unquestioned support.

Other Race Businesses Feeling the Pinch

Baseball was not the only node in the African American ecosystem with a vested interest in segregation that failed to move beyond marketing race pride. The race film industry faced challenges similar to those of Negro League baseball. Like black baseball, race films experienced significant popularity during the early decades of the century, only to decline significantly by the end of the war years. Even then, the black press questioned the efficacy of race pride as the foundation on which to build a business, foreshadowing Frazier by more than twenty years. As the *New York Age* noted as early as 1920, "The day of expecting charitable considerations in business even of our own people just because we are Negroes is past."[53]

Race film, like race baseball, experienced a resurgence during the late 1930s. Early examples of the form, such as pioneer Oscar Micheaux's *The Homesteader*, addressed the social and political themes of the day free from Hollywood constraints.[54] In contrast, what might be defined as the second generation of race films more closely mirrored the mainstream Hollywood product, much as Johnson's publications had. Black filmmakers responded to demand by producing films with all-black casts in popular genres such as gangster pictures and Westerns, some featuring Herb Jeffries, race film's original singing cowboy.[55] But white incursion was more of an issue for the race film industry than for the Negro Leagues or for publishing. While a certain percentage of black baseball's owners had always been white, and while white business interests—booking agents, for example—had significant financial interest in the sport's operations, white incursion into race film took a different turn. Seeing that the black product appealed to a certain demographic, Hollywood got into the business in the 1930s and made films with all-black casts meant to appeal to audiences of color. Indeed, two critically acclaimed 1943 box office successes with significant crossover appeal, *Cabin in the Sky* and *Stormy Weather*, were produced by Metro-Goldwyn-Mayer and Twentieth Century Fox, respectively. In this regard, race film went even further than either baseball or publishing in terms of exploiting its audience, particularly with regard to the issue of race pride. As a white-controlled industry with an African American target audience, filmmaking relied on the race dollar without ever recycling profit into the community. While, as Bunche contends, black-owned business might have been a "will-'o-the-wisp," enriching only a select few within the ecosystem, Hollywood-produced race film for the most part enriched only Hollywood.

In many ways, race film resembled black baseball in that both business models were undermined, at least in part, by advances made by African American soldiers during and after the war. "World War II," notes film historian Thomas Cripps, "having raised the prospect of Double V, rendered race movies an anachronism, turned black critics against them, and forced black audiences to opt for joining or not in the spirit of the times. After all, how could a segregated movie serve the cause of a war that slowly took on among its aims the self-determination of all peoples and the integration of blacks into the fabric of American life?" Race filmmakers, he concludes, "had simply lost part of their reason for survival and thus their future place in American movie culture in which the war had begun to redefine a black place."[56]

Indeed, Cripps points directly to black baseball as an analogue of the film industry. Black baseball "would die because its pool of talent, and its number of fans were finite as well as vulnerable to proselytizing by white parallel leagues in search of both black players and fans."[57] Micheaux made his final film in 1948, the second consecutive year in which a Major League team featuring two former Negro Leaguers appeared in the World Series. And in 1948, that team, the Cleveland Indians, won.

The race recording industry, however, represented an alternate model of a business with a vested interest in segregation. The race recording industry differed fundamentally from either film or sport in that recording had always fallen under the domain of white corporate ownership. Following the sale of Black Swan's catalog to Paramount in 1924, Harry Pace left the recording industry and moved into the insurance business. According to Pace's protégé, publisher John H. Johnson, "After Pace put Black artists and Black record buyers on the business map, White-owned corporations, in moves strikingly similar to the recent acts of White-owned insurance, cosmetics and publishing companies, started issuing 'race catalogs' in a generally successful effort to destroy Black entrepreneurs." And as Juliet E. K. Walker explains, "With the end of Black Swan Records in the late 1920s, black record companies remained on the periphery, as the white companies expanded in the 1930s and 1940s."[58]

Despite the fact that race record ownership was neither small nor centrally located in the African American ecosystem, it remained an inextricable part of the ecosystem. By design, race records were marketed to an African American consumer base that for the most part resided in urban areas. Major labels such as RCA Victor's race subsidiary, Bluebird; Columbia; and Okeh depended first and foremost on the segregated dollar.

But in 1946, Gladys Hampton, yet another New New Negro, stepped in to fill a niche that had remained empty since the demise of Black Swan. The wife of bandleader Lionel Hampton, himself a swing-era integrator who had played with some of Benny Goodman's depression-era orchestras, Gladys Hampton founded the Hamp-Tone label, becoming the first African American woman to own a record company. Hampton sought to "crack through this highly competitive field" and to capture a market share in a space where the other record companies were predominantly, if not entirely, white-owned.[59] Again like *Ebony*'s Johnson, who wanted consumers to buy his product because it was the best available, Hampton attempted to build a more far-reaching enterprise than even Pace might have imagined, offering big-name artists and new talent in a wide range of musical styles and genres. That Hampton's vision for her business was more akin to Johnson's is reinforced by the fact that in addition to her ongoing associations with the black weeklies, she regularly took out quarter-page ads in *Billboard*, the organ of the mainstream recording industry.

Yet although Hampton may have aimed at a wider consumership than traditional race businesses, attention in the black press still positioned Hamp-Tone firmly within the confines of the African American ecosystem. Noted the *Pittsburgh Courier*, "A study of economics reveals that advancement can be made if a business or enterprise can sell as well as consume marketable goods. The Negro's economic status can be raised if the Negro sells and consumes its own products. That's how Hamp-Tone records enters the picture. Negroes need not only buy Hamp-Tone records, Negroes can distribute them. . . . Desirous of giving the Negro business man a slice of pie, the company urges all record shops operated by Negroes to carry the Hamp-Tone label."[60] In this regard, Hamp-Tone attempted to do what Bunche argued black businesses could not do: create a structure with the potential not only to enrich a select few within the ecosystem but also to spread the wealth to a series of constituent businesses. While Hamp-Tone did not and could not solve the problem of the color line, it joined Johnson Publishing in offering an alternative model for a race business that did not depend entirely on segregation for continued success. Hamp-Tone was not the first or the only black-owned record label founded in 1946: Leon Rene's Exclusive Record Company had two *Billboard* hits, and Imperial Music had a biracial ownership similar to that of the Philadelphia Stars.

Hamp-Tone and by extension its founder enjoyed economic and artistic success. The recording industry was hardly a stable environment for aspiring entrepreneurs; labels, like black ball clubs, came and went, often rapidly. But savvy operators such as Hampton, who remained in the recording industry well into the 1960s with Glad Records (later Glad-Hamp), started new enterprises when their others folded. Moreover, Hampton and the other successful black recording entrepreneurs in the immediate postwar era were such important figures because they moved beyond the often narrow confines of business as typically practiced in the African American ecosystem, setting the stage for the arrival of even more ambitious forays into the music business by black entrepreneurs in the decade to follow.

Postwar Local Ecosystems

The changes in black baseball and other race entertainment enterprises, all of which had a regional or national reach, led to a redefinition of what Cripps identifies as black cultural and economic places on the local level as well. Local businesses had often trumpeted their connection to black baseball and other segments of the race entertainment industry, exclaiming loudly in their advertising the patronage of local celebrities. With the breaching of the color line, Bedford-Stuyvesant's Silver Rail Bar and Grill, which billed itself as "The No. 1 Bar in Brooklyn," proudly advertised its "Jackie Robinson Gift Party" in the *New York Amsterdam News*, noting in very small print that Robinson would not be present.[61] Using Robinson's name—in essence, his brand—as a calling card, the Silver Rail and other small businesses relied on a proven marketing strategy: value transfer. By associating the business with a particular celebrity, bar operators were, in effect, transferring the qualities associated with Robinson—athletic ability, grace, and most significantly, courage under fire—with their establishment. Even small businesses could be seen as facing cultural changes by appealing to a consumer base adapting to the same changes. Robinson's ascension to the Major Leagues signaled the increasing enfranchisement of African Americans as citizen consumers. This emerging consumer citizenry was for the first time not only able but also ready and willing to spend money in previously unavailable establishments. The Silver Rail and other small businesses had no choice but to adapt, taking whatever measures necessary to keep pace with the spirit of the times.

This strategy did not work for all business establishments, however. The continued success of such neighborhood joints as the Silver Rail did not necessarily reflect other local business developments. Nightclubs, which were central nodes in local ecosystems, faced different challenges that were not so easily met. The *Chicago Defender*'s sports and entertainment editor, Al Monroe, wrote of the economic hardships that arose in the nightclub business in the first years after the war: "Of the clubs in Harlem, still doing business, but on a smaller scale, only Small's Paradise comes up with a show. The rest are gone." The larger theaters, like the historic Apollo, were still drawing fans, but the Savoy and Renaissance Ballrooms, which had previously swung to the music of the big bands, "create no unusual stir around the box office." Moreover, the Harlem venues' problems were symptomatic of a national trend, "since local Broadway is the barometer by which all things theatrical are measured."[62]

Technological changes also had major economic implications for the local African American economy. While commercial television, still in its infancy, had yet to affect local business receipts, radio remained the more important electronic medium. Long a fixture in American homes, radio provided a link between the private sphere and the public, including music venues and sporting establishments, especially Major League ball-parks. But radio's impact was fundamentally altered by the commercial development and accessibility of the transistor. As journalist John Leland explains, "The transistor radio, invented in 1947 by Walter Brattain and Robert Gibney, made sets portable and cheap, well suited to the budding car culture. They let young people take their music away from the super-vision of adults. Radio broadcasts served different needs than nightclubs. They had to entertain and stimulate audiences, not challenge them; to flat-ter, not provoke. These media craved repetition and novelty more than intricacy and ambiguity."[63] That the transistor radio was introduced to the buying public the same year that Robinson crossed the color line appears to be a coincidence, but it was not. Both developments were the products of wartime innovations and fundamental changes in postwar America. The transistor radio affected the culture of mainstream America as well as throughout the African American ecosystem, where it perhaps had even more of an impact.

Such changes in technology further underscored changing consump-tion patterns, leading to problems in other heretofore successful black-owned industries. Black hotels, which relied for much of their business on traveling ballplayers and musicians, took a huge hit from the combination of the ascendance of portable entertainment and the fading color line. Still, white hotels did not desegregate overnight. Traditional black hotels such as New York's Theresa, Chicago's Grand, and Detroit's Gotham, therefore, did not go downhill quickly. The persistence of Jim Crow in certain parts of the country provided black hotels with a ready-made clientele, but this situation was becoming increasingly fluid, especially in cities with Negro League baseball franchises.

In December 1946, Love B. Woods, president of the National Negro Hotel and Restaurant Association, told the *Chicago Defender* that occu-pancy rates in Harlem and similar communities had fallen by an alarming 25 percent. Woods, a long-time hotelier and owner of Harlem's famous Woodside, an establishment favored by ballplayers and musicians, blamed the decrease in clientele on the dismantling of war industries and the demobilization of the armed forces.[64] But a series of cases in which large Downtown hotels settled out of court after denying rooms to people of color belied Woods's argument. The management of Philadelphia's Ben Franklin Hotel, for example, made a very public statement in the *Pittsburgh Courier* affirming the establishment's policy of nondiscrimination after accommodations were denied to an integrated college track team in town for the Penn Relays, known to some as the "Negro Olympics," which had been integrated since the event's inception in 1895.[65] Similarly, less than one week before Robinson first stepped onto the field in Brooklyn, the Boston Sheraton was faced with paying twenty-five thousand dollars in damages for refusing to rent a ballroom to a black women's social club.[66] That newly desegregating hotels, especially well-regarded hotels like the Ben Franklin and the Boston Sheraton, would have appealed to consumers of color was borne out by a letter written to the *Chicago Defender* by reader W. Washington, who decried shoddy conditions in black hostelries: "While reading through several newspapers of our race recently I became interested in numerous advertisements of Negro hotels. I have thought about colored hotels a lot the past few years, wondering why rotten systems and conditions are permitted to slide merrily on down thru the years."[67] Thus, while the black press routinely sang the praises of the more luxurious establishments, the black hotels, which became monuments to the segregation in which they had a vested interest, were soon obsolete.

The Decline of the East-West Classic

Black hotels as well as dining establishments, saloons, and nightclubs had long been the beneficiaries of the influx of fans, players, and to a lesser extent media flooding into Chicago for the annual East-West Classic. By the late 1940s, the East-West Classic had become the showplace for Negro baseball and its centerpiece promotion. In 1941, an item on the front page of the *Chicago Defender* trumpeted that the game was expected to draw more than fifty thousand fans from around the country, including five hundred who would be arriving on a special train from Memphis, home of the NAL's president, Martin.[68] The extreme popularity and the potential for profit of the all-star promotion led to the addition of a second game at various points throughout the 1940s. In 1946, the *Pittsburgh Courier's* Wendell Smith reported that "a cheering throng of 45,474 partisan fans" watched the western NAL team defeat the eastern NNL players.[69] A week earlier, 16,268 fans had gathered at Washington's Griffith Stadium to see a smaller-scale version of the Classic.[70]

While the Washington game drew decent crowds for a local attraction, its impact was small in comparison to the main event at Chicago's Comiskey Park. Of course, the game took center stage, but, as in the past, corollary events helped fuel the engines of the local economy. According to the *Defender*, among these events were soirees intended to appeal to Bronzeville's bourgeoisie. In 1946, the ancillary events included the crowning of a beauty queen, "Miss East-West 1946," as well as an "East-West Coronation Dance" at the Parkway Ballroom, owned and operated by Metropolitan Mutual's Robert Cole, former owner of the American Giants.[71] Such events demonstrated the central position of the East-West game in Bronzeville's social and business life as well as relied heavily on black Chicago's service economy, providing an economic boon. The East-West Classic thus was much more than just an exhibition game. It was a showcase for its product aimed at an audience far broader than those who could afford to attend the game, a society event, a celebration of entrepreneurial ingenuity, and a very public demonstration that African Americans were the captains of their own leisure industry.

The 1947 East-West Classic drew 48,112 spectators, among whom were several Major League scouts, while a sister promotion a few days earlier at New York's Polo Grounds drew what Dan Burley referred to as a "vast Tuesday night throng" of 38,402, equaling the crowds of the boom years of World War II.[72] The *New York Amsterdam News* opined, "There are many reasons which explain the growth and success of our baseball in recent months. Much is due to the acceptance and showing of Negro players on the Big Leagues, such as Jackie Robinson, Brooklyn Dodgers; Larry Doby, Cleveland Indians; Roy Campanella, Montreal Royals, and [Willard] Brown and [Hank] Thompson of the St. Louis Browns. Our players have made good in the National and International Leagues. They were recruited from the All-Star players, and their games are looked upon as the training and recruiting grounds from which the best Negro players are to be found for the Big Leagues."[73]

Certainly, it is feasible that the healthy attendance for the 1947 East-West promotions were due, in large part, to the fact that African American players were making good on the big stage. Consumer interest by what were, for all intents and purposes, the big league fans of tomorrow, appeared to have helped drive attendance figures for these big games. But attendance figures for regular season league games and even big promotions were down. According to Adrian Burgos Jr., the 1947 Negro League World Series between the Cuban Giants and the Cleveland Buckeyes was an economic failure. On the field, the games were entertaining and competitive. In both the stands and the press box, however, the series generated little interest. Given the scant coverage and poor attendance, it was a box office bust, with Cuban Giants owner Alex Pompez claiming twenty thousand dollars in losses.[74] And attendance continued to plum-met. The same year, according to Lanctot, "at Yankee Stadium, only 63,402 fans turned out for black baseball promotions, a drop of nearly 95,000 fans from 1946, and attendance at Newark fell from 120,293 to 57,119." The numbers were even more bleak in Philadelphia and Washington, D.C.[75]

Competition from the heretofore segregated white sport was beginning to negatively affect the business of black baseball. As Dan Burley noted in the *New York Amsterdam News*, there had been an "overnight conver-sion of at least 4,000,000 Negroes into baseball fans. And that's the truth." Before Robinson joined the Dodgers, "only an infinitesimal portion of the 25,000,000 of us . . . had any interest in big league baseball or in any sort of baseball." Continued Burley, "With characteristic disregard of conse-quences, Negroes wrecked their own version of organized baseball and went crazy over the Dodgers. That, however, is definitely excusable see-ing that we haven't had much to holler about over the years and the idea seemed to hover around that some day we'll go back and get Negro Base-ball and build it up."[76] As had been the case with boxing, not until African Americans had success in the white sporting world did black fans have a sense of race pride strong enough to bring even formerly disapproving church deacons and their wives into the fold. These changes dramatically altered black baseball's prospects as a going concern.

The forces that had been set in motion following Robinson's debut and subsequent success left Negro League baseball exposed and primed for failure, short of some miraculous turnaround. Attendance figures for the 1948 East-West Classic exposed the problem: The game's 42,099 specta-tors represented a drop of almost 15 percent from the preceding year.[77] Even more startling were the numbers for the sister promotion at Yankee Stadium, which attracted a scant 17,928, far short of expectations.[78]

Writing in the *New York Amsterdam News*, Swig Garlington claimed that ticket sales had been unusually brisk in response to an announcement by NNL president the Reverend Dr. John Howard Johnson (not to be con-fused with *Ebony* publisher John Harold Johnson) that the 1949 auxiliary all-star game would be played in Philadelphia and that it would move to other cities in subsequent years. Indeed, Garlington had predicted that paid attendance might reach 50,000.[79] But clearly this prediction was off the mark.

How could promoters, the leagues and the press have miscalculated attendance figures so dramatically? The weather was not a factor, since another baseball game in New York City had no trouble attracting fans.

On the same day as the Yankee Stadium game, over in Brooklyn, Robinson and the Dodgers were playing in front of a sellout crowd in Brooklyn as part of a three-game midweek series against the Boston Braves that drew 100,006 paid admissions, a fact that was not lost on the *New York Times*'s Roscoe McGowen.[80] This is not to suggest that spectators in Brooklyn were all people of color, or even that a majority of the fans were. What it does suggest is that there was another, more visible option available for African American baseball fans that day. In a broader sense, the scheduling conflict highlights Negro League officials' failure to perceive the implications that the desegregation of the Major Leagues held for their product.

That competition from the Major Leagues may have contributed to slumping attendance at both East-West games was also apparent on the *Chicago Defender*'s Morgan Holsey. He noted that on August 13, a week before the Classic, the White Sox drew 51,013 fans for a Friday game against the Cleveland Indians, who featured not only Larry Doby in centerfield but Satchel Paige on the mound. "On that night," Holsey wrote, "fully 15,000 were unable to get inside the park," where, as Holsey strongly suggests, they had gone en masse not to watch the Sox play the Indians nor even Doby patrolling centerfield but, rather, specifically to see the presumably forty-two-year-old rookie Paige in a Major League uniform.[81] According to Fay Young, so many fans wanted to see Paige pitch that twenty people were injured trying to push through the turnstiles.[82]

The contrast between fans' eagerness to see Paige and their relative indifference to the most important Negro League promotion of the year signaled a huge problem in the making for black baseball's entrepreneurs. In direct contrast, Bill Veeck, the Cleveland owner responsible for bringing Paige to the majors, seemed to recognize his potential gold mine. And with the help of Abe Saperstein, who scouted and secured black talent for Veeck and whose relationship with Paige went back decades, Veeck had a unique ability to exploit Paige's presence. As Rebecca Alpert explains, "Paige and Veeck both named Saperstein as the person who was responsible for persuading Veeck to bring Paige to the majors. Paige believed that Veeck was skeptical about whether he could still pitch and credited Saperstein with encouraging Veeck to sign him. For his efforts, Saperstein received a $20,000 bonus after Cleveland won the World Series, with Paige, who went 6–1 on the season, making an important contribution. Encouraging Veeck to take Paige seriously may have been Saperstein's greatest (and single most lucrative) contribution to blacks in baseball."[83]

While tension had always existed between Negro League owners and booking agents, Saperstein was especially disdained. The owners collectively were suspicious of Saperstein's motives, joining with the black press in accusing him of lining his pockets at the expense of the leagues. But by the time the color line was breached, writers in the black press had begun to reassess their position.

In a 1946 column, Burley called Saperstein "my good friend" and described him as a "dominating force in accomplishment in Negro Baseball in the West." Burley contrasted a subtle gesture of goodwill that Saperstein made to the writer on a flight to Chicago for the East-West Classic with what Burley perceived as the misbehavior of the Negro League owners that week: "Not being invited inside the inner sanctum of Tom (Baltimore Elites) Wilson's room 205, I know not which way the fussing was being directed; neither do I have verification for the reports of sundry individuals who gumshoed their way up and down the corridor, listening at the door and peeking through the keyhole or over the transom at the stacks upon stacks of greasy greenbacks and clanking silver and copper and at the sport-shirted, cigar smoking gentry on their hands and knees dividing up the gold."[84] Using language once reserved by the black press and black owners for white—particularly Jewish—interlopers, Burley characterized black baseball's owners and operators as greedy, underhanded money-grubbers. He characterized the players as the victims, benefiting less from the promotion than they should have while the owners divided the spoils. Burley and many other black journalists later put a positive spin on Saperstein's role in scouting players for Veeck and Indians general manager Hank Greenberg. The sea change in the black press's attitude, coupled with falling numbers at the turnstiles, heralded the beginning of the end for Negro League baseball as a business and particularly as a race enterprise with a vested interest in segregation.

Indeed, following the financially disastrous 1947 Negro League World Series and mounting losses during the 1948 season, Negro League baseball could no longer be thought of as a healthy part of the African American ecosystem. According to a short piece that appeared in the *Atlanta Daily World* in December 1948, "The advent of Jackie Robinson, Larry Doby and Leroy 'Satchel' Paige into organized baseball has proven fatal to the financially insecure Negro National League and continuing revenue losses have led to the dissolution of the league."[85]

In the grand scheme of things, it was not that unusual for teams or even whole leagues to fold even after a single season. But these were not just any teams, and this was not just any league. This was Negro baseball's senior circuit. Bowing out were the once vital Washington/Homestead Grays and the perpetually undercapitalized New York Black Yankees. Left with no choice, the talent-rich Newark Eagles (later the Houston/New Orleans Eagles) as well as the Philadelphia Stars, Baltimore Elite Giants, and New York Cubans took refuge in the NAL, the junior circuit.

The demise of the NNL was unfortunate for black baseball. The attrition that began with the older league was a bellwether for a certain type of race business that fueled the African American ecosystems established during the first and second waves of the Great Migration. Black baseball from the start was built on the shaky foundation of Jim Crow segregation. And like all businesses built on less-than-solid footing, black baseball was bound to fail.

6

Black Baseball's Post-Robinson Challenge, 1949–1963

Introduction

In June 1949, Effa Manley, never one to shrink from a fight, addressed a meeting of the National Negro Publishers Association and made an impassioned plea to save Negro baseball:

> Organized colored baseball today stands at the crossroads. The success or failure of the teams to draw this year may determine the future of our colored leagues. The past two seasons have seen our colored fans desert our ballparks to follow the exploits of Jackie Robinson and Roy Campanella of Brooklyn and Larry Doby of the Cleveland Indians.
>
> This season the trend of our fans is toward the major league parks, and unless a real campaign is launched to retain their interest in colored baseball, our leagues may be unable to continue operating.
>
> It is this situation which impels me to release to the colored publishers this statement as an individual who has owned a team in baseball for the past 15 years. I am firmly convinced that if colored baseball is to be saved, the colored press will have to save it. This poses the question "Is Colored baseball worth saving?"[1]

The black press struggled with this question throughout the next decade. Manley did not. She and her husband, Abe, abandoned the business following the 1948 season, when they sold their Newark franchise to W. H. Young of Memphis and Hugh Cherry of Blytheville, Arkansas, who then moved the team to Houston. Young and Cherry, previously partners in a Blytheville dental practice, were associates of Negro American League (NAL) president J. B. Martin, whose brother, B. B., was a member of the purchasing syndicate.[2] In fact, B. B. Martin, who had a personal as well as professional relationship with Young and Cherry, had been trying to interest Young in buying a Negro League franchise for the better part of a decade.[3]

Now free of any financial connections to the Negro Leagues that had perhaps caused her to measure her words and keep her criticism behind closed doors, Effa Manley asserted herself publicly, much to the chagrin of several of those still involved in black baseball. As she told the publishers' association, "Fortunately, I have no monetary interest in baseball. . . . [T]herefore my interest at this point is only in the future of the sport. I have no selfish interest."[4] Manley shifted her vitriol, previously aimed at her fellow owners as well as at the game's promoters and booking agents, toward the press. Her disenchantment with the fourth estate and her resentment of what she perceived as its role in driving the sport closer to insolvency was palpable.

Manley's public excoriation of the black press was by no means lost on the editors and columnists whom she attacked. Their responses varied, especially with regard to her assertion that the press, rather than other forces, including the actions of her fellow owners, had driven her from the sport. The *Chicago Defender*'s Fay Young deflected Manley's criticism by pointing out her inability effectively to run her franchise. From Young's perspective, the Newark Eagles' owners should have focused on keeping their own house in order rather than pointing fingers elsewhere. He claimed that the Manleys failed to recognize several facts about doing business in the shadow of the New York metropolitan area: "Mrs. Manley had too many high priced ball players for a town which supported her club so niggardly. Also Newark is too close to New York and Brooklyn. When Jackie Robinson and the Dodgers were away, the Newark fans journeyed to Manhattan to see Joe DiMaggio and the Yankees." Young continued, "Since some of our newspapers have been very fair to negro baseball, we regret the blast as a unit. Those which haven't been fair should be named. Economic conditions have hurt attendance at all sports event this year. The golden era is gone."[5]

In his fairly measured response, Young expressed what many journalists appeared to be thinking: Effa Manley was too busy laying blame to notice that the economics of Negro baseball in the region prevented her enterprise from prospering, a contention borne out by the New York Black Yankees' departure from organized baseball. Even before desegregation, staging black baseball in the New York metropolitan area had typically been a dicey proposition. Young also blasted Manley and the other owners for failing to adequately publicize their product, laying some of blame for lack of interest from the fan base squarely on her shoulders. In his opinion, "A fine ball club which looked and played like Major Leaguers wasn't well known west of the Hudson River. Had the same club represented New Orleans, Dallas, or Chitterling Switch, Miss., it would have 'packed them in.'"[6]

Sam Lacy, sports editor of the *Baltimore Afro-American*, was far less polite in expressing his displeasure at Manley's continued voice in the game even after her financial connection to the leagues had been severed. Lacy accused her of having had a direct hand in the circuit's inability to construct a working relationship with the Major Leagues regarding any future role for black baseball and control over the disbursement of its talent. And he worried that if Manley continued to act as the self- appointed voice of the Negro Leagues, especially as a self-proclaimed disinterested outsider, the Major Leagues would be unwilling to work in partnership with black baseball. Lacy accused Manley of sabotaging the efforts of a 1945 committee made up primarily of Major League representatives that had been constituted at Lacy's urging and charged with figuring out how best to integrate the Major Leagues without materially harming the Negro Leagues. Though Lacy charged that Manley had refused to meet with the Major League appointees, other evidence shows that Larry MacPhail, the new owner of the New York Yankees and the American League's representative on the committee, was not interested in desegregation for financial reasons and that his position had a much greater role in the committee's ineffectiveness.[7] Nevertheless, given what Lacy perceived to have been Effa Manley's reluctance to go along with his plan, thereby subverting the all-important work of the committee, Lacy angrily asserted that the Manleys "weren't going to permit a weekly newspaper to tell them how to run their business." According to Lacy, though Manley was officially gone from the league, she continued to publicly dominate the discourse: "The applause was premature. . . . [B]aseball still has Mrs. Effa Manley."[8]

But Lacy's ire was not reserved for Manley alone. He also took potshots at the other usual suspects, including Abe Saperstein and Branch Rickey.[9] Of course, Rickey was also the well-known object of Manley's scorn for his practice of poaching players. And Saperstein, the perpetual fly in the ointment, who had once been in Rickey's place as the most despised man within Negro League circles, was yet another of the favorite targets of both

Manley and Lacy. Thus, while Lacy and Manley waged a war of words with one another throughout much of this period, they also shared many of the same enemies. In this regard, they often appeared to be working from essentially the same script, though publicly they remained at odds.

At the same time, Saperstein, whom Lacy and Manley continued to vilify, was gaining stature among some sports columnists for his role in scouting and ultimately signing black talent for the Major Leagues and for dealing fairly with both players and journalists. But while Saperstein may have continued to be regarded with suspicion in some quarters, he was generally supplanted by Rickey as the most controversial figure to be associated with the NAL, especially in the area of Rickey's disregard for the league and its franchises when it came to the matter of player contracts. And Manley and Lacy were hardly alone in their disdain.

T. Y. Baird, who became sole owner of the Kansas City Monarchs after buying out J. L. Wilkinson in 1948, had the most legitimate complaint against Rickey's tactics in the handling of the Robinson affair. Indeed, Baird took Rickey to task for signing his shortstop with no regard for the Kansas City ownership. Baird, who rightfully claimed Robinson as property of the Monarchs under the rules that governed both the black and white sports, had every reason to contest Rickey's actions but chose not to pursue any legal claims. According to the *Atlanta Daily World*, "When asked why he didn't take Rickey to court[,] Baird answered that he would have been 'on the spot.' 'We welcomed Jackie's advancing in baseball[,] and [it] would have been okay with us—having intimated that we didn't want a Negro player integrated into big time baseball.'" What Baird desired from Rickey was not fair remuneration for Robinson's services, but he did want something. As Baird explained "Whatever he might have offered would have been okay with us."[10] Baird's concerns were political rather than solely financial. Caught in an unenviable bind, Baird and his cohort did not wish to appear as if they were trying to impede progress. Added to the equation was the fact that the Kansas City owners had always been white, making their passivity in the Robinson signing essential, if only for public relations purposes. That Rickey regarded the Negro Leagues contemptuously was without question: In 1945, Rickey referred to black baseball's structure as functioning "in the zone of a racket."[11] Regardless, the Negro League owners certainly were left holding the short end of the financial stick when it came to losing their talent, a matter that was routinely addressed in column after column in the black weeklies.

All the sniping between the black press and some of black baseball's owners as well as the growing vilification of the Major Leagues for poaching black talent indicated the changing times and the changing nature of the sport and its place in the African American ecosystem. Above all else, the backbiting pointed to a fading industry and a business model that had quite quickly become obsolete. Black baseball's future would be the topic of fairly regular columns and other items in the weeklies, which printed articles with titles such as "Negro Baseball in Throes of Death; Can Anything Save It?" and "Is Negro Baseball Doomed?"[12] After all, even Manley herself had asked whether Negro baseball was worth saving. In the late 1940s, the response appeared to be that salvaging the business was worth a try, if for no other reason than it had a role to play in bringing talented young players of color to the attention of Major League scouts. Saving black baseball as a going concern, however, would require a substantial retrenchment as well as a considerable redefinition of the business model itself. The final decade of organized black baseball would demonstrate the extent to which changes in the sociopolitical as well as the economic climate affected urban enclaves with a stake in black baseball. With integration on the rise, however slowly, the segregated dollar could no longer play a central role in the business of African America, and black baseball stood squarely on the border between the past and the future.

An Evolving Zeitgeist

While Negro League baseball had been built on a business model that was becoming increasingly obsolete, much of African America looked toward a future in which its residents would no longer be enclosed within the narrow confines of the African American ecosystem. With the end of war came changing expectations, not only for blacks but for all Americans. Indeed, issues raised during the war resulted directly in an ongoing redefinition of what it meant to be an American. On one hand, Joe DiMaggio's exploits on the field as well as his product endorsements helped gather Italian Americans into the wider fold, essentially erasing the Old World distinction, now making them simply Americans. In this sense, the notion of "American" was beginning to broaden in the late 1940s and the early 1950s in ways that the most ardent nineteenth-century Americanist or proponent of Muscular Christianity might never have fathomed. On the other hand, a new postwar Red Scare, expressed most notably in the establishment of the House Un-American Activities Committee, which had a devastating effect on the entertainment industry, at least temporarily attempted to narrow the definition of *American.*

Removing the ethnic signifier was not as easy for nonwhite populations as it was for Americans of other ethnicities. Although the dominant culture earlier in the century did not classify Italians as white, they assimilated more thoroughly into the mainstream after the war, aided by the images not only of DiMaggio but also of Yogi Berra, Frank Sinatra, and Dean Martin (born Dino Paul Crocetti), among others. But skin color prevented African Americans from seamlessly blending into the mainstream.[13] Despite the fact that in many northern and midwestern cities—Chicago, Detroit, New York, and even Kansas City—African Americans made up powerful voting blocs, often courted by political machines, black Americans did not become fully enfranchised for two decades after the war. But any full investiture in American life could not have happened without changes to the social and political atmosphere that began to take shape when black soldiers returned triumphantly from the war as Jackie Robinson and other black athletes and entertainers became part of the wider media fabric.

One of the most visible expressions of the changing zeitgeist in postwar America could be found—and heard—in the music industry. In popular music, the mingling of black and white tastes and styles eventually led to a substantive hybridization. This was not the first time the dominant culture had embraced black musical styles. Swing had filtered onto the mainstream airwaves from black nightclubs and ballrooms, some of them black and tans. While swing had such white ambassadors as Benny Goodman, Glenn Miller, and Artie Shaw, black bandleaders Duke Ellington, Count Basie, and Lionel Hampton gained significant followings among both white and black listeners. Despite economic and stylistic cross-fertilization, the emergence of swing had no lasting social or political impact, and many people, including some older African American musicians, thought jazz's next major shift, bebop, too detached and too inaccessible to mainstream audiences and markets.[14] Other popular postwar music styles, however, had significant sociopolitical impacts, particularly in the construction of youth culture.[15]

The rise of a range of new popular musical genres among African Americans was largely predicated on the dramatic demographic shift brought about by the Great Migration. In many ways, these new consumer citizens were searching for some positive reminders of their former lives—that is, without the specter of either Jim Crow or lynching. This impetus was tinged with more than a touch of nostalgia. Nevertheless, its cultural impact was tangible. Not attracted to the citified sounds of jazz and what came to be known as urban blues, the migrants, with newly expanded disposable incomes along with a nascent sense of their importance as an economic force, demanded satisfaction. Former rural musicians including Muddy Waters, Willie Dixon, Louis Jordan, and Ray Charles adapted their styles to fit their new surroundings, energizing a stagnating scene.[16] These performers' musical styles melded with existing citified sounds, creating new styles and new markets. This cross-fertilization led to the birth of rock and roll as well as a wealth of subgenres that had racialized connotations.

But the continuing influx of migrants and the general expansion of the African American ecosystem further hastened white flight. Though the process was gradual, more and more former urban dwellers were moving into new subdivisions that were located just outside the cities and that remained closed to people of color. According to David Halberstam, "At the core of it was owning one's own house—and as Henry Ford's invention and a rapidly improving network of roads and highways opened up the vast spaces of farmland surrounding American cities, the vision started to become a reality: Suburbia."[17] What started with Levittowns outside New York and Philadelphia spread exponentially on a national level, hastened by the Federal-Aid Highway Act of 1956 and its creation of the interstate highway system. The burgeoning car culture, coupled with suburbanization, led to a change in the ways in which Americans did business. Retailers became less interested in investing in inner cities, and what has come to be known as suburban sprawl slowly replaced traditional clustered urban retail districts, resulting in a broad shift in the social patterns of American life.[18]

Traditional residential patterns were also changing in the African American ecosystem. Initially heralded in the black press as the solution to increasingly overcrowded conditions in black enclaves, public housing projects offered urban dwellers the opportunity to move out of neighborhoods with growing slum conditions and into modern apartments. A small, seemingly inconsequential item that appeared in the *New York Amsterdam News* in November 1949 announced that in Chicago, "the new Dearborn homes housing project now being built to replace a near South side slum area, will open early in December."[19] Such developments rearranged and disrupted established demographic patterns, and the continuing practice of building projects and the attendant "slum clearance" began to receive more criticism than praise from both journalists and local community activists. Conversely, the expansion of African American enclaves as a result of such new construction led to new business opportunities within the changing ecosystem. On Chicago's Near West Side, for example, new housing meant a new business district, but not without costs to the old one. Indeed, the well-established economic heart of Bronzeville, centered on South State Street, Grand Avenue, and South Parkway, lost a great deal of its former luster. At the same time that Negro League baseball was in its death throes, so, too, was the Bronzeville business district, victim to many of the same forces that led to the decline in the sport.[20]

Television also revolutionized American life. Even with the new medium in its infancy, it was clear that television would have a major effect on the business of baseball, including the Negro Leagues. According to the *New York Times*, baseball and television were a match made in heaven, with "armchairs becom[ing] box seats," assuming that the economics could be worked out. That electric eye in the sky, the *Times* claimed, showed viewers just how popular the Major League sport was.[21] Following a protracted fight about standards, the Federal Communications Commission authorized the commencement of commercial television beginning in July 1941, and the first television commercial spot aired during a Brooklyn Dodgers game.[22] The development of commercial television, however, was derailed by World War II. But as returning war veterans changed the general face of American consumption, so, too, did the reintroduction of television and most specifically baseball on television change the way in which sport was consumed and marketed. Though there were fewer than five hundred sets in the New York metropolitan area, the television industry's first stronghold, the Dumont Network made a deal to broadcast the first regular season games starting in 1947, Robinson's rookie year. That same year, the Dodgers, early adopters of the new medium, played the New York Yankees in the World Series in front of an expanding television audience.[23] With individual set ownership a rarity, the sport's television viewers generally gathered in local watering holes, to some extent re-creating the communal experience inside stadiums and reaffirming the marriage of beer and baseball. According to James R. Walker and Robert V. Bellamy, "Taverns without TVs quickly got one; one despairing saloon keeper reportedly rushed into a Queens appliance store crying, 'I've got to have a set now, today or I'm ruined.' At this point, baseball's owners considered 'tavern ball' a more serious threat to attendance than in-home viewing."[24] And if "tavern ball" threatened Major League attendance to a small extent, it stood to undermine completely whatever small market share black baseball had left.

By the early 1950s, television was moving inside people's homes, a phenomenon underscored by William Levitt's offer of a free television, along with a Bendix washing machine, with each new home purchase, firmly tying television to suburbanization.[25] The social change wrought by this technological advance allowed Americans to bring their entertainment away from the public sphere and into the private, thereby disrupting the communal spirit of fandom. This disruption was further reinforced by the availability of other new and affordable technologies. Mass production of home appliances contributed to the shift, while advances in the uses of cryotechnology led to the introduction of the TV dinner in 1954.[26] But even more important in terms of the ways in which Americans lived was the increasing popularity of in-home air-conditioning. Where once city residents had spent summer days and evenings on their streets and stoops, necessarily interacting with one another and reinforcing existing and potentially expanding social networks and thereby reaffirming communal ideals, air-conditioning led to a further erosion of traditional patterns of social exchange.[27] The increasing privatization of the formerly public sphere deepened the racial divide in major metropolitan areas and further institutionalized de facto segregation at a time when de jure segregation was under scrutiny and facing serious challenges in both state and federal courts.[28] The great irony of the Supreme Court's 1954 *Brown v. Board of Education* decision was that it occurred at a time when these changing housing patterns, accompanied by technological advances, led to further segregation of the general population. It is also ironic that as African Americans were further ghettoized in terms of their options, they were increasingly entering the mainstream as consumers. The rapid technological, social, and economic changes that occurred during the first decade after the war transformed the African American ecosystem, writ large, as well as affected individual local economies.

The Postwar State of Black Business

The decline of Negro League baseball dealt a major blow to the aspirations of a handful of black entrepreneurs still working within the confines of the segregated economy. Unquestionably, the desegregation of the Major Leagues played the central role in black baseball's demise, but other, unrelated factors were often involved, and their ramifications were felt throughout black business circles for decades. Just as the rise of black baseball served as a bellwether for the expansion of the African American ecosystem during both waves of the Great Migration, the ecosystem's fade from the larger equation provided a harbinger for the future of the segregated economy.

Among these factors were new attitudes that dramatically altered traditional African American consumer practices, especially in terms of the tendency to express race pride via spending. No longer were people of color constrained by the expectation to "buy black," a practice that produced questionable results under the best of circumstances. For these increasingly enfranchised consumer citizens, spending money within the narrow confines of the ecosystem was no longer an expression of independence. Rather, progress was increasingly measured by the collective ability to buy where one's interests were best served.

An attempt to exploit this new outlook was exemplified by Peters Department Store, a "new interracial venture" that opened on 125th Street in Harlem in December 1948. Peters was intended to compete directly with traditional neighborhood retailers, and its opening was heralded in both the black and white press as indicative of the broadening of economic frontiers. Though the owners touted their "million-dollar corporation" as representing "the first step toward the economic independence of colored people," not everyone was convinced. The New York branch of the National Urban League, for example, charged that the company was "out to make money and not to solve any social problems or to give colored people a chance in business."[29] In its criticism of the Peters experiment, the Urban League was reaching backward, reviving the old rhetoric of the race dollar. But Peters was banking on the fact that the buying public did not share the organization's concern, and the National Association for the Advancement of Colored People (NAACP) vocally supported the experiment.

Central to the idea behind Peters was that in addition to training black and white clerks side by side, the store would offer high-quality merchandise at competitive prices. This business strategy hinged on the sale of products that would appeal to consumers regardless of color or politics. The emphasis on quality was borne out in Peters's print advertising, which consisted of cleanly designed images and text that touted high-end products, such as the GE Model 835 Daylight Television, to local shoppers; more conventional advertising targeting people of color focused on cut-rate products and prices.[30] The experiment failed after the owners realized that they could make more money by relying solely on the old reality of white ownership and black patronage. In so doing, Peters proved the Urban League to be correct.[31] Regardless of the failure, however, the attempt to construct a business based on a model of interracial cooperation signified that postwar challenges to the segregated dollar were beginning to make visible inroads.

Peters was not alone in attempting to forge a new interracial business model. By 1950, any number of smaller and ultimately more successful such attempts had emerged. Chicago's Baldwin Ice Cream, for example, reported an annual revenue of seventy-five thousand dollars. In Harlem, Allied Custom Hatters, jointly owned by B. J. Kutchser and H. H. Christmas, were grossing in excess of thirty thousand dollars annually by 1950. Note Robert H. Kinzer and Edward Sagarin, "The negro-white partnership, of which Allied Custom is an example, constitutes a bridge between the separate and the integrated business worlds."[32] Allied Hatters, though small in relation to the Peters experiment, proved that such a bridge was indeed possible; indeed, the Harlem hatter remained in business into the twenty-first century.

Nevertheless, by the late 1940s and early 1950s, black urban businesses faced many of the same problems that the Negro Leagues faced—most significantly, the steady erosion of their consumer base. Given the choice of purchasing a superior product, whether entertainment or clothing, black consumers, like enfranchised consumers of all ethnicities, had begun to look beyond their own ecosystems. As former Negro Leaguer and Major League Hall of Famer Monte Irvin explains, having spent most of his professional life Uptown, he suddenly found himself Downtown on a much more regular basis.[33] In this case, Irvin's spatial designations were closely tied to shifting patterns of consumption, which ultimately allowed lifelong Harlemites—or residents of Bronzeville, the Hill, or Indiana Avenue—to spread their money and with it their influence elsewhere.

The black press, itself a business dependent almost solely on the race dollar, remained unconvinced that a move toward the mainstream marked the way forward. Echoing an old refrain, the weeklies repeatedly urged African American business leaders to narrow the gap between their enterprises and mainstream businesses. The market, too, compelled black businesses to provide equal goods and services at equal prices to consumers of every ethnicity. To enlarge their enterprises, black entrepreneurs would have to appeal directly to consumers outside the ecosystems. Black baseball and other entertainment venues, particularly the black and tan nightclubs so popular in the 1920s and 1930s, had always done so—quietly. Effa Manley, for example, did not trumpet the fact that her Eagles deliberately attempted to appeal to potential spectators outside the race, though records clearly indicate the team's efforts in that direction. Manley made private overtures to retailers as early as 1939 in which she stated her intent to attract white fans to Eagles' games.[34] Doing business in African America required black enterprises to try to appeal to a broader market. But as America gradually desegregated, the press asserted, black entrepreneurs had no choice but to become more aggressive in courting those outside the ecosystem.

In a July 8, 1950, piece in the *Pittsburgh Courier*, editor P. L. Prattis echoed sociologist E. Franklin Frazier by issuing a call to arms for black businesses to change the way they operated. Prattis accused black business owners of having a vested interest in segregation, singling out black baseball for criticism: "But what to do to destroy the label of jim-crow business? What plans do we have for the big competition? Jackie Robinson was helped over the hurdle from Negro baseball to major league baseball. What about major league business? Are Negro businessmen only competent to cater to a trade based on race prejudice?"[35] Fifteen months later, another *Courier* editorial, "Fenced In," underscored the ecosystem's unwillingness to look beyond its traditional boundaries, printing certain words in all capital letters for emphasis:

IT IS A GREAT MISFORTUNE that to a large extent Negro business is fenced in and NOT appreciably expanding.

This week the National Negro Business League is holding its fifty-first annual convention in Washington, DC, and it is to be hoped that it will DISCUSS this phenomenon in detail.

It is asserted that Negro business is FENCED IN because it is a FACT that most Negro businesses are catering only or largely to NEGROES and not going out for the larger market.

If Chinese catered only to Chinese, there would be practically no Chinese business—and yet the amount of Chinese business is far GREATER than the sum of Negro business, although Negroes in this country outnumber Chinese 100 to 1.

If the Jews catered ONLY to Jews, there would be very LITTLE Jewish business, and only in the sections largely populated by Jews; whereas Jews have more businesses in Negro districts than Negroes themselves!

Obviously neither Irish, Germans nor any OTHER of the many groups making up our nation go into business just to buy and sell to THEMSELVES.

Why is it, then, that Negroes ALONE make little or no effort to do business with other than themselves, and in their own sections?

Naturally, there are OBSTACLES to Negroes doing business outside their areas; but obstacles are a challenge which is supposed to be met; and the fact that SOME Negro businesses have met the challenge PROVES that others might do so if they TRIED.

There is a suspicion that the CHIEF obstacles are not outside, but INSIDE the group.

It is INERTIA, indifference, incompetence, IGNORANCE more than race prejudice and color discrimination that prevent Negroes from entering the general market.

There are a thousand OPPORTUNITIES which white people are not preventing Negro business men from exploiting.

Negroes have let the restaurant and hotel business almost go by DEFAULT except in their own districts, and even there some of the best places are owned and/or operated by whites or Chinese.

There was never very MUCH objection to the establishment of such Negro businesses outside Negro areas, and white patrons have ALWAYS been available. Moreover Negroes have had over 150 years' experience in it.

Would other people REFUSE to patronize a "downtown" movie theatre if it was known a Negro owned it? Scarcely, and yet where is there one?

Even in parts of the deepest South where racial tensions are strongest, there ARE Negroes with grocery stores and meat markets who have considerable, even predominantly, white patronage.

Why are there so FEW? Would there be hostility toward such businesses in OTHER parts of the country?

Once we had a great foothold in the barbering, shoeshining and cleaning businesses in the general market, but NOT today.

Why have the Greeks and Italians surpassed us?

If by INGENUITY we are able to get residences outside Negro districts why do we not use it to obtain BUSINESS places outside?

Why do not our insurance companies seek more WHITE business, since our record of failures is as good as that of the whites?

Our businesses have got to learn to PIONEER, to familiarize themselves more with the intricacies of commerce, to give service inferior to NONE and to venture into new areas if we are going to amount to much in the business world which, after all, is the AMERICAN world.[36]

Evidence to support the sentiments printed in this editorial could be seen throughout the African American ecosystem and beyond. Mainstream business increasingly understood that black consumer citizens voted with their pocketbooks and with their feet, an idea reinforced by the fact that the black press depicted Jackie Robinson as both an athlete and a product endorser for major national advertisers that had previously eschewed the black weeklies as not worth the investment. Old Gold Cigarettes, for example, seemed to have realized that their product could appeal to black as well as white consumers. And after he joined the Major League New York Giants in 1949, Irvin appeared in ads hawking Rheingold Beer. A case study in an advertising industry publication of the period exclaimed, "Today the Negro rightfully wants to be advertised to. Possibly the greatest sale clincher of all is whether the manufacturer has advertised in a Negro medium. Negroes want to know that their business is earnestly desired."[37]

Liggett and Myers, the makers and marketers of Chesterfield Cigarettes, understood this trend particularly well. Beginning in 1950, Chesterfield sponsored twelve ten-minute documentaries meant to be shown in black-owned theaters and on campuses of traditional black colleges. The films showcased African American advances in a variety of spheres, including entertainment, sports, and business. More than three million consumers saw each of these films—and received cigarette samples. Later in the decade, the tobacco company produced a new series including interviews with Ralph Bunche as well as jazz greats Lionel Hampton and Sarah Vaughan, among others. In what amounted to an all-out marketing blitz, Chesterfield also advertised with point-of-purchase displays that featured Robinson; his Dodger teammate, Roy Campanella; and rising Giants star and former Birmingham Black Baron Willie Mays.[38]

These tobacco companies and other advertisers as diverse as Kimberly-Clark, Pepsi-Cola, Pillsbury, Colgate-Palmolive-Peet, and Esso Standard Oil were banking on reports of dramatic increases in buying power among ethnic and racial minorities, making them untapped markets ripe for exploitation. According to a 1950 government bulletin, the median income among nonwhites had moved steadily upward from a low of 38.1 percent of white income in 1939 to 52.2 percent of white income in 1950.[39] These numbers gave rise to corporate understanding that nonwhite buying power would continue to increase. More significantly, the average income for nonwhites more than quadrupled over this period, growing far more rapidly than whites' income. While race-based income inequality was hardly about to become a thing of the past, African Americans and other consumers of color had become a significant and untapped market.

A general upturn in the economy as part of the long postwar boom no doubt drove this and other changes. And African Americans had of course experienced prosperity during earlier eras. But unlike the boom period of the 1920s, after World War II, businesses outside the ecosystem began to recognize the economic clout of African American consumers. As African Americans were moving outside their ecosystem, they developed a sense of legitimacy about their place on a much larger economic stage. They also began to realize that they had the power to effect changes not only in the economy but also in the sociopolitical realm. Thus, the move to lay claim to black dollars pushed African Americans that much closer to a level of the consumer citizenship that previous generations had worked hard to achieve and helped make them a genuine force in larger economic circles. As Marcus Alexis indicates, while buying power alone would not have been enough to engineer rapid social change for the African American population, their gradual move into the mainstream economy nevertheless offered them a degree of consideration that put their consumption patterns on the economic map.[40]

The growing power of the postwar African American dollar was similarly not lost on the National Negro Business League (NNBL) and particularly its president, Cincinnati real estate and hotel mogul Horace Sudduth. According to Sudduth, the "tremendous buying power of Negro America . . . estimated at $12,000,000,000 yearly . . . would open up the doors to private employment if intelligently directed and channeled." To that end, he announced that the NNBL would conduct a study of "what the Negro buys and from whom he buys it . . . and why." Addressing a business league meeting, Sudduth put forth "Four Cardinal Principles" for the development of successful business:

(1)—Through technical knowledge, plus the training of an efficient staff.
(2)—Ability to compete, price-wise and quality-wise with your competition, by buying as a group and meeting the challenge of bargain prices.
(3)—Abandonment of the fallacious belief that "hate" campaigns, built on the antiquated "buy black" slogan, is the answer to solving our economic business problems.

(4)—Continuation of business organizations in EVERY community, with paid personnel, to do detailed work, and a sincere effort to solicit the assistance of the church and civic groups in implementing a positive program.[41]

These points touch on a number of themes that had developed in the rhetoric surrounding African American business. His assertion that those entering the world of business required technical training directly referred to the admonitions of Booker T. Washington as far back as the Atlanta Compromise Speech. Indeed, the Tuskegee Institute had been founded on precisely this principle. In contrast, the notion that business organizations outside the ecosystem, "in EVERY community," ought to become involved in furthering the positive program of economic progress echoed W. E. B. Du Bois's contention that only by joining in the larger project of America could black citizens become fully enfranchised. So, too, did Sudduth's admonition to abandon "hate campaigns" couched in the language of race pride as grounds on which to conduct business. Finally, by urging black businesses to buy as a group—in effect, to set up purchasing cooperatives—Sudduth predicted the ways in which various ethnic groups would conduct business into the twenty-first century.

An Ecosystem in Transition

The segregated business model had remained virtually unchanged since the first wave of migrants arrived in the urban North and Midwest. In Harlem, Bronzeville, 18th and Vine, North Philadelphia, and other such communities, businesses were established to fill niches created by the mainstream's lack of interest, disregard, or refusal to exploit the segregated dollar.

The major shift in the postwar economics of urban African America is evident in the fortunes of a major contributor to the Bronzeville ecosystem, Robert A. Cole. In 1951, insurance giant Metropolitan Life sued Cole's Chicago Metropolitan Mutual Assurance Company (CMMAC), formerly the Metropolitan Funeral Systems Association, one of Bronzeville's largest and oldest black-owned businesses, over ownership of the word *Metropolitan*.[42] Under Cole's proprietorship, CMMAC had become one of Bronzeville's most diversified businesses. In addition to an insurance company, its holdings included the Parkway Amusement Company, which oversaw the operation of the elegant Parkway Ballroom and the Parkway Dining Room, two of Bronzeville's most vibrant establishments. According to CMMAC historian Robert E. Weems Jr., Parkway Amusement "was a 'paper' corporation. While it ostensibly supplied the Parkway Ballroom with liquor and the Parkway Dining Room with food, Chicago Metropolitan actually financed these facilities' operating expenses."[43]

That a large, national corporation sued a smaller one—though big by Bronzeville standards—was not at all unusual. But that a large white corporation sued a smaller race business told a different story. By suing CMMAC, Met Life was issuing a challenge, putting Cole on notice that it was going after the Bronzeville business that had belonged exclusively to CMMAC and its primary competitor, Supreme Liberty Life, as well as smaller black insurance companies. Met Life, like other mainstream businesses, had begun to realize that when it came to consumer dollars, the only important color was the color of money. Though Met Life eventually lost the suit, it became a stiff competitor for black consumers shopping for insurance, which had previously been the largest race industry in the ecosystem.

Moreover, according to Weems, "During the company's first 29 years, Chicago Metropolitan, along with other black-owned firms, provided a sizable percentage of the clerical and professional positions available to black Chicagoans. Yet, by the mid-50s, several mainstream Chicago corporations began to abolish the historic discrimination practiced against Bronzeville's citizens. Consequently, blacks now had opportunity to work downtown in capacities other than janitors, elevator operators, or cleaning women."[44] Celebrities such as Irvin were not the only African Americans who found themselves "downtown." The growth of a desegregated economy, however limited, appears to have represented progress to Bronzeville's residents in a way in which participation in a race business never could. Writes Weems, "Besides providing economical insurance coverage to Chicago's black community, the old Metropolitan Funeral Systems Association (and its later derivatives) sought to exert a positive influence on other sectors of African American life. Robert A. Cole, sometimes using personal gambling winnings, promoted the company's involvement in a myriad of community enhancement activities. Ironically, at the time of his death, Black Chicagoans, optimistic about implications of racial integration, had begun to abandon some of the community based institutions that Cole and Company had created or supported."[45] One of the businesses created and to some extent supported by Cole and his company was the Chicago American Giants of the NAL.

Indeed, Cole's interests suffered from the steady erosion of Bronzeville's once vibrant economy, compounded by poor personal choices. In 1955, Cole's wife, Mary, a licensed mortician who ran one of CMMAC's subsidiaries, was arrested for allegedly participating in an extortion ring that targeted, among others, Horace G. Hall, a top CMMAC executive, one of her husband's most trusted colleagues, and Robert Cole's replacement as the majority owner of the American Giants.[46] While the case against Mary Cole was ultimately dismissed on legal technicalities, the smear on the Cole name could not be wiped clean, forcing both her and her husband out of the social limelight.[47] By the time of his 1956 death, Cole had long been out of the black baseball business and had become "a sickly recluse."[48] Hall, the alleged victim, had also long since divested himself from race sports, having sold the American Giants more than a decade earlier to a syndicate headed by J. B. Martin. But the suit was not at the root of the demise of Cole's empire, but rather, a symptom of it. Personal indiscretions aside, had the ecosystem remained strong, Cole's subsidiary businesses could have weathered this storm.

One place in which the changes to the ecosystem could be seen most clearly was in black America's luxury hotels. In the first years after the war, the black hotel industry was still going strong, and despite some very public lawsuits against mainstream establishments in Philadelphia and Boston, there was, as Juliet E. K. Walker suggests, no reason to believe that the full integration of white hotels was imminent.[49] In fact, some of the older black hotels had begun renovations to provide better services for well-heeled clients. Toward this end, the owners of black hotels, not all of them people of color, organized the National Hotel Association. Headed up by William H. Bloom, manager of the largest and one of the most luxurious of the black hostelries, Harlem's Hotel Theresa, the organization sought to encourage owners of hotels, motels, tourist courts, and guesthouses to continue to make physical improvements as well as to improve service. Writes Walker, "Excluded from the white trade associations, the organization also saw itself providing a service in the collection and dissemination of vital information concerning trends, statistics, and the latest techniques."[50] The hotel association's aim was very much in keeping with the Washingtonian precepts of the NNBL as expressed by Sudduth. Although the association did not place the notion of appealing to consumers outside the ecosystem high on its list of priorities, it did emphasize the need to provide services equal to or better than those found in the segregated downtown hotels.

But the miniboom in black hotel renovation came to a screeching halt in the mid-1950s. To a great extent, the rapid decline of the industry may be traced to the 1954 *Brown* decision. According to Hotel Theresa historian Sondra Kathryn Wilson, the Court "didn't abolish legal segregation in restaurants, hotels, and parks, but it did send forth a signal. A few hotels downtown saw the writing on the wall and began discreetly permitting black patronage. In the mid-1950s, downtown hotels began chipping away at the Theresa's clientele."[51] Even in the South, certain white hoteliers understood that money could be made by integrating their businesses. In Carthage, Missouri, for example, a white tourist court hotel announced in 1953 that it would gladly accept patrons of color. "This is an all-American establishment," claimed the owner, "and I want Negro tourists to know that if there is space available, they will be accommodated here."[52]

Of course, the changing nature of the hotel industry related directly to the businesses of both sports and entertainment, both of which required substantial travel and thus depended on the ability to secure appropriate accommodations for their participants. By 1954, Jackie Robinson, the specter whose presence in Jim Crow Florida during the early years of his Major League career helped precipitate the construction of Dodgertown, Branch Rickey's modern spring training facility in Vero Beach, was staying in the same hotel as his white teammates.[53] Moreover, in the case of one of St. Louis's premier white hotels, the Chase, Robinson served once again as the desegregator. But while the Chase permitted Robinson to lodge there in 1954, he was barred from the restaurant and the swimming pool and was not allowed to spend time in the lobby.[54] Robinson's acquiescence to the hotel's strictures caused something of a stir in the black press, but Fay Young explained Robinson's decision: "Jackie was given a clean slate for his stand in the St. Louis hotel incident. Investigation showed according to our informers that the white hotel's door had always been open to the Dodger ball players. Jackie stayed there because he didn't want to Jim Crow himself and others by openly showing they preferred the Negro hotel where Roy Campanella and the other Dodger 'spooks' hurried off to enjoy the big steaks the owner had for them[,] the use of the owner's high powered automobile[,] and the fun that could be had in the wee hours of the morning without being known to have broken training rules which they were doing."[55] To remain in business, black hotels, confronted with the loss of their celebrity clientele, had to find a way to induce their traditional client base to continue to patronize their establishments. But steaks, fast cars, and the promise of broken curfews could only go so far. That St. Louis's

Negro hotel offered these services to Campanella and other players suggests that the business was going to great lengths to retain its high-profile customers in the face of desegregation. A year later, the Chase bowed to pressure when entertainer Nat King Cole appeared there and opened its public facilities to all guests regardless of color, although Henry Aaron has contended that African American players did not receive the best rooms.[56] And this increasingly the case throughout the hospitality industries. As Irvin remembers, where once he had spent the majority of his leisure time rubbing elbows with Harlem's elite at Smalls Paradise and the Skyline Ballroom at the Hotel Theresa, by the 1950s he was welcome in such New York hotspots as Toots Shor's and the Copacabana. He may not have had the best table in the room—those went to white marquee players such as Joe DiMaggio and Mickey Mantle—but at least Irvin got in the door.[57]

As the mainstream business community continued to open its doors ever more widely to black dollars, businesses catering solely to black consumers could no longer bank on the use of the dated rhetoric of race pride to appeal to their celebrity clientele. And where celebrities went, other well-to-do patrons followed. Indeed, some celebrities had grown hostile to the race pride message, especially as the traditional centers continued to deteriorate. As the nightlife in Harlem continued to fade, so too did the once-stately Theresa. According to Wilson, as the 1950s progressed, "Mainly pimps and prostitutes were frequenting the Theresa's bar."[58] In 1953, for instance, Harlem's own Sammy Davis Jr. bypassed the Theresa and stayed at the world-class Sherry-Netherland on Fifth Avenue while performing at the Copacabana, quipping, "They [blacks] haven't made a hotel that's [as] luxurious as I want to live in." Davis was also known to frequent the Waldorf-Astoria or "wherever anyone else with my fame and financial ability would be able to stay."[59] Perhaps even more tellingly, the Negro Publishers Association, a race organization, held its 1951 annual meeting not at the Theresa but at the integrated McAlpin Hotel in Herald Square.[60]

Though hardly representative of the views of the typical African American consumer, Davis's attitude was shared by Negro League baseball's dwindling fan base. These new citizen consumers ultimately voted with their feet, leaving black baseball's entrepreneurs without their ready-made market. To stay afloat, the owners had no choice but to embrace a business strategy of selling their assets—players—a necessarily finite approach that led to a downward spiral of product quality and consumer demand.

Facing Change

From a baseball standpoint, perhaps the most ominous sign of increasingly difficult times for the segregated economy was the demise of the sports and entertainment empire of Pittsburgh's Gus Greenlee, whose Crawford Grill No. 1 was destroyed by fire in 1951. According to managing editor William G. Nunn's 1952 obituary for Greenlee, which appeared on the *Courier*'s front page, "Creditors began closing in on his other partnerships and the U.S. Government sued him for unpaid income taxes." Greenlee, the Hill's erstwhile numbers king, who "played the game of life hard, fast and clean," could no longer meet his obligations.[61] His financial ruin constituted yet another indicator of how deeply troubled the traditional economy had become. When insurance adjusters were unable to contact the parties responsible for the burnt-out Crawford Grill after the fire, the *Courier*'s John L. Clark, once Greenlee's publicity man, was moved to observe that "buyers for taverns and hotels are not plentiful nowadays," another sign of the increasingly rapid deterioration of the postwar ecosystem.[62]

Those in the black press charged with the task of framing the larger African American narrative struggled with the significance of such apparently transformative moments, producing varying assessments of what such matters meant in terms of the present as well as what the future held. This phenomenon was most apparent in the journalists' response to the plight of the Negro Leagues. Nowhere was their response more impassioned on both sides as when they commented on the fate of the Negro Leagues' biggest promotion, the annual East-West Classic. Nunn was particularly disturbed by the dwindling interest in the 1953 exhibition, which drew a mere ten thousand spectators:

> Gone . . . in the game, were the tremendous crowds which formerly crammed every nook and cranny of the historic South Side Park.
>
> Gone . . . in the game, were the "names" which once thrilled the countless thousands as they yelled their defiance to the invisible color barrier which kept their athletes from participation in organized baseball.
>
> Gone . . . was the finesse and promotional skill which had nursed the famous diamond classic from a modest 7,500 start . . . to the acme of the entertainment which once saw 51,000 people pay to enter the gates, while another 4.000 clamored for admission outside.[63]

Gone, too, was Abe Saperstein, who had handled promotion for the Classic throughout the 1940s, though he remained connected to the game by virtue of his stake in the Chicago American Giants, which he purchased from J. B. Martin in 1951. He also continued to serve as a scout for Bill Veeck, who had taken over the St. Louis Browns (and who in late 1953 would move the franchise to Baltimore and rename them the Orioles). According to Saperstein's obituary in *Jet*, the booking agent turned scout and owner/operator of the Harlem Globetrotters even had a minority stake in the Browns' franchise.[64] Saperstein also had the ear of Hank Greenberg, general manager of the Cleveland Indians, who remained on the job after Veeck's departure. According to Rebecca Alpert, "Greenberg, who continued to bring African American talent to the Indians, saw Saperstein as a conduit to Negro League owners and the person who had opened his eyes to the talent of the Negro Leagues," showing him that players of color were not "'just a bunch of clowns' as he had been 'brainwashed' to assume."[65]

Saperstein was not the only executive with ties to the Negro Leagues to market his expertise in black baseball to the Major Leagues. Alex Pompez, former owner of the New York Cubans, parlayed his vast knowledge of black ball into a job as a big league scout. Following the 1950 season, the Cubans disbanded, but Pompez remained in the game. Even before his exit from league ownership, however, Pompez organized barnstorming tours featuring Major League stars such as Robinson, Campanella, and Mays.[66] He also provided a link between the New York Giants, from whom he rented the Polo Grounds as the Cubans' home field, and the Negro Leagues. As Adrian Burgos Jr. reports, Pompez was instrumental in the Giants' acquisition of Monte Irvin following Effa Manley's contract dispute with Branch Rickey, who, because he continued to ignore contractual arrangements within the Negro Leagues, refused to compensate the Eagles for the loss of Irvin, one of their most marketable stars.[67] Once his Cubans disbanded, Pompez went to work for the Major League Giants in an official capacity, consulting with Carl Hubbell, the team's scouting director. Pompez was directly involved in the Giants' acquisition of Mays from the Birmingham franchise, though Pompez lost out on bringing Henry Aaron to the Giants following a protracted negotiation with Clowns owner Syd Pollock, who eventually sold his rising young star to the Boston Braves for a lot more money than the Giants were willing to offer.[68]

Pompez's greatest contribution to the Giants franchise and Major League Baseball as a whole was his creation of an impressive pipeline between the big leagues and Latin America. Among the emergent talent he scouted and ultimately signed were future Hall of Famers Orlando Cepeda and Juan Marichal as well as brothers Felipe, Matty, and Jesus Alou.[69] Beyond acting as a liaison between black and Latino baseball and the Major Leagues, Pompez and to a lesser extent Saperstein followed the new pattern established by the players whose careers they helped make, forsaking the Negro Leagues for the Majors once the opportunity presented itself.

Send in the Clowns

By 1952, the NAL was down to six teams, and by the middle of the decade, only four remained: the Birmingham Black Barons and the Memphis Red Sox in the Deep South and Mid-South, respectively, where the segregated dollar still held sway; the Kansas City Monarchs, also technically a southern franchise; and the lone northern team, the Detroit Stars. After the 1954 season, Syd Pollock's Indianapolis Clowns, described by Neil Lanctot as the only franchise that "managed to maintain anything near the financial vitality of the prior decade," left the league and became independent. According to Lanctot, "While the team benefited from outstanding (and relentless) promotion, the success of the Clowns (and basketball's Harlem Globetrotters) lay in their strong appeal among whites who found the blend of comedy and athleticism irresistible."[70]

Pollock's continued financial success indeed depended, at least in part, on the Clowns' appeal to white audiences, especially on barnstorming tours of the Upper Midwest and Canada, where the team was particularly popular. But the Clowns also drew crowds when they played against the remaining league teams, whose fan base, however diminished, was still overwhelmingly African American. In fact, Pollock's aggregation drew especially well in the South, where segregation persisted and translated into decent if not spectacular numbers at the gate.[71]

Pollock's operation was above all else a barnstorming operation. But in this regard, the Clowns were not alone. Even before the NAL ceased to exist in all but name, barnstorming once again emerged as a mainstay of black baseball, filling out the schedule between official league contests. If Negro League franchises had relied solely on scheduled league games, the enterprise would have folded long before it did. Certain elements in the black press, wanting to boost an enterprise that sought to entertain African American fans and by extension supported other black businesses, touted the continuing popularity of the Clowns and their opponents, both within and outside the NAL. And to an extent, they were not wrong. The Clowns continued to be a consistent draw, whether they were playing league opponents or whether their opponents were independent or semiprofessional.

As Lanctot suggests, relentless promotion contributed significantly to the Clowns' success. Pollock peppered the sports pages of the black weeklies with regular game announcements, touting the Clowns' "international fame" and massive popularity. In a 1950 promotional piece, Pollock bragged about a crowd of 6,500 at Shibe Park in Philadelphia, a respectable attendance figure, especially in light of the fact that the Major League Athletics, Shibe's primary occupants, averaged only 4,023.[72] Wrote Pollock, "This, and other record crowds, prove that the Clowns are still the number one attraction in Negro baseball. The fun-making 'Imps of the Diamond' are all business once the game gets underway, yet King Tut and Spec Bebop, the club's comics, offer the fans plenty of buffoonery on the sidelines, in sufficient portions to whet the appetite of most any baseball fan."[73] Pollock also placed advertising for the Clowns in mainstream newspapers. For the most part, the same promotional copy that appeared in the *Chicago Defender*, the *Pittsburgh Courier*, and the *Indianapolis Recorder* also was found in papers from Benton Harbor, Michigan, to Del Rio, Texas, and points beyond.

But while advertisements and advertorials for the Clowns appeared on the sports pages of the black press, the mainstream papers often placed such items elsewhere. Hearkening back to the nineteenth century, when announcements for games by colored nines were sandwiched between ads for Buffalo Bill's Wild West Show and for reenactments of the Sack of Rome and the eruption of Mount Vesuvius, positioning the games as theater and spectacle rather than as baseball contests, Clowns' promotional material often appeared on the entertainment or even the funny pages of small-town newspapers.[74] A 1954 ad in the Missouri's *Chillicothe Constitution-Tribune* appeared directly under an ad for *The Egg and I*, a film starring Claudette Colbert and Fred MacMurray, and simply reads "Baseball, Clowns vs. Monarchs, Girl Players, Clowns, Negro Acrobats."[75] The ad's inclusion of "Girl Players"—Toni Stone, Connie Morgan, and Mamie "Peanut" Johnson—pointed to the lengths to which Pollock and Monarchs' owner T. Y. Baird would go to draw a respectable gate. This was ironic given the fact that Pollock's outfit was the same club that the league had once tried to ban in response to its minstrel-like performance aesthetic, But by the mid-1950s, other teams came to count on Pollock's traveling circus to keep the circuit afloat with cash infusions from ticket sales.

Pollock's press promotions and print advertising frequently emphasized appearances by black baseball's few remaining celebrities. In 1954, the team's final season in the NAL, Pollock signed former Negro League great Oscar Charleston to manage the Clowns. Charleston's appeal to non–African American audiences was in all probability negligible. Moreover, Charleston, unlike other black baseball stars, most specifically Satchel Paige, was not noted for showboating in any way, shape, or form. Hiring Charleston indicated that the Clowns remained serious about playing competitive ball, though they continued to showcase their antics between innings. Although Charleston seemed an unlikely fit as leader of the Clowns, his hiring proved to be a shrewd promotional move. Not only did he lead the team to the NAL championship, but he was a drawing card, attracting members of Pollock's primary audience in much the same way that the retired Babe Ruth drew fans as a coach for the 1938 Brooklyn Dodgers. But in the case of Charleston, who made a real impact with the Clowns, the move proved to have far better on-field results.

The Clowns also made money barnstorming with the Jackie Robinson All-Stars, a team that included a number of former Negro Leaguers who had made the leap to the big leagues. But aging Negro League stars were not the only celebrities to profit from Pollock's promotional machine. When off-season earnings were at stake, even the generally buttoned-down Robinson was not beyond appearing with a novelty baseball team, even with its minstrel show elements. Four-time Olympic gold medalist Jesse Owens got in on the act, too, racing against Henry "Speed" Merchant, the Clowns' fastest runner, as well as giving motivational speeches about his victories in the 1936 games.[76] But Pollock's most audacious promotional move of the 1950s was the signing of Marcenia Lyle "Toni" Stone, which infused some much-needed capital into the cash-strapped business.

In marketing this move, using language typical of Pollock, a June 20, 1953, *Defender* advertorial trumpeted, "Promoters are claiming that with the assistance of the weatherman, the crowd" for a doubleheader with the Monarchs at Detroit's Briggs Stadium "will exceed 30,000. Continuing to make the headlines is the Clowns 22-year-old second baseman, Toni Stone, first girl infielder to be signed and break down the prejudice against women players in the NAL."[77] And indeed, the games drew 20,399 fans, a significant gate for a Negro League promotion.[78]

According to Alan Pollock, Syd's son, Stone received her nickname based on the popularity of Toni Home Permanents, a claim that is certainly in keeping with Pollock's tendency to link baseball with marketing.[79] Although Stone's biographer, Martha Ackmann, contends that Stone was already known as Toni when she joined the team, the moniker nevertheless linked her to the Ethiopian Clowns and their practice of assigning stereotypical nicknames to their players and performers, reaffirming the franchise's connection to the traditions of minstrelsy.[80]

Pollock sold Stone to the Monarchs before the 1954 season, replacing her with two more female players, infielder Connie Morgan and pitcher Mamie "Peanut" Johnson. While hardly important as a baseball-related transaction, Stone's move to the Monarchs suggests a great deal about the role of novelty in terms of keeping black baseball teams solvent. The Monarchs were so desperate to draw fans that what had been the premiere African American ball club, one that managed to survive the breakup of Rube Foster's original NNL and the Depression, was reduced to employing the same tactics used by black baseball's former pariahs. But as more female players appeared, the less of a novelty they became.

Truth be told, Monarchs' owner Baird had embraced a Clowns-like approach even before 1954. A 1953 correspondence between Baird and Oscar Rico, manager of the Cuban Giants, another of Baird's baseball enterprises, points to the owner's growing appreciation for the value of novelty baseball even before purchasing Stone's contract. The Cuban Giants, who were, in fact, actually Cuban, unlike the original black professional team that bore the name and so many "Cuban" teams that followed, Pompez's ventures notwithstanding, toured America that summer. Arranging for promotion, Baird told Rico in no uncertain terms that his side needed a gimmick to survive. Rico's answer was something he billed as a "Rhumba Show," which included the "penguin dance" and the "crippled baseball dance."[81] But Baird did not think Rico's plan went far enough and told the manager that the "Cuban Giants could be made a good attraction if they . . . do things to make them popular with the fans. Just straight baseball will not make the team, you, or players money. Can you get a comedian something like Tut of the Clowns?"[82] It was clear that by this point that even the owner of the once-august Monarchs realized that black baseball had become a hard sell without a healthy dose of *shtick*.

Baird was also not above paying members of the mainstream press to promote the Monarchs, a practice that was far from uncommon but certainly not aboveboard. Recalling the relationship between Effa Manley and Newark broadcaster Jocko Maxwell, Baird also engaged in the practice of payola, but on an extremely smaller scale. Writing to his publicity agent, Matty Brescia, in March 1952, Baird offered to pay the paltry sum of ten dollars for a mention of the Monarchs by Meryl Hereford, assistant sports editor of the *Dallas Morning News*.[83] But even publicity in such a high-profile, mainstream newspaper would not help the business, which was reaching the end of its run, something that even the Clowns began to recognize. Following their 1954 departure from the NAL, the Clowns again ratcheted up their theatrics, reintroducing such outrageous routines as the "Saturday Night Whore," among others. They were eventually joined by the Monarchs, both in defection from league ball and on tour. The Clowns also reached into Saperstein's Globetrotter playbook, often traveling with a team of patsies contracted to lose to Pollock's outfit. Perhaps as an offhanded tribute to James Semler's futile New York outfit, the Clowns' touring companions were usually known as the Black Yankees.[84] By the mid-1950s, competitive black baseball—baseball by African Americans for African Americans—was for all intents and purposes dead.

Denouement

Negro League baseball officially died in 1963, when the NAL folded. By that point, Detroit Stars' owner Ted Raspberry controlled what was left of the circuit. Syd Pollock's Clowns remained in the business, though in 1965 Pollock sold his majority share of the organization to his road manager and partner, Ed Hamman, who had long worn other hats with the team.[85] For years, Hamman had regularly appeared as an entertainer, wearing traditional white clown makeup and even replacing Spec Bebop in the "dentist's chair." Under Hamman's direction, the outfit, reduced both in size and by circumstances, limped along for another ten-plus years, offering a degree of hope for marginal players who had been previously ignored by scouts. A stint with Hamman's Clowns could still mean the possibility of a minor league contract, however remote. But by all measures, the Clowns too had become a relic, carrying the torch for a business that had long since served its purpose.

One notable aspect of the Clowns under Hamman's ownership was that the team was no longer solely African American but began featuring white players alongside its black core. In fact, this was not the first instance of desegregation in black baseball, the experiment having been attempted first in Cleveland and then in Chicago in the late 1940s and early 1950s in an unsuccessful effort to broaden the fan base.[86] By signing a few white players for the sake of novelty, the new-look Clowns represented what might be construed as an alternative version of black baseball. On one hand, the team remained a business that catered to and employed African Americans, serving the needs of black consumers while benefiting white ownership. On the other, the Clowns had grown beyond the segregated dollar. Even in its death throes, the enterprise attempted to present an idealized vision of what the country could be by offering a fully integrated business playing to a similarly integrated audience that looked like America. But it was a case of too little, too late.

While organized black baseball had ceased to exist as a viable enterprise, its audience was primed to make the transition to Major League fandom, at least in part because of its exposure to the sport via the Negro Leagues. By the late 1950s, black southerners as well as northerners were enjoying the opportunity to hear their favorite Major League players on the radio and increasingly to watch them on television in bars and restaurants. Walter O'Malley, the later reviled Brooklyn Dodgers owner, who forced Branch Rickey out of the organization in 1950 and later moved the team to Los Angeles, made Major League Baseball accessible to southern fans when he established the Dodger Radio Network. The network featured games re-created by announcer Nat Albright, who spiced up his broadcasts with a wide range of realistic sound effects that brought his play-by-play to life.[87] The network could be heard in various southern locations as well as in California, making new Dodgers fans in areas of the country that lacked Major League clubs and cutting even further into what remained of the audience that continued to follow black baseball.[88] Tom Hayes, owner of the Birmingham Black Barons, warned fans of the potential economic consequences of the failure of black baseball, citing the "thousands of dollars we spend in Negro cafes, hotels, newspapers, and similar enterprises," which would suffer without the business.[89] And while Hayes was certainly correct, the die had long since been cast. In 1966, Major League Baseball came to the South when the Milwaukee Braves, complete with Aaron, the former Clown, as their star attraction, moved to Atlanta.

One race enterprise bucked the trend, however. The Chitlin' Circuit, the last major African American industry, built on the tested principles of barnstorming, followed black baseball's lead by offering entertainment to primarily African American audiences by largely African American performers. In many of the same small southern towns where the Clowns continued to appear until they folded in 1983, Chitlin' Circuit–affiliated roadhouses and juke joints jumped to live music by Jimmie Lunceford, Clarence "Gatemouth" Brown, Roy Brown's Good Rockin' Revival, the Isley Brothers, and a young, pompadoured Little Richard, who at one point featured a similarly pompadoured Jimmy (later Jimi) Hendrix in his road band.[90] In fact, much of the early story of the Chitlin' Circuit parallels that of black baseball. Following the collapse of the Theatre Owners Booking Association, the white-run black vaudeville circuit that operated until the Great Depression, entertainment promoters brought swing and other bands as well as comedy acts to the segregated South and led to the development of the Chitlin' Circuit, which included primarily small towns.[91]

The brainchild of Indianapolis sportsman and mogul Denver Ferguson and his brother, Sea, the Chitlin' Circuit made an end run around mob-controlled nightclubs in the big cities. The Fergusons resembled many Negro League owners in that they raised their start-up capital in the numbers rackets and developed a vast network of venues along with promoters who advertised the appearances of affiliated artists in beauty parlors and barbershops, bars and cafés, and the small-town press, black and mainstream, alike, following the practices of the Clowns and other black barnstorming troupes. Ferguson, like Pollock, often issued promotional materials that exaggerated the acts' quality.[92] Touting a 1943 tour featuring two of his top acts, Ferguson wrote, in an advertorial worthy of Pollock himself, "The Mills Brothers, world's greatest singing combination, and the Carolina Cotton Pickers, world's greatest swinging combination . . . will invade the West, bringing to the theatres and ballrooms the biggest attraction to hit the road in years. The Mills Brothers, noted for their close harmony and melodic singing are fresh from Hollywood and radio commercials. The Carolina Cotton Pickers under the leadership of Leroy Harding, featuring Wesley Jones, singer of sweet songs and Dwight 'Gate Mouth' Moore, blues singer, are known from coast to coast for their syncopated style of swing."[93] Though the Mills Brothers were budding stars, the ad's use of hyperbole certainly inflated the popularity of all these acts. Ferguson's infectious enthusiasm, as reflected in the ad copy, served to drum up the support he needed to make his nascent circuit viable.

In many ways, life on the Chitlin' Circuit was like barnstorming with the Clowns and their touring companions. Performers spent much of the year on the road, living out of buses or caravans of station wagons that were always in danger of breaking down, often in places where black performers did not want to be stranded. And though this circuit may have been lucrative for the Fergusons and the handful of promoters who worked in management, the performers, it continued to be, like the TOBA circuit that preceded it, "tough on black asses."[94] The musicians and comedians, like the ballplayers, depended upon the necessity of drawing a decent-sized audience, since they too were paid solely based on the gate. Writes Preston Lauterbach, "Though the chitlin' circuit touring model—one-night stands, revolving through promoters' respective hubs and spokes—was built to sustain itself, Ferguson's big bands operated with little room for error. Bus fuel and maintenance, the band's food, clothes, and instruments, and salaries for a crew of twenty, not to mention makeup and high-heel repair for the queens, required steady cash. A single cancellation—and there were always cancellations—stranded bands. And many a *good* day left them threadbare."[95] Cancellations, transportation woes, and similar complications also constantly concerned traveling black ball clubs, even during the industry's heyday. But like black baseball, the circuit provided some performers with a stepping-stone to bigger and better opportunities.

By the 1950s, big bands found that playing the Chitlin' Circuit was no longer cost-effective, in no small part as a consequence of the dwindling popularity of the big-band sound. Performers began to travel in smaller groups, meaning that their visits provided considerably less money for the local economy in the towns where they appeared. Unlike black baseball's failure to recognize the nature of the changing times, however, the emergent entertainment circuit embraced the possibilities represented by a dramatically shifting zeitgeist. Indeed, Ferguson and his stable of small-town promoters as well as his competitors remained at the forefront of popular tastes. Performers such as B. B. King and Little Esther Phillips were among the pioneers of rock and roll. Comedians Bill Cosby and Richard Pryor cut their teeth on the Chitlin' Circuit, where their popularity was supported rather than hurt by emerging technologies.

In contrast, technological advances constituted a body blow to barnstorming black baseball and to all non–Major League baseball. Radio, jukeboxes, and later television helped bring the Chitlin' Circuit's products out of the predominantly rural shadows. Since the early 1940s, radio broadcasts of rural performers had provided a boon to the stations themselves as well as to performers, who used the medium to promote live performances and recordings. The second Sonny Boy Williamson (aka Aleck "Rice" Miller); his sponsor, the Interstate Grocer Company; and the Helena, Arkansas, radio station KFFA, for example, were responsible for the creation and success of the vaunted *King Biscuit Time*, the first regularly scheduled broadcast of its kind in the region, showing the way to a coming generation of rural-based artists of color.[96]

The Chitlin' Circuit was organized in a way that could withstand fundamental changes in the economy, both narrowly defined and broadly conceived, as well as changes in the sociocultural landscape. The circuit essentially followed the model of the Major League farm system, functioning as a vertically integrated business that showcased talent, some of which would make its way to the biggest stages of American entertainment, most literally "the show." Minor league baseball found itself battling many of the same forces that were battering the Negro Leagues. Although minor league attendance briefly spiked immediately after the war, it had dropped precipitously by the early 1950s. In 1949, for example, close to forty-two million spectators attended games played by 464 teams in fifty-nine different minor leagues, but attendance dropped by seven million each of the next two years. According to historian Ron Briley, by the end of the decade, there were a mere twenty-one minor leagues that drew a total of twelve million fans. While these numbers are huge compared to the Negro Leagues even at their zenith, in light of the relative market shares of the two industries, the decline in the minor leagues was similar in scope to that of Negro League baseball. In Briley's words, "Baseball officials and publications like the *Sporting News* blamed [minor league] baseball's attendance woes upon a multiplicity of factors including: television, air conditioning, growing availability of Major League broadcasts, and increased suburbanization."[97] But while black baseball had no parent industry to which to look for support, the vertically integrated farm system, introduced by Branch Rickey during the depression, served as a conduit for talent to the Major Leagues and had Major League financial backing.[98]

The Chitlin' Circuit was just such a conduit. Acts embarked on the circuit with the hopes of landing on the stages of such bigger black showcases as Harlem's Apollo Theater, the Handy Theater in Memphis, and the Howard in Washington, D.C., and eventually on even more public stages such as Don Cornelius's *Soul Train*, which aired nationally for thirty-five years beginning in 1971.[99] And like the Major League clubs that had a stake in the minor league talent they developed, the Ferguson brothers and other Chitlin' Circuit promoters retained a financial interest in the acts they managed at all levels.

The efficacy of the Chitlin' Circuit as a model black business outlived the Ferguson brothers. Indeed, like minor league baseball, the circuit continues to exist into the twenty-first century and has undergone something of a renaissance, as has the minor league sport.[100] But with dwindling audience and no room to grow, black baseball, even in the organized Negro Leagues, could not respond to changing times. Perhaps had it integrated vertically under the auspices of the Major Leagues, black baseball might have remained viable for a few more years. But as it was, black baseball no longer served a purpose. Its business model was hopelessly anachronistic, trapped behind the color line, where the Washingtonian act of "casting down your buckets" was no longer economically viable. While a Du Boisian model in which African American business enterprises could take their rightful place within the mainstream remained years away, the tide had irrevocably begun to turn. Negro League baseball, an industry built on the shifting foundations of Jim Crow and predicated on race pride and the segregated dollar, would have folded under any circumstances. The Negro Leagues and similar race businesses, all with a vested interest in segregation, simply had no economic future.

POSTSCRIPT

What Has the Promise Wrought?

In a 1998 article reflecting on the significance of Jackie Robinson's ascension to the Major Leagues, Gerald Early observes,

> Last year's celebration of the fiftieth anniversary of Jackie Robinson's breaking
> the color line in major league baseball was one of the most pronounced and
> prolonged ever held in the history of our Republic in memory of a black man
> or of an athlete. It seems nearly obvious that, on one level, our preoccupation
> was not so much with Robinson himself—previous milestone anniversaries of
> his starting at first base for the Brooklyn Dodgers in April 1947 produced little
> fanfare—as it was with ourselves and our own dilemma about race, a problem
> that strikes us simultaneously as being intractable and "progressing" toward
> resolution; as a chronic, inevitably fatal disease and as a test of national char-
> acter that we will, finally, pass.[1]

He continues,

> If nothing else, Robinson, an unambiguous athletic hero for both races and
> symbol of sacrifice on the altar of racism, is our most magnificent case of
> affirmative action. He entered a lily-white industry amid cries that he was
> unqualified (not entirely unjustified, as Robinson had had only one year of
> professional experience in the Negro Leagues, although, on the other hand,
> he was one of the most gifted athletes of his generation), and he succeeded,
> on merit, beyond anyone's wildest hope. And here the sports metaphor is a
> perfectly literal expression of the traditional democratic belief of that day: If
> given the chance, anyone can make it on his ability, with no remedial aid or
> special compensation, on a level playing field. Here was the fulfillment of our
> American Creed, to use Gunnar Myrdal's term (*An American Dilemma* had

183

appeared only a year before Robinson was signed by the Dodgers), of fair play and equal opportunity. Here was our democratic orthodoxy of color-blind competition realized. Here was an instance where neither the principle nor its application could be impugned. Robinson was proof, just as heavyweight champion Joe Louis and Olympic track star Jesse Owens had been during the Depression, that sports helped vanquish the stigma of race.[2]

In the twenty-first century, Major League Baseball (whose acronym, MLB, has become its brand) and more specifically MLB Properties have embraced the legacy of Jackie Robinson. MLB celebrated the fiftieth anniversary of Robinson's Major League debut by declaring that his number, 42, would not be reissued and would ultimately be retired once the last of the current players who wear the number retires. Starting with Ken Griffey Jr.'s personal tribute to Robinson on what has come to be known as Jackie Robinson Day, MLB first allowed players to sport the number 42 on the field on April 15 and then in 2009 mandated that all players and on-field personnel do so. With this action, MLB basically attempted to erase the legacy of a half-century of segregation, simultaneously creating revenue-generating opportunities by licensing and selling jerseys, T-shirts, and other Robinson-branded souvenirs and memorabilia.

Irrespective of such commercial avenues, Robinson represented a true exemplar of W. E. B. Du Bois's Talented Tenth, and not just on the field of play. As if directly heeding Du Bois's call, Robinson attended UCLA, fulfilling the admonition to become educated as an equal within the mainstream. And his education—in the classroom, in the barracks, and more particularly on the field—afforded Robinson the opportunity to step up to the plate and ultimately succeed with the Dodgers.

Perhaps more significantly, after his playing days ended, Robinson's career provided him with a springboard into the American power structure, even though he would have been excluded under virtually any other circumstances. As a vice president and personnel director of Chock Full o'Nuts, a company with a considerable nonwhite workforce, Robinson continued to grow outside the narrow confines of the African American ecosystem, operating directly within the broader American economy. His full entry into the mainstream is best exemplified by his enthusiastic embrace of Richard Nixon and the Republican Party in the 1960s, much to the chagrin of those who looked on Nixon and his party as part of the problem. As Early writes,

Both the left and the right have used Jackie Robinson for their own ends. The left, suspicious of popular culture as a set of cheap commercial distractions constructed by the ruling class of postindustrial society to delude the masses, sees Robinson as a racial martyr, a working-class member of an oppressed minority who challenged the white hegemony as symbolized by sports as a political reification of superior, privileged expertise; the right, suspicious of popular culture as an expression of the rule of the infantile taste of the masses, sees him as a challenge to the idea of restricting talent pools and restricting markets to serve a dubious privilege. For the conservative today, Robinson is the *classic, fixed* example of affirmative action properly applied as the extension of opportunity to all, regardless of race, class, gender or outcome. For the liberal, Robinson is an example of the *process* of affirmative action as the erosion of white male hegemony, where outcome is the very point of the exercise.[3]

The fact that the whole of the political spectrum has attempted to claim Robinson as an iconic figure attests to his personal success in entering the mainstream, if only as a figurehead for progress.

If baseball's desegregation narrative had followed the feel-good course claimed by MLB's Robinson mythmakers—after April 15, 1947, African Americans entered that most American of sports, leading directly to the *Brown* decision, the Montgomery Bus Boycott, and equal rights for all—there would have been no lynching of Emmett Till, no assassination of Medgar Evers, no 16th Street Baptist Church bombing, and no other violence associated with the struggle for full enfranchisement of African Americans not just as consumer citizens but as American citizens. The reality of MLB's Robinson narrative is considerably uglier than the organization would have twenty-first-century fans believe. A dozen years passed between Robinson's debut and the desegregation of the last Major League team. And desegregation is not integration, which took still longer and is part of a much more complex discussion.

In a way, the pendulum did not swing to the other side until September 1, 1971, when, in Gus Greenlee and Cum Posey's hometown, the Pittsburgh Pirates became the first team to take the field with a lineup comprised entirely of players of color. Ironically, however, the victory by the team that would go on to win that year's World Series was preserved by a white reliever from Texas.[4] That several of those in the starting lineup that day, including Roberto Clemente, who was brought to Pittsburgh by Branch

Rickey, were Latino rather than African American is beside the point. To negate the fact that a proportion of Latinos with darker skin were excluded from the Major Leagues prior to 1947 under the same rationale as other players of color is to negate the work of Alex Pompez, who facilitated the flow of Latinos into the Major Leagues in his post–Negro League years. It is also to negate the intransigence of those who maintained MLB's pre-Robinson color line.

According to the Institute for Diversity and Ethics in Sports's annual "Racial and Gender Report Card," Major League Baseball's 2011 opening day player rosters were "61.5 percent white, 27 percent Latino, 2.1 percent Asian, 0.4 percent Native American or Native Alaskan, and 0.3 percent Native Hawaiian or Pacific Islander." The percentage of African American players dropped from 10 percent in the 2010 season to 8.5 percent a year later, the lowest since 2007 and the third-lowest in several decades. Although MLB may be defined as a racially diverse industry in terms of labor, this is not the case with ownership. As of 2011, Arturo Moreno of the American League's Anaheim franchise was the only person classified as an owner of color, and that classification may be disputed. While Moreno is certainly ethnically Latino, it is unlikely that by pre-Robinson MLB standards, he would have been labeled a Negro and thereby excluded. As was true of many Major League players prior to 1947, his ethnicity rather than his color marks him as different from his fellow billionaire owners.[5]

Using color alone as a yardstick, no Major League Baseball franchise had an African American owner until 2012, when basketball Hall of Famer Earvin "Magic" Johnson purchased a share of Robinson's former team, the Dodgers. Basketball preceded all American franchise sports when Michael Jordan became a minority owner as well as director of basketball operations of the Washington Wizards in 2000. As part of the purchase agreement, he also bought a minority stake in Washington's National Hockey League franchise, the Capitals. But majority ownership of a major American sports franchise proved elusive to a person of color until 2002, when Robert L. Johnson of Black Entertainment Television (BET) was awarded the majority share of the expansion Carolina Bobcats, which began play in 2004. From the outset, Johnson was flanked by Jordan, who held a minority stake in the Carolina franchise after he was publicly and unceremoniously dumped by Wizards/Capitals owner Abe Pollin. Then in 2010, Jordan headed a group that purchased a majority stake in the Charlotte team from Johnson.[6]

By all measures, BET's Johnson was one of the most successful American entrepreneurs of his generation, regardless of color. But his success in the entertainment business as an African American was not without precedent. Well before African Americans became successful owners of mainstream sports franchises or television networks, a group of young black entrepreneurs showed what could be done in the music business. Following the lead of Gladys Hampton and indirectly Harry Pace as well as the Ferguson brothers, Chicago's Vee-Jay Records and Detroit's Motown family of labels were black-owned enterprises built in the spirit of John H. Johnson's publishing empire. In fact, Vee-Jay and Motown moved beyond Johnson Publishing's model by producing high-quality products that appealed not only to the race but also to a broad spectrum of young people worldwide.

Neither of these enterprises emerged in a vacuum. Vee-Jay, founded in the early 1950s, worked from virtually the same script as other small, independent labels—specifically, white-owned Chess Records in Chicago and Atlantic Records in New York, which was founded by a pair of Turkish immigrant brothers. And Motown had Vee-Jay and the other ventures as a ready-made template for success. Leonard and Phil Chess and Atlantic's Ahmet and Nesuhi Ertegun drew the blueprint for the way in which independent, niche labels could crack the larger marketplace, an approach Vee-Jay's Vivian Carter and her husband, Jimmy Bracken, aided by visionary company stalwart Ewart Abner, embraced wholeheartedly.[7]

Though Vee-Jay initially found success with its blues and jazz catalogs, it branched out by hiring white promoters as well as talent scouts and developers to uncover new artists around the country in various popular genres that moved the label away from the traditional expectations of a black record company. Vee-Jay not only signed the Four Seasons as well as various country and western and folk acts but was also the first American label to hold exclusive rights to the Beatles, though Vee-Jay lost those rights in a lawsuit, one of several factors that ultimately led to the company's liquidation in 1966.[8] Regardless of the unfortunate outcome, Vee-Jay's aspirations ran as high or even higher than Gladys Hampton's efforts to create a full-service label beginning in the late 1940s. Vee-Jay embodied the admonitions to black-owned enterprises made by Horace Sudduth, president of the National Negro Business League, in the 1950s: To make a real impact, black-owned business had to compete outside the ecosystem, on equal footing with other businesses, by appealing to consumers regardless of color or ethnicity.[9]

Berry Gordy Jr.'s Motown venture built on Vee-Jay's vision for a black-owned and -operated record label and ultimately moved in a different direction. Whereas Vee-Jay consciously ignored the color of its artists and the racial connotations of its products as long as the talent could generate income, Gordy sought to retain the culturally specific nature of his largely African American catalog while ensuring that his acts were palatable to an increasingly mainstream youth market.[10] In this regard, he synthesized the seemingly antithetical concepts behind the Du Bois–Washington divide. Motown successfully bridged this divide by offering the sounds of black America to the youth market writ large, essentially making sure that his artists were unthreatening to white audiences and to white retailers. By sending his artists to charm school and insisting on etiquette training, Gordy created an operation that fit squarely within the parameters of Washingtonian ideals as exemplified by the theories that informed his Tuskegee Institute. At the same time, by taking a place among white entrepreneurs in the broader marketplace and permitting artists to express a social conscience, Gordy embraced the Du Boisian notion that economic gain without a political foundation was a hollow experience antithetical to progress.

Motown also took vertical integration to a whole new level. Gordy's Hitsville, USA was run almost like a factory. From within its walls, Gordy controlled virtually every aspect of the music-making process from songwriting and publishing to promotion and distribution; like the larger labels, Motown featured a house band for the purposes of quality control.[11] Taken together, Motown and Vee-Jay represent the modernization of the notion of race business, setting the stage for other independent, black-owned labels such as Death Row. Moreover, by getting into the film production and distribution business in the 1970s, releasing, among other films, *Lady Sings the Blues* (1972) and *The Bingo Long Traveling All-Stars and Motor Kings* (1976) both of which featured former Chitlin' Circuit comedian Richard Pryor in some of his earliest screen roles, Motown diversified.

In 1983, in what would generally be considered the denouement of an American success story, Motown was acquired by MCA Universal, which also purchased the Chess catalog as well as those of a host of other small and midsized labels. Consequently, Motown is no longer a black-owned enterprise. In that respect, it is linked to the BET network, which Robert Johnson sold to Viacom for three billion dollars in 2001.[12] But while Motown and BET are now owned by large, multinational corporations, John H. Johnson's publishing empire, producers of *Ebony* and *Jet* as well as Fashion Fair cosmetics, remains ostensibly family operated, though J. P. Morgan Chase became an equity partner in the firm in 2012.[13]

In perhaps a final twist of fate, Abe Saperstein's Harlem Globetrotters remain a fixture on the American entertainment circuit, often playing to fully integrated audiences in large, mainstream venues such as New York's Madison Square Garden and Chicago's United Center. Indeed, Saturday morning cartoons and a guest appearance on the popular television sit-com *Gilligan's Island*, preserved in perpetuity through reruns, introduced new generations to the Globetrotters in the 1960s, 1970s and 1980s.

In 2003, former player Mannie Jackson purchased the Globetrotters and moved the team's offices from Chicago, where they had always been located, to their namesake Harlem. Following the lead of Berry Gordy and Robert Johnson, however, Jackson sold 80 percent of his business to a large corporation, Shamrock Holdings, an investment fund operated by Roy Disney. Shamrock also purchased the perennial Globetrotter foils, the Washington Generals, which began life as booking agent and Negro League owner Ed Gottlieb's all-white SPHAs, named for the South Phila-delphia Hebrew Association. Jackson, retaining 20 percent of the venture, remains the public face of the Harlem Globetrotters, making them a black sports and entertainment venture with a global reach.

On the surface, Jackson's Globetrotters remain a black business, an increasingly visible image of black entrepreneurship built for the twenty-first century. But under the surface, the story is far more complicated. In some ways, the Globetrotters' narrative resembles that of Negro League baseball. Both were products of segregation and the demand for race-based entertainment. And both were products of a narrowly conceived ecosystem. But while the team that Saperstein founded has been rescued from insolvency and transformed into a financially viable corporate entity with strong mainstream backing and a multihued international fan base, no such fate awaited the Negro Leagues. They, like the economy that pro-duced them and other race businesses, depended largely on the segregated dollar. Thus, Negro League baseball as designed had no future.

ACKNOWLEDGMENTS

Project Origins

This project resulted from a chance meeting at the 2005 Cooperstown Symposium on Baseball and American Culture at the National Baseball Hall of Fame and Museum. On the sidelines, while watching a rousing game of town ball, we first broached the subject of entangling our complementary interests in baseball and African American life, the culture that gave birth to it, and what resulted. In discussing these matters in greater detail over the next few years, we realized that there was a gap in the literature needing to be closed, particularly in terms of the way Negro League baseball functioned in the context of the larger American economy. While volumes of excellent work had already been done on segregated sport both as pastime and as cultural institution, little had been written about the socioeconomic impact of segregated baseball and its relationship to urban African America writ large.

Our ongoing discussions kept returning to the contention that the aftermath of the Jackie Robinson moment was unproblematic, a matter that we debated at our second encounter at the annual *NINE* conference in Tucson the following spring. In fact, the original working title of this project (and there have been many!) was *After Jackie*, but ESPN had already claimed it for a celebratory volume dealing rather uncritically with Robinson's impact on American culture and the game. It became increasingly clear that our work was never going to center on Robinson or on the years following his ascent to the Major Leagues in 1947. And because the Robinson story and its reverberations had already been told so many times that it had entered the realm of myth and hagiography, we soon discovered that to fully flesh out baseball's desegregation narrative, we would need to leave Robinson behind, at least to some extent. We quickly recognized that our challenge was to look beyond the lines of the game and its mythology, focusing instead on the relationship between the segregated sport and the various communities that supported it from its turn-of-the-twentieth-century origins. We increasingly shifted our focus to the business and cultural institutions that provided black baseball with its economic underpinnings and that it in turn supported. Yet we continued to return to the same question: What happened economically in black America when the stars of the segregated sport were lured to the white game? What we found was a thread of inquiry that wove through a complex tapestry of American life from the onset of the Great Migration through the late 1950s.

When we finally committed to the project a year later, we spent a week on a beach near Rincón, Puerto Rico, fueled alternately by local coffee and a potent concoction made of dark rum and the meat of mangos gathered from the roadside. We thus thank the men and women of Yauco's coffee plantations and the anonymous people of the west end of the island who had the foresight to plant all those trees, keeping us liquid while we pondered the liquidity of the Negro Leagues. Appropriately hydrated, we immersed ourselves in the subject matter, finally putting our far-flung and admittedly overly ambitious thoughts on paper. Five years later, fittingly, we celebrated the project's conclusion at the 2012 American Studies Conference in San Juan, bringing our collaboration full circle.

A Note on Methodology

As we moved closer to the writing stage, following years of extensive research conducted both individually and together, we realized that the conventional means of collaboration—dividing the chapters between us and subsequently editing each other's work—could not produce the single narrative voice we sought. We thus faced a logistical challenge: How could we shorten the distance between Brooklyn and Allentown, not to mention individual forays as far afield as Nevada, Texas, Minnesota, Alabama, and even China and West Africa, without enriching the coffers of oil companies and highway authorities more than was absolutely necessary?

Here, technology was our friend. Skype and Google Docs enabled us to work as if we were in the same room. We were further aided by frequent sessions at the microfilm reader and by such effective research tools as Proquest Historical Newspapers, Newspaper Archives, and Google Scholar, to name but a few. Our reliance on the proper functioning of the information superhighway posed its own set of problems—occasionally sketchy internet connectivity, the odd power outage, and unfortunate bouts of equipment failure. Nevertheless, we pushed through, averaging between four and eight hours a day with our voices in each other's heads. Perhaps this is how we ended up finishing each other's sentences by the end of our run. It is also how we came to discover that almost anything we had to say apart from our actual writing could be summed up simply by quoting baseball's preeminent cultural text, *Bull Durham.* For this, we acknowledge Ron Shelton and his cast and crew.

In Gratitude

A work such as this never happens in a vacuum. Indeed, the list of those who helped us bring this project to fruition is extensive.

First, we express our heartfelt appreciation to Monte Irvin, who addressed all of our questions with a smile on his face, and Earl Smith, who read every word of the manuscript from start to finish. Certainly worthy of equally special mention are Jean Hastings Ardell and Dan Ardell for introducing us to each other in between their at-bats at the town ball game in Cooperstown. We also thank the men and women who organize and participate annually in the Cooperstown Symposium, specifically Tim Wiles, Jim Gates, and Bill Simons; the annual participants and organizers of the *NINE* Spring Training Conference, in particular Trey Strecker, Geri Strecker, and the late, great Bill Kirwin; the editors and publishers of *NINE: A Journal of Baseball History and Culture*; Elizabeth A. Parsels, who provided tireless research assistance; Moravian College's SOAR program, which gave generous financial assistance; the Youseloff Foundation of the Society for Baseball Research, which provided seed money; New York University's Liberal Studies Program, most notably Dean Fred Schwarzbach and the various grant committees that provided time and funding for this project as well as the precious gift of time to write; Ray Doswell, curator of the Negro Leagues Baseball Museum in Kansas City, Missouri; the participants in the 2011 Jerry Malloy Negro Leagues Conference in Indianapolis; the staff at the National Baseball Library and Giamatti Research Center in Cooperstown, New York, at the Newark Public Library's New Jersey Room, at the Moorland-Spingarn Research Center at Howard University, and at the Kenneth Spencer Research Library at the University of Kansas; Neil Lanctot, whose painstakingly detailed work was invaluable to this project; Arlene Kutner Newman, for her sociological insight; and Mark S. Gutentag, for his care and legal counsel.

We also thank the following individuals (in no particular order) for their support and encouragement: Ed Grupsmith, Evan Grupsmith, Marya Fisher, Clark Fisher, Mauri Newman, James and Cathy Newman, Gabriele L. Gutentag, Stanley and Ida Rosen, Jerry and Lillie Weissman, David and Marcie Weissman, Craig and Pat Gordon, Pam Irvin Fields, Lisa Doris Alexander, James E. Brunson III, David C. Ogden, Bruce Markusen, Rebecca Alpert, Steve Gietscher, John Thorn, James Overmyer, Larry Hogan, Adrian Burgos Jr., Leslie Heaphy, Larry Lester, Herb Douglass, Bill White, Mal Whitfield, Debra Wetcher-Hendricks, Lori L. Boyle, Debbi Gaspar, Nancy Strobel, Davarian Baldwin, Thabiti Lewis, Rusty and Kris Torres, Alberto Ramos Sr., Helen Churko, Ellen Price, Emily Bauman, George Gmelch, Daniel Nathan, Maureen M. Smith, Peter Fogo, James F. Payne, Jack Lule, Lee Lowenfish, Larry Gerlach, Dick Crepeau, Gary Mitchem, Stephanie Fleet Licio, and Claudette Raines.

And lastly, we are profoundly grateful to Craig Gill, Anne Stascavage, Katie Keene, Ellen Goldlust, and the entire staff at the University Press of Mississippi. From start to finish, they have ably shepherded this project through to its happy conclusion.

—Roberta J. Newman and Joel Nathan Rosen

NOTES

Chapter 1

1. Ivan Light and Stephen J. Gold, *Ethnic Economies* (San Diego: Academic, 2000), 188.

2. Ibid., 4.

3. Ibid., 15.

4. Joel Nathan Rosen, *From New Lanark to Mound Bayou: Owenism in the Mississippi Delta* (Durham, N.C.: Carolina Academic Press, 2011).

5. "Black Businesses: They Began before the Revolution," *Ebony*, August 1975, 117.

6. Juliet E. K. Walker, *The History of Black Business in America: Capitalism, Race, Entrepreneurship* (New York: Macmillan, 1998), 109.

7. Isabel Wilkerson, *The Warmth of Other Suns: The Epic Story of America's Great Migration* (New York: Vintage, 2011), 9.

8. Ibid., 11.

9. Ibid., 9.

10. *The Black Press: Soldiers without Swords*, directed by Stanley Nelson, PBS, transcript, accessed July 18, 2012, http://www.pbs.org/blackpress/film/fulltranscript .html.

11. Robert Abbott, "Advice to Migrants," *Chicago Defender*, May 9, 1925, 4.

12. "Take Heed and Make Good at Your Work," *Chicago Defender*, August 19, 1916, 8.

13. Jack, "Railroad Rumblings by Jack," *Chicago Defender*, October 30, 1915, 5.

14. Ibid., November 6, 1915, 5.

15. Adam McKible, "Our Country," in *The Black Press: New Literary and Historical Essays*, ed. Todd Vogel (New Brunswick, N.J.: Rutgers University Press, 2001), 126.

16. Robert W. Bagnall, "Michigan—The Land of Many Waters," in *These "Colored" United States: African American Essays from the 1920s*, ed. Tom Lutz and Suzanna Ashton (New Brunswick, N.J.: Rutgers University Press, 1996), 16.

17. Robert Abbott, "Advice to Migrants," 4.

18. Catherine Silva, "Racial Restrictive Covenants: Enforcing Neighborhood Segregation in Seattle," *Seattle Civil Rights and Labor History Project*, accessed February 16, 2012, http://depts.washington.edu/civilr/covenants_report.htm#_edn3.

19. Dominic A. Pacyga, *Chicago: A Biography* (Chicago: University of Chicago Press, 2010), 207.

20. Ibid., 106.

21. Juliet E. K. Walker, *History of Black Business*, 199.

22. Jessie Carney Smith, ed., *Encyclopedia of African American Businesses: K–Z* (Westport, Conn.: Greenwood, 2006), 651.

23. Light and Gold, *Ethnic Economies*, 185.

24. St. Clair Drake and Horace R. Cayton, *Black Metropolis: A Study of Negro Life in a Northern City* (Chicago: University of Chicago Press, 1945), 198.

25. Light and Gold, *Ethnic Economies*, 186.

26. Neil Lanctot, *Negro League Baseball: The Rise and Ruin of a Black Institution* (Philadelphia: University of Pennsylvania Press, 2004), 4.

27. Adam Green, *Selling the Race: Culture, Community, and Black Chicago, 1940–1945* (Chicago: University of Chicago Press, 2007), 96.

28. This term represents culturally contextual economic activity. It first came into use during the 1990s after its introduction into the popular lexicon by FUBU, a clothing manufacturer that targeted young African American consumers.

29. Juliet E. K. Walker, *History of Black Business*, 193.

30. Sol White, *Sol White's History of Colored Base Ball, with Other Documents on the Early Black Game, 1886–1936* (Lincoln: University of Nebraska Press, 1995), 7.

31. Roberta Newman, "Pitching behind the Color Line: Baseball, Advertising, and Race," *Baseball Research Journal* 8, no. 36 (2007): 81–90.

32. Jerry Malloy, "The Birth of the Cuban Giants: The Origins of Black Professional Baseball," in *Out of the Shadows: African American Baseball from the Cuban Giants to Jackie Robinson*, ed. Bill Kirwin (Lincoln: University of Nebraska Press, 2005), 5–6.

33. Newman, "Pitching behind the Color Line," 82.

34. "Barnstormers," U.S. Centennial of Flight Commission, accessed June 3, 2013, http://webarchive.library.unt.edu/eot2008/20080916072334/http://centennialofflight.gov/essay_cat/12.htm.

35. Manning Marable, *Malcolm X: A Life of Reinvention* (New York: Viking, 2011), Kindle edition, chapter 1.

36. Booker T. Washington, "The Atlanta Compromise," in *Ripples of Hope: Great American Civil Rights Speeches*, ed. Josh Gottheimer (Cambridge, Mass.: Civitas, 2003), 129–31.

37. "Plessy v. Ferguson, 163 U.S. 537 (1896)," Find Law, accessed February 20, 2012, http://caselaw.lp.findlaw.com/scripts/getcase.pl?court=us&vol=163&invol=537.

38. National Negro Business League, *Proceedings of the National Negro Business League: Its First Meeting, Held in Boston, Massachusetts, August 23 and 24, 1900* (Boston: Hamm, 1901), 1.

39. W. E. B. Du Bois, *The Souls of Black Folk* (1903; Rockville, Md.: Arc Manor, 2008), 41.

40. Ibid., 41.

41. Ibid., 42.

42. Ibid., 44.

43. Marable, *Malcolm X*, chapter 1.

44. Alain Locke, "Enter the New Negro," *Survey Graphic* 6, no. 6 (1925): 662–63.

45. Gerald Early, "The New Negro Era and the Great African American Association," *American Studies* 48, no. 4 (2007): 14.

46. Joel Nathan Rosen, *The Erosion of the American Sporting Ethos: Shifting Attitudes toward Competition*, (Jefferson, N.C.: McFarland, 2007), 84–87.

47. E. Franklin Frazier, "Human, All Too Human: The Negro's Vested Interest in Segregation," *Survey Graphic* 36, no. 1 (1947): 100.

Chapter 2

1. "Baseball Magnates Hold Conference," *Chicago Defender*, February 4, 1920, 11.

2. "Bolden Made Chairman of Eastern Colored Baseball League," *New York Amsterdam News*, March 7, 1923, 4.

3. Charles S. Johnson, "Illinois: Mecca of the Migrant Mob," in *These "Colored" United* States, ed. Lutz and Ashton, 111.

4. Ibid., 113.

5. "Historical Census Browser, Illinois, Cook County," accessed February 27, 2012, http://mapserver.lib.virginia.edu/php/county.php.

6. Charles S. Johnson, "Illinois," 112.

7. Drake and Cayton, *Black Metropolis*, 78–79.

8. Charles S. Johnson, "Illinois," 112.

9. James A. Merone, *Hellfire Nation: The Politics of Sin in America* (New Haven: Yale University Press, 2004), 271.

10. Karen Abbott, *Sin in the Second City: Madams, Ministers, Playboys, and the Battle for America's Soul* (New York: Random House, 2008), 58.

11. Ron Chepesiuk, *Black Gangsters of Chicago* (Fort Lee, N.J.: Barricade, 2007), 9.

12. Ibid., 7.

13. Ivan Light, "Numbers Gambling among Blacks: A Financial Institution," *American Sociological Review* 42, no. 6 (1977): 894.

14. Juliet E. K. Walker, *History of Black Business*, 238.

15. "Games on the 'Levee' Wide Open," *Chicago Tribune*, June 18, 1897, 2.

16. "Games Go Gaily On," *Chicago Tribune*, July 31, 1897, 1.

17. Davarian L. Baldwin, *Chicago's New Negroes* (Chapel Hill: University of North Carolina Press, 2007), 46. Baldwin asserts that the nickname "Mushmouth" resulted from Johnson's liberal use of profanity.

18. William Howland Kenney, *Chicago Jazz: A Cultural History, 1904–1930* (New York: Oxford University Press, 1994), 17.

19. "Binga-Johnson Wedding the Most Brilliant Ever Held in Chicago," *Chicago Defender*, February 24, 1912, 1.

20. Beth Johnson, "Binga Bank and the Development of the Black Metropolis," in *Racial Structure and Radical Politics in the African Diaspora*, ed. James L. Conyers Jr. (New Brunswick, N.J.: Transaction, 2009), 2–3.

21. Ibid., 4.

22. "Negro Banks and Where Located," *Chicago Defender*, September 3, 1910, 1.

23. Cynthia M. Blair, *I've Got to Make My Livin': Black Women's Sex Work in Turn-of-the-Century Chicago* (Chicago: University of Chicago Press, 2010), 24.

24. Ibid., 24.

25. Paul Oliver, *The Story of the Blues* (Boston: Northeastern University Press, 1997), 81.

26. "Patronize Worthy Race Enterprises Along 'the Stroll,'" *Chicago Defender*, May 8, 1915, 4.

27. Blair, *I've Got to Make My Livin'*, 170.

28. Chepesiuk, *Black Gangsters*, 21.

29. "Citizens to Banquet the American Giants," *Chicago Defender*, April 24, 1915, 7.

30. Chicago Commission on Race Relations, *The Negro in Chicago : A Study of Race Relations and a Race Riot* (Chicago: University of Chicago Press, 1922), 192.

31. Robert C. Puth, "Supreme Life: The History of a Negro Life Insurance Company, 1919–1962," *Business History Review* 43, no. 1 (1969): 3; internal citations omitted.

32. Drake and Cayton, *Black Metropolis*, 608.

33. Q. C. Gilmore, "The Negro in Baseball, Part II," *Kansas City Call*, February 1, 1924, 6.

34. Charles E. Coulter, *Take Up the Black Man's Burden: Kansas City's African American Communities, 1865–1939* (Columbia: University of Missouri Press, 2006), 62.

35. Ibid., 24; Kenneth Marvin Hamilton. *Black Towns and Profit: Promotion and Development in the Trans-Appalachian West, 1877–1915* (Urbana: University of Illinois Press, 1991).

36. "Meat Packing Gave City Large Industry," *Kansas City Kansan*, November 24, 1985, 2A, accessed July 10, 2012, http://www.kckpl.lib.ks.us/documents/meatpacking .pdf; Kevin Hillstrom and Laurie Collier Hillstrom, eds., *The Industrial Revolution in America: Communication, Agriculture, and Meatpacking, Overview/Comparison* (Santa Barbara, Calif.: ABC/Clio, 2007), 184.

37. Coulter, *Take Up the Black Man's Burden*, 68.

38 "Meat Packing Gave City Large Industry."

39. Asa Earl Martin, *Our Negro Population: A Sociological Study of the Negroes of Kansas City* (Kansas City, Mo.: Hudson, 1913), 43.

40. Coulter, *Take Up the Black Man's Burden*, 99.

41. Sherry Lamb Schirmer, *A City Divided: The Racial Landscape of Kansas City, 1900–1960* (Columbia: University of Missouri Press, 2002), 168.

42. Coulter, *Take Up the Black Man's Burden*, 114.

43. Schirmer, *City Divided*, 169.

44. Lyle W. Dorset, "Kansas City Politics: A Study of Boss Pendergast's Machine," *Journal of the Southwest* 8, no. 2 (1966): 111.

45. "Julius Rosenwald and the Negro," *The Crisis*, September 1921, 203.

46. "Plan to Entertain League," *Chicago Defender*, February 6, 1920, 11.

47. "Defender Editor Speaks," *Chicago Defender*, February 21, 1920, 16.

48. "Many Democrats in Western Cities," *Baltimore Afro-American*, June 15, 1912, 3.

49. Ralph W. Tyler, "Race Thrift in an Indiana City," *Baltimore Afro-American*, January 31, 1914, 3.

50. "Historical Census Browser, Indiana, Marion County, 1900, 1920," accessed March 15, 2012, http://mapserver.lib.virginia.edu/php/county.php; Emma Lou Thornborough, *Indiana Blacks in the Twentieth Century* (Bloomington: Indiana University Press, 2000), 36.

51. Tyler, "Race Thrift," 3.

52. Stanley Warren, "The Monster Meetings at the Negro YMCA in Indianapolis," *Indiana Magazine of History* 91, no. 1 (1995): 58.

53. Adia Harvey Wingfield, *Doing Business with Beauty: Black Women, Hair Salons, and the Racial Enclave Economy* (Lanham, Md.: Rowman and Littlefield, 2008), 33.

54. "History and Education, Madame Walker Theatre Center," accessed July 10, 2012, http://www.walkertheatre.com/history-education.

55. Bob Ostrander and Derrick Morris, *Hoosier Beer: Tapping into Indiana Brewing History* (Charleston, S.C.: History Press, 2011), 121.

56. Ibid., 122.

57. Michael E. Lomax, "Black Entrepreneurship in the National Pastime: The Rise of Semiprofessional Baseball in Black Chicago, 1890–1915," *Journal of Sport History* 25, no. 1 (1998): 51.

58. Neil Lanctot, *Fair Dealing and Clean Playing: The Hilldale Club and the Development of Black Professional Baseball, 1910–1932* (Syracuse, N.Y.: Syracuse University Press, 1994), 38.

59. Ibid., 73.

60. Frank A. "Fay" Young, "Sport Editorial: A Case of Good Judgment," *Chicago Defender*, February 12, 1921, 6.

61. Detroit African-American History Project, Wayne State University, accessed July 10, 2012, http://www.daahp.wayne.edu/1900_1949.html.

62. Bagnall, "Michigan," 161.

63. Walter F. White, "Success of Negro Migration," *The Crisis*, January 1920, 113.

64. Elizabeth Anne Martin, "Detroit and the Great Migration, 1916–1929," Bentley Historical Library, University of Michigan, accessed March 16, 2012, http://bentley.umich.edu/research/publications/migration/ch1.php.

65. Paul Finkelman, *Encyclopedia of African American History, 1896 to the Present* (New York: Oxford University Press, 2009), 56.

66. Richard Bak, *Turkey Stearnes and the Detroit Stars: The Negro Leagues in Detroit, 1919–1933* (Detroit: Wayne State University Press, 1994), 57–59, 179.

67. "Tenney Blount in Town," *Chicago Defender*, April 23, 1921, 11.

68. Bak, *Turkey Stearnes*, 57; internal citations omitted.

69. "Big Baseball Scandal Grows," *Pittsburgh Courier*, December 27, 1924, 1.

70. Lanctot, *Fair Dealing and Clean Playing*, 91.

71. Ibid., 91.

72. Robert Peterson, *Only the Ball Was White: A History of Legendary Black Players and All-Black Professional Teams* (New York: Oxford University Press, 1992), 86.

73. Lanctot, *Fair Dealing and Clean Playing*, 93.

74. W. E. B. Du Bois, Elijah Anderson, and Isabel Eaton, *The Philadelphia Negro: A Social Study* (Philadelphia: University of Pennsylvania Press, 1899), 5.

75. "Historical Census Browser, Pennsylvania, Philadelphia County," accessed February 21, 2021, http://mapserver.lib.virginia.edu/php/county.php.

76. Ibid.

77. Robert Gregg, *Sparks from the Anvil of Oppression: Philadelphia's African Methodists and Southern Migrants, 1890–1940* (Philadelphia: Temple University Press, 1998), 25.

78. Lanctot, *Fair Dealing and Clean Playing*, 43.

79. Gregg, *Sparks from the Anvil of Oppression*, 29.

80. Lanctot, *Fair Dealing and Clean Playing*, 50.

81. W. Rollo Wilson, "Brown and Stevens Have Pioneer Bank of North," *Pittsburgh Courier*, October 6, 1923, 1.

82. Abram Lincoln Harris, *The Negro as Capitalist: A Study of Banking and Business among American Negroes* (New York: Ardent Media, 1936), 130.

83. Ibid., 143.

84. Ibid., 130.

85. "Dunbar Theater Sold," *Baltimore Afro-American*, September 5, 1921, 8.

86. "T.O.B.A. Doings," *Chicago Defender*, June 25, 1921, 7.

87. Neil Lanctot, "Fair Dealing and Clean Playing: Ed Bolden and the Hilldale Club, 1910–1932," *Pennsylvania Magazine of History and Biography* 117, nos. 1–2 (1993): 21.

88. Lanctot, *Fair Dealing and Clean Playing*, 66.

89. Lanctot, "Fair Dealing and Clean Playing," 21.

90. Du Bois, *Souls of Black Folk*, 73.

91. "Ed Bolden Explains Dallas Selection," *Baltimore Afro-American*, April 11, 1924, 7.

92. Rebecca T. Alpert, *Out of Left Field: Jews and Black Baseball* (New York: Oxford University Press, 2011), 11.

93. Jules Tygiel, "Unreconciled Strivings: Baseball and Jim Crow America," in *The American Game: Baseball and Ethnicity*, ed. Lawrence Baldassero and Richard A. Johnson (Carbondale: Southern Illinois University Press, 2002), 82.

94. Sol White, *Sol White's History*, 79.

95. "To Break Nat Strong in Baseball: Hebrew Said to Control One Hundred and Fifty Amusement Parks and Hundreds of Colored Ball Players," *Baltimore Afro-American*, February 11, 1921, 7; *The Black Press: Soldiers without Swords*).

96. William I. Thomas, "The Definition of the Situation," in *Self, Symbols, and Society: Classic Readings in Social Psychology*, ed. Nathan Rousseau (Lanham, Md.: Rowman and Littlefield, 2002), 103–15.

97. Light and Gold, *Ethnic Economies*, 6.

98. Marcy S. Sacks, *Before Harlem: The Black Experience in New York City before World War I* (Philadelphia: University of Pennsylvania Press, 2006), 66.

99. Harry D. Wintz and Paul Finkelman, *Encyclopedia of the Harlem Renaissance* (New York: Routledge, 2004), 2:884–85.

100. Juliet E. K. Walker, *History of Black Business*, 199.

101. "Historical Census Browser, New York, New York County," accessed March 22, 2012, http://mapserver.lib.virginia.edu/php/county.php.

102. E. Franklin Frazier, *The Black Bourgeoisie* (1957; New York: Free Press, 1997).

103. "N.Y.'s Elite Open Urban League Drive," *Baltimore Afro-American*, May 26, 1926, 14.

104. H. Binga Dismond, "New York Society," *Pittsburgh Courier*, February 6, 1926, 6.

105. Ron Chepesiuk, *Gangsters of Harlem: The Gritty Underworld of New York's Most Famous Neighborhood* (Fort Lee, N.J.: Barricade, 2007), 21–36.

106. Jitu K. Weusi, "The Rise and Fall of Black Swan Records," *Red Hot Jazz Archive*, accessed February 29, 2012, http://www.redhotjazz.com/blackswan.html.

107. Puth, "Supreme Life," 8–9.

108. Weusi, "Rise and Fall"; Marybeth Hamilton, *In Search of the Blues* (New York: Basic Books, 2008), 9, 13.

109. Lester Walton, "Race's Failure to Enter Trade Seen as Mistake," *Pittsburgh Courier*, September 16, 1924, 4.

110. Colin Grant, *Negro with a Hat: The Rise and Fall of Marcus Garvey* (New York: Oxford University Press, 2008), 89.

111. Ibid., 235.

112. "The Sportive Spotlight," *New York Amsterdam News*, June 23, 1926, 4.

113. Adrian Burgos Jr., *Cuban Star: How One Negro-League Owner Changed the Face of Baseball* (New York: Hill and Wang, 2011), 34.

114. Ibid., 35.

115. Ibid., 21.

116. Ibid., 31.

117. Lanctot, *Negro League Baseball*, 60.

118. "1924 World Series," *Baseball Reference*, accessed March 31, 2012, http://www.baseball-reference.com/bullpen/1924_Negro_World_Series.

119. Lanctot, *Negro League Baseball*, 36.

120. A. D. Williams, "Behind the Curtain of Negro Baseball: Some Facts of the 'Ups and Downs' of the Game the Past Seven Years, and Why the Game Hit the Skids in the West," *Kansas City Call*, December 16, 1927, A4.

121. Paul Debono, *The Indianapolis ABCs: History of a Premier Team in the Negro Leagues* (Jefferson, N.C.: McFarland, 1997), 3.

122. "Rube Foster, Baseball Magnate, in Sanitarium," *Chicago Defender*, September 4, 1926, 1.

123. Peterson, *Only the Ball Was White*, 114.

124. Ibid., 113.

125. "Ballpark Fire Injures 100," *Chicago Defender*, July 13, 2012, 1.

126. Bak, *Turkey Stearnes*, 186.

127. "Fans Plan Boycott of Detroit Park," *Baltimore Afro-American*, September 2, 1930, A14.

128. Raymond Drake, "Negro Baseball Needs Shakeup, Opines Fan," *Pittsburgh Courier*, June 8, 1929, 17.

129. "Better Service," *Pittsburgh Courier*, September 7, 1929, 12.

130. John Kenneth Galbraith, *The Great Crash: 1929* (New York: Houghton Mifflin, 1997), 6.

131. Ibid., 9.

132. Juliet E. K. Walker, *History of Black Business*, 182.

133. "Failures in Negro Business," *Pittsburgh Courier*, January 21, 1928, A8.

134. Kelly Miller, "Failure of Negro Leaders," *New York Amsterdam News*, December 17, 1930, 20.

Chapter 3

1. Galbraith, *Great Crash*, 88.

2. Ibid., 108.

3. Ibid., 90.

4. Daniel Roland Fusfeld and Timothy Mason Bates, *The Political Economy of the Urban Ghetto* (Carbondale: Southern Illinois University Press, 1984), 38.

5. "The 1930s: The Great Depression," *New Jersey Information Digital Collections*, Unit 11, accessed April 3, 2012, http://slic.njstatelib.org/NJ_Information/Digital_Collections/AAHCG/unit11.html.

6. Joe William Trotter, introduction to *The Great Migration in Historical Perspective: New Dimensions of Race, Class, and Gender*, ed. Trotter (Bloomington: Indiana University Press, 1991), 10.

7. Drake and Cayton, *Black Metropolis*, 608.

8. Light, "Numbers Gambling among Blacks," 896.

9. Juliet E. K. Walker, *History of Black Business*, 236.

10. Drake and Cayton, *Black Metropolis*, 486.

11. Ibid., 483–44.

12. Ibid., 474.

13. *Pittsburgh Courier*, September 25, 1937, 18.

14. Ibid., November 18, 1933, A7.

15. Light and Gold, *Ethnic Economies*, 72.

16. Larry Tye, *Satchel: The Life and Times of an American Legend* (New York: Random House, 2010), 36.

17. "Gus Greenlee," *Pittsburgh Music History Home Page*, accessed April 4, 2012, http://sites.google.com/site/pittsburghmusichistory/pittsburgh-music-story/managers-and-promoters/gus-greenlee.

18. Burgos, *Cuban Star*, 43.

19. John N. Ingram and Lynne B. Feldman, *African-American Business Leaders: A Biographical Dictionary* (Westport, Conn.: Greenwood, 1994), 299.

20. "Head New Booking Agency," *Pittsburgh Courier*, November 28, 1925, 2.

21. "Appearing at Re-Opening of Paramount Inn," *Pittsburgh Courier*, May 22, 1926, 8.

22. *Pittsburgh Courier*, August 23, 1930, 9.

23. I.F., "Greenlee Is Lauded by Uptowner," *Pittsburgh Courier*, September 7, 1929, 9.

24. "Arrests Made in Lottery Raid," *Pittsburgh Courier*, July 13, 1929, 8.

25. Laurence Glasco, "Double Burden: The Black Experience in Pittsburgh," in *City at the Point: Essays on the Social History of Pittsburgh*, ed. Samuel P. Hays (Pittsburgh: University of Pittsburgh Press, 1989), 70.

26. Ibid., 70.

27. Juliet E. K. Walker, *History of Black Business*, 182–83.

28. Rob Ruck, *Raceball: How the Major Leagues Colonized the Black and Latino Game* (Boston: Beacon, 2011), 17–18.

29. "Crawfords Set Lively Pace in Local Industrial Loop," *Pittsburgh Courier*, July 2, 1927, A4.

30. Ruck, *Raceball*, 152–53.

31. Thomas Harding, "Crawfords Called Best Money Could Buy: Team of 1935 Ranks Second in History of Black Baseball," *mlb.com*, accessed April 5, 2012, http://mlb.mlb.com/news/article.jsp?ymd=20070219&content_id=1807855&vkey=news_mlb&fext=.jsp&c_id=mlb.

32. Ingram and Feldman, *African-American Business Leaders*, 293.

33. "'Cum' Posey, Manager of Homestead Grays, and League Bosses, Agree to Disagree as Sequel to Hard Fought Battle of Wits," *Pittsburgh Courier*, January 16, 1926, 12.

34. Rob Ruck, "Baseball and Community: From Pittsburgh's Hill to San Pedro's Canefields," in *Out of the Shadows*, ed. Kirwin, 53.

35. Finkelman, *Encyclopedia of African American History*, 150.

36. Brian McKenna, "Cum Posey," *SABR Baseball Biography Project*, accessed April 6, 2012, http://sabr.org/bioproj/person/ff7b091e.

37. John L. Clark, "Wylie Avenue," *Pittsburgh Courier*, October 7, 1933, 7.

38. Philip J. Lowry, *Green Cathedrals: The Ultimate Celebration of Major League and Negro League Ballparks* (New York: Bloomsbury, 2006), 190.

39. John L. Clark, "The Rise and Fall of Greenlee Field," *Pittsburgh Courier*, December 10, 1938, 17.

40. "Greenlee Field!," *Pittsburgh Courier*, July 23, 1938, 6.

41. Neil Lanctot, *Negro League Baseball: The Rise and Ruin of a Black Institution* (Philadelphia: University of Pennsylvania Press, 2004), 17.

42. Romeo L. Dougherty, "Sports by Romeo L. Dougherty," *New York Amsterdam News*, December 15, 1934, 11.

43. Burgos, *Cuban Star*, 73.

44. Ibid., 82.

45. Romeo L. Dougherty, "Sports," *New York Amsterdam News*, February 23, 1935, 11.

46. Rufus Schatzberg, *Black Organized Crime in Harlem, 1920–1930* (New York: Garland, 1993), 19.

47. Burgos, *Cuban Star*, 98.

48. A. M. Wendell Malliet, "Dewey Calls Alex Pompez," *New York Amsterdam News*, August 20, 1938, 1.

49. "Bankers Didn't Quit Racket as Trial Went On!," *New York Amsterdam News*, October 15, 1938, 1.50. *New York Amsterdam News*, December 22, 1934, A23.

51. Bessye Bearden, "Cuban Stars, Brooklyn Join League: Death of Nat Strong Chills First Meeting Held in N.Y.," *Chicago Defender*, January 19, 1935, 17.

52. "Yanks Defy New League: Semler Says That His Team Is Ready and Will Meet Best in Association," *New York Amsterdam News*, February 16, 1935, 11.

53. Jim Bankes, *The Pittsburgh Crawfords* (Jefferson, N.C.: McFarland, 2001), 81.

54. "Admit Black Yanks into the League at N.Y. June Meeting: Morton Affects This Reconciliation," *Chicago Defender*, June 27, 1936, 13.

55. Willie Collins, "Savoy Ballroom," *St. James Encyclopedia of Pop Culture*, accessed April 10, 2012, http://findarticles.com/p/articles/mi_g1epc/is_tov/ai_2419101066/.

56. "Connie's Inn," *NYC Ago*, accessed April 10, 2012, http://www.nycago.org/Organs/NYC/html/ConniesInn.html.

57. James Rian, "Harlem: As Seen under the Caption of 'The Inky Way' in the *Brooklyn Eagle*," *New York Amsterdam News*, November 27, 1929, 8.

58. Theophilus Lewis, "The Harlem Sketch Book," *New York Amsterdam News*, April 9, 1930, 9.

59. "Nightlife Problem," *New York Amsterdam News*, September 20, 1938, 6.

60. Romeo L. Dougherty, "Sports Whirl," *New York Amsterdam News*, August 10, 1935, 10.

61. Lanctot, *Negro League Baseball*, 41.

62. Frank Tucker, "Jersey Sports," *Baltimore Afro-American*, November 9, 1935, 10.

63. Ibid., October 19, 1935, 21.

64. Lanctot, *Negro League Baseball*, 51.

65. James Overmyer, *Queen of the Negro Leagues: Effa Manley and the Newark Eagles* (Lanham, Md.: Scarecrow, 1998), 9.

66. "Negro Clerks for 125th Street Store," *New York Age*, June 9, 1934, 1; Drake and Cayton, *Black Metropolis*, 84.

67. "Blumsteins to Hire Negro Clerks," *New York Age*, August 4, 1934, 1.

68. Roberta J. Newman and Joel Nathan Rosen, "Playing in the Gray Area: Black Baseball and Its Jewish 'Middleman' Economy," in *The Cooperstown Symposium on*

Baseball and American Culture, 2009–2010, ed. William M. Simons (Jefferson, N.C.: McFarland, 2011), 172–80.

69. Cheryl Lynn Greenberg, *"Or Does It Explode?": Black Harlem in the Great Depression* (New York: Oxford University Press, 1991), 117.

70. "Negro Chain Store Reveals Expansion," *New York Times*, April 29, 1930, 50.

71. *New York Amsterdam News*, April 2, 1930, 2.

72. "The CMA Stores," *Pittsburgh Courier*, January 18, 1930, 10.

73. "CMA Stores to Feature Negro-Manufactured Goods," *New York Amsterdam News*, July 22, 1931, A8; "What's Wrong with the CMA?," *Pittsburgh Courier*, August 12, 1933, 10.

74. Kenneth Winter and Michael J. Haupert, "The East-West Game: All Stars and Negro League Finances," in *Cooperstown Symposium, 2009–2010*, ed. Simons, 158.

75. Jules Tygiel, *Baseball's Great Experiment: Jackie Robinson and His Legacy* (New York: Oxford University Press, 1997), 24.

76. Emil Roth, "40 Years Ago—The First All-Star Game," *Baseball Digest* 32, no. 7 (1973): 45.

77. Jules Tygiel, *Past Time: Baseball as History* (New York: Oxford University Press, 2000), 91.

78. Lanctot, *Negro League Baseball*, 23.

79. "150,000 Vote on Negro All-Star Baseball Teams," *Chicago Tribune*, August 19, 1933, 14.

80. David M. Fletcher, "Never on a Friday: The Baseball Palace of the World Turns 100 Years Old," *Chicago Baseball Museum*, accessed April 25, 2012, http://www.chicagobaseballmuseum.org/chicago-baseball-museum-Comisky-Park.php.

81. Robert Peterson, *Only the Ball Was White*, 114.

82. Suzanne E. Smith, *To Serve the Living: Funeral Directors and the African American Way of Life* (Cambridge: Harvard University Press, 2010), 101.

83. Robert E. Weems Jr., "The Chicago Metropolitan Mutual Assurance Company: A Profile of a Black-Owned Enterprise," *Illinois Historical Journal* 86, no.1 (1993): 3.

84. Drake and Cayton, *Black Metropolis*, 454.

85. Suzanne E. Smith, *To Serve the Living*, 101.

86. Weems, "Chicago Metropolitan Mutual Assurance Company," 5.

87. Ibid.

88. Green, *Selling the Race*, 83; internal citations omitted.

89. Robert E. Weems Jr., *Black Business in the Black Metropolis: The Chicago Metropolitan Assurance Company, 1925–1985* (Bloomington: Indiana University Press, 1996), 24.

90. "Giants Park Is Sold to Local Business Men," *Chicago Defender*, February 20, 1932, 1.

91. Weems, "Chicago Metropolitan Mutual Assurance Company," 7; "Giants Lose Ball Grounds: Old Schorling Park Will Be Home of Dogs," *Chicago Defender*, March 3, 1933, 8.

92. "They're No Longer Called Orphans," *Chicago Defender*, February 17, 1934, 9.

93. Lanctot, *Negro League Baseball*, 47.

94. Ibid., 46.

95. "Alderman Jackson's Success Is Real Inspiration to Race," *Pittsburgh Courier*, August 10, 1935, A3.

96. "Horizons," *The Crisis*, November 1916, 35; "Chicago City Council," *The Crisis*, June 1933, 135.97. "American League Moguls Close Last Meet of Year," *Chicago Defender*, December 18, 1937, 8.

98. Gilmore, "Negro in Baseball," 6.

99. Jules Tygiel, *Extra Bases: Reflections on Jackie Robinson, Race, and Baseball History* (Lincoln: University of Nebraska Press, 2002), 61.

100. "Hutchinson to See Night Baseball," *Hutchinson News*, September 27, 1930, 3.

101. Burgos, *Cuban Star*, 129.

102. "Expect New Field to Pep Up Yankees," *New York Amsterdam News*, July 9, 1938, 4A.

103. *New York Amsterdam News*, July 23, 1938, A4; "Black Yanks, Cubans to Share Yankee Diamond," *Chicago Defender*, March 4, 1939, 8.

104. "Black Yanks, Cubans to Share Yankee Diamond," *Chicago Defender*, March 4, 1939, 8.

105. Lanctot, *Negro League Baseball*, 61.

106. John L. Clark, "The Rise and Fall of Greenlee Field," *Pittsburgh Courier*, December 10, 1938, 17.

107. Peter Rutkoff, "The Style of Black Baseball: Birmingham and Pittsburgh," in *The Cooperstown Symposium on Baseball and American Culture, 2005–2006*, ed. William Simons (Jefferson, N.C.: McFarland, 2007), 28.

108. Kevin Kirkland, "Greenlee Field Site Earns Place in History," *Pittsburgh Post-Gazette*, September 17, 2009, accessed April 24, 2012, http://www.post-gazette.com/stories/sports/uncategorized/greenlee-field-site-earns-place-in-history-349838/.

Chapter 4

1. Wilkerson, *Warmth of Other Suns*, 45.

2. James T. Patterson, *Grand Expectations: The United States, 1945–1974* (New York: Oxford University Press, 1996), 19.

3. Lanctot, *Negro League Baseball*, 147.

4. Wilkerson, *Warmth of Other Suns*, 218.

5. Drake and Cayton, *Black Metropolis*, 726.

6. Green, *Selling the Race*, 21.

7. Ibid., 21.

8. Ibid., 38–39.

9. Drake and Cayton, *Black Metropolis*, 443–44.

10. Light and Gold, *Ethnic Economies*, 127.

11. Effa Manley to Seward Posey, August 1, 1941, Newark Eagles Papers, Charles F. Cummings New Jersey Information Center, Newark Public Library, Newark, N.J.

12. Wendell Smith, "The Sports Beat," *Pittsburgh Courier*, February 2, 1946, 26.

13. Cum Posey, "Posey Defends Use of White Records Agency," *Pittsburgh Courier*, March 25, 1944, 14.

14. Wendell Smith, "The Sports Beat," *Pittsburgh Courier*, January 11, 1947, 18.

15. "Edward 'Ed' Gottlieb," Naismith Memorial Basketball Hall of Fame, accessed May 3, 2012, http://www.hoophall.com/hall-of-famers/tag/edward-ed-gottlieb.

16. Frank A. "Fay" Young, "The Stuff Is Here: Past-Present-Future, *Chicago Defender*, July 27, 1940, 23.

17. Promotional Expenses for the 1943 East-West Game, Comiskey Park, Sunday, August 1, 1943, T. Y. Baird Papers, 414:2:2, Kansas Collection, Kenneth Spencer Research Library, University of Kansas, Lawrence.

18. Alan J. Pollock, *Barnstorming to Heaven: Syd Pollock and His Great Black Teams*, ed. James A. Riley (Tuscaloosa: University of Alabama Press, 2006), 46.

19. Ibid., 83.

20. Lanctot, *Negro League Baseball*, 109.

21. Harold Seymour and Dorothy Z. Seymour, *Baseball: The People's Game* (New York: Oxford University Press, 1991), 271.

22. C. Oren Renick and Joel Nathan Rosen, "Inextricably Linked: Joe Louis and Max Schmeling Revisited," in *Fame to Infamy: Race, Sport, and the Fall from Grace*, ed. David C. Ogden and Joel Nathan Rosen (Jackson: University Press of Mississippi, 2011), 105.

23. Robert C. Toll, *Blacking Up: The Minstrel Show in Nineteenth-Century America* (New York: Oxford University Press, 1974), 28.

24. Wendell Smith, "Smitty's Sports Spurts," *Pittsburgh Courier*, July 15, 1944, 12.

25. Mel Watkins, "Blackface Minstrelsy," *The American Experience: Stephen Foster*, accessed July 16, 2012, http://www.pbs.org/wgbh/amex/foster/sfeature/sf_minstrelsy_5 .html.

26. Donn Rogosin, *Invisible Men: Life In the Negro Leagues* (Lincoln: University of Nebraska Press, 2007), 142. Tut's persona alludes directly to a stock minstrel character, Zip Coon.

27. Pollock, *Barnstorming to Heaven*, 13.

28. Ibid., 135.

29. E. B. Rea, "Down My Street," *Baltimore Afro-American*, January 10, 1942, 20.

30. Buck Leonard quoted in Lanctot, *Negro League Baseball*, 138.

31. Ethiopian Clowns advertisement, ca. 1941, Newark Eagles Papers.

32. Real Times, Inc., accessed July 28, 2012, http://www.fundinguniverse.com/ company-histories/real-times-inc-company-history.html.

33. Tygiel, *Past Time*, 119.

34. "A Separate World," accessed May 9, 2012, http://www.pbs.org/blackpress/ educate_event/separate.html.

35. W. E. B. Du Bois, "Du Bois Finds Race Papers Free from the Shackles of Big Business Advertisers," *Chicago Defender*, February 27, 1943, 13.

36. Green, *Selling the Race*, 83.

37. Roland Marchand, *Advertising the American Dream: Making Way for Modernity, 1920–1940* (Berkeley: University of California Press), 64.

38. *New York Amsterdam News*, September 13, 1941, 4.

39. "Cincy-Indianapolis Clowns, Black Crax, Set for Crucial Series at Poncey Park," *Atlanta Daily World*, August 3, 1945, 5.

40. Ledger entry, May 14, 1941, Newark Eagles Papers; "Measuring Worth," accessed May 9, 2012, http://www.measuringworth.com/uscompare/relativevalue.php.

41. Ledger entry, July 10, 1941, Newark Eagles Papers.

42. Lanctot, *Negro League Baseball*, 191.

43. Bruce Weber, "Sherman L. Maxwell, 100, Sportscaster and Writer, Dies," *New York Times*, July 19, 2008, accessed May 9, 2012, http://www.nytimes.com/2008/07/19/sports/19maxwell.html.

44. Jocko Maxwell to Effa Manley, May 1, 1940, Newark Eagles Papers.

45. Effa Manley to Jocko Maxwell, May 1, 1942, ibid.

46. Oliver "Butts" Brown to Effa Manley, April 4, 1940, ibid.

47. Effa Manley to Jerome Kessler, February 25, 1944, ibid.

48. Effa Manley to Murray Halpern, March 24, 1939, ibid.

49. Donald Spivey, "Satchel Paige's Struggle for Selfhood in the Era of Jim Crow," in *Out of the Shadows: A Biographical History of African American Athletes*, ed. David K. Wiggins (Fayetteville: University of Arkansas Press, 2006, 106.

50. Ibid., 107.

51. Cum Posey to Effa Manley, August 8, 1941, Newark Eagles Papers.

52. Ric Roberts, "Paige Magnet for Spectators," *Baltimore Afro-American*, August 2, 1941, 21.

53. "Race Employment Biggest in History: Discrimination Felt to Be at All-Time 'Low,'" *Pittsburgh Courier*, November 28, 1942, 5; "Employment Gains 33% in Less Than 6 Months," *Pittsburgh Courier*, March 13, 1943, 8.

54. "Employment Jumps as Fifteen New Firms Weekly Drop Color Bars," *Baltimore Afro-American*, April 11, 1942.

55. "Pepsi Cola Gives Jobs to Negroes," *Chicago Defender*, January 30, 1943, 22.

56. George Q. Flynn, "Selective Service and American Blacks during World War II," *Journal of Negro History* 69, no. 1 (1984): 20.

57. Lanctot, *Negro League Baseball*, 118–39.

58. Dan Burley, "Crowds in East Eclipse Chicago's Sport Classic," *New York Amsterdam News*, July 5, 1942, 11.

59. Delores Calvin, "Benny Decides to Travel by Train," *Atlanta Daily World*, July 27, 1942, 2; "Lionel Hampton, Traveling by Train, Plays to 8,000 Whites at Miami Beach," *Pittsburgh Courier*, July 4, 1942, 21.

60. Lanctot, *Negro League Baseball*, 133.

61. "U.S. Ban Lifted for Three Month Trial," *Pittsburgh Courier*, September 5, 1942, 21.

62. Lanctot, *Negro League Baseball*, 134.

63. Preston Lauterbach, *The Chitlin' Circuit and the Road to Rock 'n' Roll* (New York: Norton, 2011), 23.

64. Ibid., 25.

65. "Lionel Hampton, Traveling by Train," 21.

66. "Nation-Wide Support Grows for Double V," *Pittsburgh Courier*, March 14, 1942, 12.

67. *The Black Press: Soldiers without Swords*.

68. Cum Posey, "Posey's Points," *Pittsburgh Courier*, August 18, 1942, 17.

69. "Readers Want Double V Made into Pins, Emblems," *Pittsburgh Courier*, February 21, 1942, 2.

70. "Nation Lauds Courier's Double V Campaign," *Pittsburgh Courier*, March 7, 1942, 12.

71. Frazier, "Human, All Too Human," 100.

72. "Race Needs Economic Leadership," *Pittsburgh Courier*, August 29, 1942, 15.

73. Seymour L. Wolfbein, "War and Post-War Trends in Employment of Negroes," *Monthly Labor Review* 60, no. 1 (1945): 1–5.

74. Ibid., 5.

75. "Negro Workers Face Severe Cut in Post-War Employment Decline," *Pittsburgh Courier*, February 3, 1945, 15.

76. Seymour L. Wolfbein, "Post-War Trends in Negro Employment," Monthly Labor Review 65, no. 6 (1947): 665.

77. Robert C. Weaver, "Negro Labor since 1929," *Journal of Negro History* 35, no. 1 (1950): 30.

78. Elmer A. Carter, "Fighting Prejudice with Law," *Journal of Educational Sociology* 19, no. 5 (1946): 301.

79. Leo Egan, "Anti-Racial Bill Signed by Dewey," *New York Times*, March 13, 1945, 38.

80. "Job Discrimination a Crime," *Wall Street Journal*, March 13, 1945, 6.

81. "New York: First Year of Ives-Quinn Law Termed Encouraging," *Pittsburgh Courier*, July 20, 1946, 6.

82. "Commission Finds Less Bias in Jobs," *New York Times*, July 9, 1946, 20.

Chapter 5

1. "Fans Okay Negroes in Big Leagues," *Pittsburgh Courier*, February 15, 1947, 17.

2. Nicholas Lemann, *The Promised Land: The Great Black Migration and How it Changed America* (New York: Random House, 2011), 5.

3. Ibid., 6.

4. Patterson, *Grand Expectations*, 5.

5. "Our Mounting Fire Tragedies," *Chicago Defender*, January 25, 1947, 14.

6. Henry Brown, "Expanding West Side Holds Relics of Past; Glimmer of the Future," *Chicago Defender*, August 21, 1948, 20.

7. "Topics of the Times," *New York Times*, October 3, 1946, 26.

8. Edwin G. Burrows and Mike Wallace, *Gotham: A History of New York City to 1898* (New York: Oxford University Press, 1998), 972.

9. Michael Shapiro, *The Last Good Season: Brooklyn, the Dodgers, and Their Final Pennant Race Together* (New York: Broadway Books, 2004), 225.

10. Ibid., 106.

11. David Halberstam, *The Fifties* (New York: Ballantine, 1993), 132.

12. Ibid., 131–33.

13. Carl E. Prince, *Brooklyn's Dodgers: The Bums, the Borough, and the Best of Baseball, 1947–1957* (New York: Oxford University Press, 1997), 113.

14. John Metzger, "Planned Abandonment: The Neighborhood Life-Cycle Theory and National Urban Policy," *Housing Policy Debate* 11, no. 1 (2000): 11.

15. William Levitt quoted in Halberstam, *Fifties*, 141.

16. Patterson, *Grand Expectations*, 5.

17. Ibid., 5.

18. Tygiel, *Baseball's Great Experiment*, 59–60.

19. "Biography," Jackie Robinson, accessed May 29, 2012, http://www.jackierobinson .com/about/bio.html.

20. John Vernon, "Jim Crow, Meet Lieutenant Robinson: A 1944 Court-Martial," *Prologue* 40, no. 1 (2008), accessed May 29, 2012, http://www.archives.gov/publications/ prologue/2008/spring/robinso n.html.

21. Alain Locke, ed., *The New Negro: Voices of the Harlem Renaissance* (1925; New York: Touchstone, 1997).

22. A. S. Young, "Black Athlete in Golden Age of Sports," *Ebony*, November 1968, 160.

23. Lee Lowenfish, *Branch Rickey: Baseball's Ferocious Gentleman* (Lincoln: University of Nebraska Press, 2009), 376.

24. Derek T. Dingle, *Black Enterprise Titans of the B.E. 100s: Black CEOs Who Redefined and Conquered American Business* (Hoboken, N.J.: Wiley, 1999), 4.

25. Green, *Selling the Race*, 132.

26. Dingle, *Black Enterprise Titans*, 13.

27. Ibid., 14.

28. Ibid., 11.

29. Ibid., 9.

30. "Gus Greenlee Forms His New Baseball Loop—U.S. League," *New York Amsterdam News*, January 6, 1945, B5.

31. Lanctot, *Negro League Baseball*, 126.

32. Wendell Smith, "Posey Balks on 'More Power' Plan for League," *Pittsburgh Courier*, January 5, 1946, 16.

33. Minutes of Joint Meeting of the NNL and NAL, June 1, 1943, Newark Eagles Papers.

34. Lanctot, *Negro League Baseball*, 290.

35. Allen Johnson to Abe and Effa Manley, January 31, [1946], Newark Eagles Papers. The letter is dated 1945, but Robinson did not meet initially with Rickey until August 1945.

36. Rufus "Sonnyman" Jackson to Abe and Effa Manley, April 20, 1946, ibid.

37. Lanctot, *Negro League Baseball*, 318.

38. Ibid., 318.

39. Drake and Cayton, *Black Metropolis*, 443–44.

40. Gunnar Myrdal, *An American Dilemma: The Negro Problem and Modern Democracy* (1944; New Brunswick, N.J.: Transaction, 1996), 2:803.

41. James Weldon Johnson quoted in ibid., 803.

42. Monte Irvin, interview by authors, July 16, 2012.

43. Ralph Bunche quoted in Myrdal, *American Dilemma*, 804.

44. Charles P. Korr, *The End of Baseball as We Knew It: The Players Union, 1960–81* (Urbana: University of Illinois Press, 2005).

45. Ralph Bunche quoted in Myrdal, *American Dilemma*, 804.

46. Robert Peterson, *Only the Ball Was White*, 135–37.

47. Lanctot, *Negro League Baseball*, 144.

48. Monte Irvin, interview by authors, October 11, 2009.

49. Effa Manley to [Monte] Irvin, February 9, 1946, Newark Eagles Papers.

50. For a discussion of Bunche's participation in *An American Dilemma*, see Ralph J. Bunche, "Conceptions and Ideologies of the Negro Problem," *Contributions in Black Studies: A Journal of African and African American Studies* 9, no. 1 (1992): 70–114.

51. Frazier, "Human, All Too Human," 100.

52. Ibid., 76.

53. Novotny Lawrence, *Blaxploitation Films of the 1970s: Blackness and Genre* (New York: Routledge, 2008), 6.

54. Ibid., 5.

55. Ibid., 6.

56. Thomas Cripps, *Making Movies Black: The Hollywood Message Movie from World War II to the Civil Rights Era* (New York: Oxford University Press, 1993), 129.

57. Ibid.

58. Juliet E. K. Walker, *History of Black Business*, 320.

59. "Hampton's Platter Mill to Begin Grinding Racy Disks," *Baltimore Afro-American*, June 8, 1946, 6.

60. "Hamp-Tone Label New Outlet for Business," *Pittsburgh Courier*, September 7, 1946, 22.

61. *New York Amsterdam News*, August 30, 1947, 15.

62. Al Monroe, "Show Business in New York Just Another Let-Down, Monroe Learns," *Chicago Defender*, September 20, 1947, 15.

63. John Leland, *Hip: The History* (New York: Harper Perennial, 2005), 135.

64. "Hotel Business Hit by General Slump," *Chicago Defender*, December 28, 1946, 3.

65. "Penn Relays," *Philly Sports History*, accessed June 18, 2012, http://phillysportshistory.com/2011/04/28/history-at-the-penn-relays/.

66. "Ask $25,000 in Boston Hotel Jim Crow Suit," *Chicago Defender*, April 12, 1947, 5.

67. W. Washington in *Chicago Defender*, January 4, 1947, 14.

68. "Paige Will Pitch in the East-West Game," *Chicago Defender*, July 26, 1941, 1.

69. Wendell Smith, "45,474 Fans See West Wallop East, 4 to 1," *Pittsburgh Courier*, August 24, 1946, 25.

70. Sam Lacy, "62,000 See East, West Split All-Star Diamond Tilts," *Baltimore Afro-American*, August 24, 1946, 16.

71. "Crowning Miss East-West 1946 to Mark Ball Game," *Chicago Defender*, July 27, 1946, 16.

72. Frank A. "Fay" Young, "50,000 and Major League Scouts See West Best East in Great Game," *Chicago Defender*, August 2, 1947, 1; Dan Burley, "86,402 See 2 Negro Baseball Classics: 38,402 in Crowd in PG Biggest Ever in East," *New York Amsterdam News*, August 2, 1947, 1.

73. "America's Greatest Pastime," *New York Amsterdam News*, August 9, 1947, 8.

74. Burgos, *Cuban Star*, 180.

75. Lanctot, *Negro League Baseball*, 317.

76. Dan Burley, "Confidentially Yours," *New York Amsterdam News*, October 11, 1947, 12.

77. Morgan Holsey, "Scalpers and Politics Mar East-West Game," *Chicago Defender*, August 28, 1948, 10.

78. "Second East vs. West Game Draws 17,928," *Chicago Defender*, September 4, 1948, 11; "Negro Nationals Score 6–1 Victory," *New York Times*, August 25, 1948, 33.

79. Swig Garlington, "40,000 Expected at 'Dream Game,'" *New York Amsterdam News*, August 21, 1948, 14.

80. "The Weather in the Nation," *New York Times*, August 25, 1948, 51; Roscoe McGowen, "Dodgers Bow to Braves in 14th and Fall to Third," *New York Times*, August 24, 1948, 27.

81. Holsey, "Scalpers and Politics Mar East-West Game," 10.

82. Frank A. "Fay" Young, "Satchel Paige Magnificently Defeats Sox," *Chicago Defender*, August 21, 1948, 10.

83. Alpert, *Out of Left Field*, 182.

84. Dan Burley, "Confidentially Yours," *New York Amsterdam News*, August 24, 1946, 12.

85. "Negro National League Loop Folds as Gate Dips," *Atlanta Daily World*, December 4, 1948, 5.

Chapter 6

1. Effa Manley, "At the Crossroads: Ex-Newark Eagles Owner Tells Story," *Baltimore Afro-American*, June 25, 1949, C5.

2. Lanctot, *Negro League Baseball*, 339–40.

3. Bob Luke, *The Most Famous Woman in Baseball: Effa Manley and the Negro Leagues* (Dulles, Va.: Potomac, 2011), 145.

4. Manley, "At the Crossroads," C5.

5. Frank A. "Fay" Young, "Fay Says," *Chicago Defender*, July 30, 1949, 14.

6. Ibid., 14.

7. Lanctot, *Negro League Baseball*, 261.

8. Sam Lacy, "From A to Z," *Baltimore Afro-American*, June 25, 1949, C3.

9. Ibid.

10. "Negro Baseball Owners Flay Branch Rickey," *Atlanta Daily World*, March 11, 1948, 5.

11. Robert Peterson, *Only the Ball Was White*, 80.

12. Julius J. Adams, "Negro Baseball in Throes of Death; Can Anything Save It?," *New York Amsterdam News*, August 13, 1948, 1; Fay Young, "Is Negro Baseball Doomed?," *Chicago Defender*, April 23, 1949, 1.

13. Stephen Steinberg, *The Ethnic Myth: Race, Ethnicity, and Class in America*, 3rd ed. (Boston: Beacon, 2001), 253–62.

14. Leland, *Hip*, 130.

15. Thomas Hine, *The Rise and Fall of the American Teenager: A New History of the American Adolescent Experience* (New York: HarperCollins, 1999), 246–57.

16. Francis Davis, *History of the Blues: The Roots, the Music, the People* (New York: Hyperion, 1995), 175–99.

17. Halberstam, *Fifties*, 13.

18. Ibid., 145.

19. "Housing Project to Open," *New York Amsterdam News*, November 12, 1949, 4.

20. "Challenges of Rebuilding Bronzeville: A Chicago Case Example," *Urban Juncture*, accessed June 30, 2012, http://www.urban-juncture.com/casestudy.html.

21. "Watching a Televised Baseball Game," *New York Times*, September 3, 1939, X10.

22. Dave Berkman, "Long before Arledge: Sports and TV, the Earliest Years, 1937–1947, as Seen by the Contemporary Press," *Journal of Popular Culture* 22, no. 2 (1990): 54; E. W. Stewart, "Imagery for Profit," *New York Times*, July 6, 1941, X1.

23. Nick Curran, "It's 25 Years Now for Baseball on TV," *Baseball Digest* 23, no. 6 (1964): 88.

24. James Walker and Bellamy, *Center Field Shot*, 37.

25. Lynn Spigel, *Welcome to the Dreamhouse: Popular Media and Postwar Suburbs* (Durham, N.C.: Duke University Press, 2001), 4.

26. "Everyday Mysteries," *Library of Congress*, accessed July 2, 2012, http://www.loc .gov/rr/scitech/mysteries/tvdinner.html.

27. Robert D. Putnam, *Bowling Alone: The Collapse and Revival of American Community* (New York: Simon and Schuster, 2001), 211.

28. Jane Jacobs, *The Death and Life of Great American Cities* (New York: Random House Digital, 1992), 72.

29. "Interracial Department Store," *Baltimore Afro-American*, January 1, 1949, 3.

30. *New York Amsterdam News*, April 2, 1949, 18.

31. "Peters Department Store Folds," *New York Age*, July 23, 1949, 32.

32. Robert H. Kinzer and Edward Sagarin, *The Negro in American Business: The Conflict between Separatism and Integration* (New York: Greenberg, 1950), 180.

33. Monte Irvin, interview by authors, May 6, 2008.

34. Effa Manley to Murray Halpern, March 24, 1939, Newark Eagles Papers.

35. P. L. Prattis, "The Horizon," *Pittsburgh Courier*, July 8, 1950, 18.

36. "Fenced In," *Pittsburgh Courier*, October 13, 1951, 20.

37. Marcus Alexis, "Pathways to the Negro Market," *Journal of Negro Education* 28, no. 2 (1959): 116.

38. Ibid.

39. Ibid., 114.

40. Ibid., 114, 127.

41. "Race's Buying Power Key to Jobs, Says Business League Head," *Pittsburgh Courier*, July 8, 1950, 2.

42. Weems, *Black Business*, 38.

43. Ibid., 96.

44. Ibid., 50.

45. Ibid., 56.

46. "Mary Cole's Own Story," *Chicago Defender*, December 17, 1955, 1.

47. "Free Mary Cole; Case Dismissed," *Chicago Defender*, June 26, 1956, 1.

48. Weems, *Black Business*, 48.

49. Juliet E. K. Walker, *History of Black Business*, 255.

50. Ibid., 257.

51. Sondra Kathryn Wilson, *Meet Me at the Theresa: The Story of Harlem's Most Famous Hotel* (New York: Atria, 2004), 144.

52. Juliet E. K. Walker, *History of Black Business*, 257.

53. Charles Fountain, *Under the March Sun: The Story of Spring Training* (New York: Oxford University Press, 2009), 43.

54. Tygiel, *Baseball's Great Experiment*, 312.

55. Frank A. "Fay" Young, "Fay Says," *Chicago Defender*, August 28, 1954, 11.

56. Tygiel, *Baseball's Great Experiment*, 313.

57. Monte Irvin, interview by authors, October 10, 2009.

58. Sondra Kathryn Wilson, *Meet Me at the Theresa*, 220.

59. Sammy Davis Jr. quoted in Sondra Kathryn Wilson, *Meet Me at the Theresa*, 21.

60. "Negro Newspapers Publishers Plan 12th Annual Convention," *Atlanta Daily World*, June 5, 1951, 1.

61. William G. Nunn, "Hundreds Mourn Gus Greenlee: Sports, Political Figure Dies Quietly at Home," *Pittsburgh Courier*, July 12, 1952, 1.

62. John L. Clark, "Wylie Ave.," *Pittsburgh Courier*, August 4, 1951, 20.

63. William G. Nunn, "East-West Game Needs an Overhauling," *Pittsburgh Courier*, August 29, 1953, 24.

64. Bobbie Barbee, "Obituary: Globetrotters' Founder," *Jet*, March 31, 1966, 54.

65. Alpert, *Out of Left Field*, 184–85.

66. Burgos, *Cuban Star*, 190.

67. Ibid., 194.

68. Ibid., 203.

69. Ibid., 200.

70. Lanctot, *Negro League Baseball*, 370.

71. Pollock, *Barnstorming to Heaven*, 1.

72. "1950 Major League Attendance," *Baseball Reference*, accessed July 5, 2012, http://www.databasebaseball.com/leagues/leagueatt.htm?yr=1950.

73. "Clowns' Antics Paying Off in Big Boxoffice," *Chicago Defender*, August 26, 1950, 19.

74. Newman, "Pitching behind the Color Line," 81.

75. *Chillicothe Constitution-Tribune*, September 3, 1954, 2.

76. Pollock, *Barnstorming to Heaven*, 167.

77. "Expect Record Attendance at Clown-Monarch Tiff," *Chicago Defender*, June 20, 1953, 22.

78. Lanctot, *Negro League Baseball*, 381.

79. Pollock, *Barnstorming to Heaven*, 242.

80. Martha Ackmann, *Curveball: The Remarkable Story of Toni Stone, the First Woman to Play Professional Baseball in the Negro League* (Chicago: Hill, 2010), 59.

81. Oscar Rico to T. Y. Baird, February 27, 1953, Baird Papers, 414:3:1.

82. T. Y. Baird to Oscar Rico, February 23, 1953, ibid.

83. T. Y. Baird to Matty Brescia, March 27, 1952, ibid., 414:2:4.

84. Pollock, *Barnstorming to Heaven*, 263.

85. Ibid., 380.

86. Stephanie M. Liscio, *Integrating Cleveland Baseball: Media Activism, the Integration of the Indians, and the Demise of the Negro League Buckeyes* (Jefferson, N.C.: McFarland, 2010), 7.

87. Lowenfish, *Branch Rickey*, 497.

88. Douglas Martin, "Nat Albright, Voice of Dodgers Games He Did Not See, Dies at 87," *New York Times*, August 15, 2011, accessed July 6, 2012, http://www.nytimes.com/2011/08/16/sports/baseball/nat-allbright-voice-of-dodgers-games-he-did-not-see-dies-at-87.html?_r=1&scp=1&sq=Nat+Allbright&st=cse.

89. Tom Hayes quoted in Lanctot, *Negro League Baseball*, 343.

90. Charles Shaar Murray, *Crosstown Traffic: Jimi Hendrix and the Post-War Rock 'n' Roll Revolution* (London: St. Martin's Griffin, 1991), 154.

91. Lauterbach, *Chitlin' Circuit*, 79.

92. Ibid., 89.

93. "Mills Brothers Join the Carolina Cotton Pickers," *Chicago Defender*, July 24, 1943, 18.

94. "Indianapolis Betting Pool Said to Be Worth $50,000: Says Ferguson Runs $50,000 Lottery," *Baltimore Afro-American*, September 26, 1931, 1.

95. Lauterbach, *Chitlin' Circuit*, 91.

96. Robert Palmer, *Deep Blues* (New York: Penguin, 1981), 185–88.

97. Ron Briley, *Class at Bat, Gender on Deck, and Race in the Hole: A Line-Up of Essays on Twentieth Century Culture and America's Game* (Jefferson, N.C.: McFarland, 2003), 302.

98. Tygiel, *Past Time*, 92.

99. Nelson George, *The Death of Rhythm and Blues* (New York: Penguin, 1988), 137–38.

100. Lauterbach, *Chitlin' Circuit*, 291.

Postscript

1. Gerald Early, "Performance and Reality: Race, Sports, and the Modern World," *The Nation*, August 10–17, 1998, 11.

2. Ibid., 12.

3. Ibid., 13.

4. Bruce Markusen, "Cooperstown Confidential: Where Are the All-Black Nine Now?," *Hardball Times*, posted September 2, 2011, accessed July 30, 2012, http://www.hardballtimes.com/main/article/cooperstown-confidential-where-are-the-all-black-nine-now/.

5. Richard Lapchick with Christina Cloud, Aaron Gearlds, Tavia Record, Elizabeth Schulz, Jake Spiak, and Matthew Vinson, "The 2011 Racial and Gender Report Card: Major League Baseball," *Institute for Diversity and Ethics in Sport*, April 21, 2011, accessed July 30, 2012, http://www.tidesport.org/RGRC/2011/2011_MLB_RGRC_FINAL.pdf.

6. "Michael Jordan Reaches Deal to Buy NBA's Bobcats," *CNN.com*, February 27, 2010, accessed August 1, 2012, http://www.cnn.com/2010/SPORT/02/27/michael.jordan.bobcats/index.html.

7. George, *Death of Rhythm and Blues*, 82–85.

8. "Curtain Down on Vee-Jay as Liquidation Is Ordered," *Billboard*, August 13, 1966, 7.

9. "Race's Buying Power Key to Jobs, Says Business League Head," *Pittsburgh Courier*, July 8, 1950, 2.

10. *Record Row: Cradle of Rhythm and Blues* (documentary), directed by Michael D. McAlpin, USA Network, February 20, 1997.

11. George, *Death of Rhythm and Blues*, 86–89.

12. "Michael Jordan Reaches Deal."

13. Johnson Publishing Company Management, accessed July 31, 2012, http://www.johnsonpublishing.com/page.php?id=4.

SELECTED BIBLIOGRAPHY

Manuscript Collections

T. Y. Baird Papers. Kansas Collection, RH MS 414, Kenneth Spencer Research Library, University of Kansas, Lawrence.

Newark Eagles Papers. Charles F. Cummings New Jersey Information Center, Newark Public Library, Newark, N.J.

Periodicals

Atlanta Daily World
Baltimore Afro-American
Billboard
Chicago Broad Ax
Chicago Defender
Chicago Tribune
Cleveland Call and Post
The Crisis
Detroit Free Press
Detroit Plain Dealer
Ebony
Indianapolis Freeman
Jet
Kansas City American
Kansas City Call
Los Angeles Sentinel
The Messenger
Michigan Chronicle
New York Age
New York Amsterdam News
New York Daily News

New York Times
Philadelphia Tribune
Survey Graphic

Books

Abbott, Karen. *Sin in the Second City: Madams, Ministers, Playboys, and the Battle for America's Soul*. New York: Random House, 2008.

Ackmann, Martha. *Curveball: The Remarkable Story of Toni Stone, the First Woman to Play Professional Baseball in the Negro League*. Chicago: Hill, 2010.

Alpert, Rebecca T. *Out of Left Field: Jews and Black Baseball*. New York: Oxford University Press, 2011.

Bak, Richard. *A Place for Summer: A Narrative History of Tiger Stadium*. Detroit: Wayne State University Press, 1998.

———. *Turkey Stearnes and the Detroit Stars: The Negro Leagues in Detroit, 1919–1933*. Detroit: Wayne State University Press, 1994.

Baldassero, Lawrence, and Richard A. Johnson, eds. *The American Game: Baseball and Ethnicity*. Carbondale: Southern Illinois University Press, 2002.

Bankes, Jim. *The Pittsburgh Crawfords*. Jefferson, N.C.: McFarland, 2001.

Bell, William K. *A Business Primer for Negroes*. New York: Bell, 1948.

Ben-Ami, Daniel. *Cowardly Capitalism: The Myth of the Global Financial Casino*. West Sussex, Eng.: Wiley, 2001.

Blair, Cynthia M. *I've Got to Make My Livin': Black Women's Sex Work in Turn-of-the-Century Chicago*. Chicago: University of Chicago Press, 2010.

Briley, Ron. *Class at Bat, Gender on Deck, and Race in the Hole: A Line-Up of Essays on Twentieth Century Culture and America's Game*. Jefferson, N.C.: McFarland, 2003.

Bruce, Janet. *Kansas City Monarchs: Champions of Black Baseball*. Lawrence: University Press of Kansas, 1986.

Brundage, W. Fitzhugh. *Beyond Blackface: African Americans and the Creation of American Popular Culture, 1890–1930*. Chapel Hill: University of North Carolina Press, 2011.

Burgos, Adrian, Jr. *Cuban Star: How One Negro-League Owner Changed the Face of Baseball*. New York: Hill and Wang, 2011.

Burrows Edwin G., and Mike Wallace. *Gotham: A History of New York City to 1898*. New York: Oxford University Press, 1998.

Carroll, Brian. *When to Stop the Cheering?: The Black Press, the Black Community, and the Integration of Professional Baseball*. New York: Routledge, 2007.

Chepesiuk, Ron. *Black Gangsters of Chicago*. Fort Lee, N.J.: Barricade, 2007.

———. *Gangsters of Harlem: The Gritty Underworld of New York's Most Famous Neighborhood*. Fort Lee, N.J.: Barricade, 2007.

Chicago Commission on Race Relations. *The Negro in Chicago: A Study of Race Relations and a Race Riot*. Chicago: University of Chicago Press, 1922.

Coulter, Charles Edward. *Take Up the Black Man's Burden: Kansas City's African American Communities, 1865–1939*. Columbia: University of Missouri Press, 2006.

Cripps, Thomas. *Making Movies Black: The Hollywood Message Movie from World War II to the Civil Rights Era*. New York: Oxford University Press, 1993.

Davies, David Randall. *The Postwar Decline of American Newspapers, 1945–1965*. Westport, Conn.: Greenwood, 2006.

Davis, Francis. *History of the Blues: The Roots, the Music, the People*. New York: Hyperion, 1995.

Debono, Paul. *The Indianapolis ABCs: History of a Premier Team in the Negro Leagues*. Jefferson, N.C.: McFarland, 1997.

Dingle, Derek T. *Black Enterprise Titans of the B.E. 100s: Black CEOs Who Redefined and Conquered American Business*. Hoboken, N.J.: Wiley, 1999.

Doak, Robin Santos, Stephen Asperheim, and Alexa L. Sandmann. *Black Tuesday: Prelude to the Great Depression*. Los Angeles: Compass Point, 2007.

Drake, St. Clair, and Horace R. Cayton. *Black Metropolis: A Study of Negro Life in a Northern City*. Chicago: University of Chicago Press, 1945.

Du Bois, W. E. B. *The Souls of Black Folk*. 1903; Rockville: Arc Manor, 2008.

Finkelman, Paul. *Encyclopedia of African American History: 1896 to the Present*. New York: Oxford University Press, 2009.

Fountain, Charles. *Under the March Sun: The Story of Spring Training*. New York: Oxford University Press, 2009.

Fox, William Price. *Satchel Paige's America*. Tuscaloosa: University of Alabama Press, 2006.

Frazier, E. Franklin. *The Black Bourgeoisie*. 1957; New York: Free Press, 1997.

Fusfeld, Daniel Roland, and Timothy Mason Bates. *The Political Economy of the Urban Ghetto*. Carbondale: Southern Illinois University Press, 1984.

Galbraith, John Kenneth. *The Great Crash: 1929*. New York: Houghton Mifflin, 1997.

George, Nelson. *The Death of Rhythm and Blues*. New York: Penguin, 1988.

Grant, Colin. *Negro with a Hat: The Rise and Fall of Marcus Garvey*. New York: Oxford University Press, 2008.

Green, Adam. *Selling the Race: Culture, Community, and Black Chicago, 1940–1945*. Chicago: University of Chicago Press, 2007.

Greenberg, Cheryl Lynn. *"Or Does It Explode?": Black Harlem in the Great Depression*. New York: Oxford University Press, 1991.

Gregg, Robert. *Sparks from the Anvil of Oppression: Philadelphia's African Methodists and Southern Migrants, 1890–1940*. Philadelphia: Temple University Press, 1998.

Halberstam, David. *The Fifties*. New York: Ballantine, 1993.

Hamilton, Kenneth Marvin. *Black Towns and Profit: Promotion and Development in the Trans-Appalachian West, 1877–1915*. Urbana: University of Illinois Press, 1991.

Hamilton, Marybeth. *In Search of the Blues*. New York: Basic Books, 2008.

Harris, Abram Lincoln. *The Negro as Capitalist: A Study of Banking and Business among American Negroes*. New York: Ardent Media, 1936.

Hays, Samuel P., ed. *City at the Point: Essays on the Social History of Pittsburgh*. Pittsburgh: University of Pittsburgh Press, 1989.

Heaphy, Leslie A. *The Negro Leagues, 1869–1960.* Jefferson, N.C.: McFarland, 2003.

Herskovitz, Melville. *The Myth of the Negro Past.* 1941; New York: Beacon, 1990.

Heward, Bill, and Dimitri V. Gat. *Some Are Called Clowns: A Season with the Last of the Great Barnstorming Baseball Teams.* New York: Crowell, 1974

Hillstrom, Kevin, and Laurie Collier Hillstrom. *The Industrial Revolution in America: Communication, Agriculture, and Meat Packing, Overview/Comparison.* Santa Barbara, Calif.: ABC/Clio, 2007.

Hine, Thomas. *The Rise and Fall of the American Teenager: A New History of the American Adolescent Experience.* New York: HarperCollins, 1999.

Hogan, Lawrence D. *Shades of Glory: The Negro League and the Glory of African-American Baseball.* Washington, D.C.: National Geographic, 2006.

Jacobs, Jane. *The Death and Life of Great American Cities.* New York: Random House Digital, 1992.

Kenney, William Howland. *Chicago Jazz: A Cultural History, 1904–1930.* New York: Oxford University Press, 1994.

Kinzer, Robert H., and Edward Sagarin. *The Negro in American Business: The Conflict between Separatism and Integration.* New York: Greenberg, 1950.

Kirwan, Bill, ed. *Out of the Shadows: African American Baseball from the Cuban Giants to Jackie Robinson.* Lincoln: University of Nebraska Press, 2005.

Korr, Charles P. *The End of Baseball as We Knew It: The Players Union, 1960–81.* Urbana: University of Illinois Press, 2005.

Lanctot, Neil. *Fair Dealing and Clean Playing: The Hilldale Club and the Development of Black Professional Baseball, 1910–1932.* Syracuse, N.Y.: Syracuse University Press, 1994.

———. *Negro League Baseball: The Rise and Ruin of a Black Institution.* Philadelphia: University of Pennsylvania Press, 2004.

Lauterbach, Preston. *The Chitlin' Circuit and the Road to Rock 'n' Roll.* New York: Norton, 2011.

Lawrence, Novotny. *Blaxploitation Films of the 1970s: Blackness and Genre.* New York: Routledge, 2008

Leland, John. *Hip: The History.* New York: Harper Perennial, 2005.

Lemann, Nicholas. *The Promised Land: The Great Black Migration and How It Changed America.* New York: Random House, 2011.

Liddick, Don *The Mob's Daily Number.* Lanham, Md.: University Press of America, 1999.

Light, Ivan, and Steven J. Gold. *Ethnic Economies.* San Diego: Academic, 2000.

Locke, Alain, ed. *The New Negro: Voices of the Harlem Renaissance.* 1925; New York: Touchstone, 1997.

Lowenfish, Lee. *Branch Rickey: Baseball's Ferocious Gentleman.* Lincoln: University of Nebraska Press, 2009.

Lowry, Philip J. *Green Cathedrals: The Ultimate Celebration of Major League and Negro League Ballparks.* New York: Bloomsbury, 2006.

Luke, Bob. *The Baltimore Elite Giants: Sport and Society in the Age of Negro League Baseball.* Baltimore: Johns Hopkins University Press, 2009.

———. *The Most Famous Woman in Baseball: Effa Manley and the Negro Leagues.* Dulles, Va.: Potomac, 2011.

Lutz, Tom, and Suzanna Ashton, eds. *These "Colored" United States: African American Essays from the 1920s.* New Brunswick, N.J.: Rutgers University Press, 1996.

Marable, Manning. *Malcolm X: A Life of Reinvention.* New York: Viking, 2011. Kindle edition.

Marchand, Roland. *Advertising the American Dream: Making Way for Modernity, 1920–1940.* Berkeley: University of California Press.

Martin, Asa Earl. *Our Negro Population: A Sociological Study of the Negroes of Kansas City.* Kansas City, Mo.: Hudson, 1913.

McNeill, William F. *Black Baseball Out of Season: Pay for Play Outside the Negro Leagues.* Jefferson, N.C.: McFarland, 2007.

Merone, James A. *Hellfire Nation: The Politics of Sin in American History.* New Haven: Yale University Press, 2004.

Mjagkij, Nina. *Organizing Black America: An Encyclopedia of African American Organizations.* New York: Garland, 2005.

Murray, Charles Shaar. *Crosstown Traffic: Jimi Hendrix and the Post-War Rock 'n' Roll Revolution.* London: St. Martin's Griffin, 1991.

Myrdal, Gunner. *An American Dilemma: The Negro Problem and Modern Democracy.* 1944; New Brunswick, N.J.: Transaction, 1996.

National Negro Business League. *Proceedings of the National Negro Business League: Its First Meeting, Held in Boston, Massachusetts, August 23 and 24, 1900.* Boston: Hamm, 1901.

Oliver, Paul. *The Story of the Blues.* Boston: Northeastern University Press, 1997.

O'Neill, William L. *American High: The Years of Confidence, 1945–1960.* New York: Free Press, 1989.

Ostrander, Bob, and Derrick Morris. *Hoosier Beer: Tapping into Indiana Brewing History.* Charleston, S.C.: History Press, 2011.

Overmyer, James. *Queen of the Negro Leagues: Effa Manley and the Newark Eagles.* Lanham, Md.: Scarecrow, 1998.

Pacyga, Dominic A. *Chicago: A Biography.* Chicago: University of Chicago Press, 2010.

Palmer, Robert. *Deep Blues.* New York: Penguin, 1981.

Patterson, James T. *Grand Expectations: The United States, 1945–1974.* New York: Oxford University Press, 1996.

Peterson, Bernard L. *The African American Theatre Directory, 1816–1960: A Comprehensive Guide to Early Black Theatre Organizations, Companies, Theatres, and Performing Groups.* Westport, Conn.: Greenwood, 1997.

Peterson, Robert. *Only the Ball Was White: A History of Legendary Black Players and All-Black Professional Teams.* New York: Oxford University Press, 1992.

Pollock, Alan J. *Barnstorming to Heaven: Syd Pollock and His Great Black Teams.* Ed. James A. Riley. Tuscaloosa: University of Alabama Press, 2006.

Prince, Carl E. *Brooklyn's Dodgers: The Bums, the Borough, and the Best of Baseball, 1947–1957.* New York: Oxford University Press, 1997.

Putnam, Robert D. *Bowling Alone: The Collapse and Revival of American Community.* New York: Simon and Schuster, 2001.

Rogosin, Donn. *Invisible Men: Life in the Negro Leagues.* Lincoln: University of Nebraska Press, 2007.

Rosen, Joel Nathan. *The Erosion of the American Sporting Ethos: Shifting Attitudes toward Competition.* Jefferson, N.C.: McFarland, 2007.

———. *From New Lanark to Mound Bayou: Owenism in the Mississippi Delta.* Durham, N.C.: Carolina Academic Press, 2011.

Ruck, Rob. *Raceball: How the Major Leagues Colonized the Black and Latino Game.* Boston: Beacon, 2011.

Sacks, Marcy S. *Before Harlem: The Black Experience in New York City before World War I.* Philadelphia: University of Pennsylvania Press, 2006.

Schatzberg, Rufus. *Black Organized Crime in Harlem, 1920–1930.* New York: Garland, 1993.

Schatzberg, Rufus, and Robert J. Kelly. *African American Organized Crime: A Social History.* New York: Garland, 1996.

Schirmer, Sherry Lamb. *A City Divided: The Racial Landscape of Kansas City, 1900–1960.* Columbia: University of Missouri Press, 2002.

Seigman, Joseph. *Jewish Sports Legends: The International Jewish Hall of Fame.* Dulles, Va.: Brassey's, 2000.

Semmes, Clovis E. *The Regal Theater and Black Culture.* Hampshire, Eng.: Palgrave Macmillan, 2006.

Seymour, Harold, and Dorothy Z. Seymour. *Baseball: The People's Game.* New York: Oxford University Press, 1991.

Shapiro, Michael. *The Last Good Season: Brooklyn, the Dodgers, and Their Final Pennant Race Together.* New York: Broadway Books, 2004.

Smith, Jessie Carney, ed. *Encyclopedia of African American Businesses, K–Z.* Westport, Conn.: Greenwood, 2006.

Smith, Suzanne E. *To Serve the Living: Funeral Directors and the African American Way of Life.* Cambridge: Harvard University Press, 2010.

Spigel, Lynn. *Welcome to the Dreamhouse: Popular Media and Postwar Suburbs.* Durham, N.C.: Duke University Press, 2001.

Steinberg, Stephen. *The Ethnic Myth: Race, Ethnicity, and Class in America.* 3rd ed. Boston: Beacon, 2001.

Thornborough, Emma Lou. *Indiana Blacks in the Twentieth Century.* Bloomington: Indiana University Press, 2000.

Toll, Robert C. *Blacking Up: The Minstrel Show in Nineteenth-Century America.* New York: Oxford University Press, 1974.

Trav, S. D. *No Applause, Just Throw Money; or, The Book That Made Vaudeville Famous.* New York: Faber and Faber, 2005.

Trotter, Joe William, ed. *The Great Migration in Historical Perspective: New Dimensions of Race, Class, and Gender.* Bloomington: Indiana University Press, 1991.

Tye, Larry. *Satchel: The Life and Times of an American Legend.* New York: Random House, 2010.

Tygiel, Jules. *Baseball's Great Experiment.* New York: Oxford University Press, 1997.

———. *Extra Bases: Reflections on Jackie Robinson, Race, and Baseball History.* Lincoln: University of Nebraska Press, 2002.

———. *Past Time: Baseball as History.* New York: Oxford University Press, 2001.

Vogel, Todd, ed. *The Black Press: New Literary and Historical Essays.* New Brunswick, N.J.: Rutgers University Press, 2001.

Walker, James, and Robert V. Bellamy Jr. *Center Field Shot: A History of Baseball on Television.* Lincoln: University of Nebraska Press, 2008.

Walker, Juliet E. K. *The History of Black Business in America: Capitalism, Race, Entrepreneurship.* New York: Macmillan, 1998.

Watkins, Mel. *On the Real Side: Laughing, Lying, and Signifying.* New York: Simon and Schuster, 1994.

Weems, Robert. E. *Black Business in the Black Metropolis: The Chicago Metropolitan Assurance Company, 1925–1985.* Bloomington: Indiana University Press, 1996.

Westcott, Rich. *The Mogul: Eddie Gottlieb, Philadelphia Sports Legend and Pro Basketball Pioneer.* Philadelphia: Temple University Press, 2008.

White, Shane, Stephen Garton, Stephen Robertson, and Graham White. *Playing the Numbers: Gambling in Harlem between the Wars.* Cambridge: Harvard University Press, 2010.

White, Sol. *Sol White's History of Colored Base Ball, with Other Documents on the Early Black Game, 1886–1936.* Lincoln: University of Nebraska Press, 1995.

Wilkerson, Isabel. *The Warmth of Other Suns: The Epic Story of America's Great Migration.* New York: Vintage, 2011.

Wilson, Sondra Kathryn. *Meet Me at the Theresa: The Story of Harlem's Most Famous Hotel.* New York: Atria, 2004.

Wingfield, Adia Harvey. *Doing Business with Beauty: Black Women, Hair Salons, and the Racial Enclave Economy.* Lanham, Md.: Rowman and Littlefield, 2008.

Wintz, Harry D., and Paul Finkelman. *Encyclopedia of the Harlem Renaissance.* New York: Routledge, 2004.

Wynter, Leon E. *American Skin: Pop Culture, Big Business, and the End of White America.* New York: Crown, 2002.

INDEX

Made in the USA
Middletown, DE
26 August 2022

72277137R00141